Historical Imagination

SOCIAL IMAGINARIES

Series Editors:
Suzi Adams, Paul Blokker, Natalie J. Doyle, Saulius Geniusas,
John W. M. Krummel, and Jeremy C. A. Smith

This groundbreaking series aims to investigate social imaginaries from theoretical, comparative, historical, and interdisciplinary perspectives. Its objective is to foster challenging research on the burgeoning but heterogeneous field of social imaginaries, on the one hand, and the related field of the creative imagination, on the other. The series seeks to publish rigorous and innovative research that reflects the international, multiregional, and interdisciplinary scope across these fields.

Titles in the Series
Ricoeur and Castoriadis in Discussion
    Edited by Suzi Adams
Productive Imagination
    Edited by Saulius Geniusas and Dmitri Nikulin
Stretching the Limits of Productive Imagination
    Edited by Saulius Geniusas
Social Imaginaries: Critical Interventions
    Edited by Suzi Adams and Jeremy C. A. Smith
The Labyrinth of Modernity: Horizons, Pathways and Mutations
    By Johann P. Arnason
The Creative Imagination: Indeterminacy and Embodiment in the Writings of Kant, Fichte, and Castoriadis
    By Jodie Lee Heap
Hate Speech against Women Online: Concepts and Countermeasures
    By Louise Richardson-Self
Debating Imaginal Politics: Dialogues with Chiara Bottici
    Edited by Suzi Adams and Jeremy C. A. Smith
Historical Imagination: Hermeneutics and Cultural Narrative
    By Paul Fairfield

Historical Imagination

Hermeneutics and Cultural Narrative

Paul Fairfield

ROWMAN & LITTLEFIELD
Lanham • Boulder • New York • London

Published by Rowman & Littlefield
An imprint of The Rowman & Littlefield Publishing Group, Inc.
4501 Forbes Boulevard, Suite 200, Lanham, Maryland 20706
www.rowman.com

86-90 Paul Street, London EC2A 4NE

Copyright © 2022 by The Rowman & Littlefield Publishing Group, Inc.

All rights reserved. No part of this book may be reproduced in any form or by any electronic or mechanical means, including information storage and retrieval systems, without written permission from the publisher, except by a reviewer who may quote passages in a review.

British Library Cataloguing in Publication Information Available

Library of Congress Cataloging-in-Publication Data
Names: Fairfield, Paul, 1966– author.
Title: Historical imagination : hermeneutics and cultural narrative / Paul Fairfield.
Description: Lanham : Rowman & Littlefield, [2022] | Includes bibliographical references and index. |
Summary: "A phenomenological and hermeneutical investigation into the nature of historical imagination. Carefully defining historical imagination, the book probes the relationship between the imaginative and the empirical, as well as the relationship between historical understanding and self-understanding"— Provided by publisher.
Identifiers: LCCN 2022010195 (print) | LCCN 2022010196 (ebook) | ISBN 9781538156537 (hardback) | ISBN 9781538156544 (epub)
Subjects: LCSH: History—Philosophy. | History—Methodology. | Historiography. | Narration (Rhetoric) | Imagination (Philosophy) | Hermeneutics.
Classification: LCC D16.8 .F315 2022 (print) | LCC D16.8 (ebook) | DDC 901—dc23/eng/20220519
LC record available at https://lccn.loc.gov/2022010195
LC ebook record available at https://lccn.loc.gov/2022010196

∞™ The paper used in this publication meets the minimum requirements of American National Standard for Information Sciences—Permanence of Paper for Printed Library Materials, ANSI/NISO Z39.48-1992.

For Gwyneth and Evangeline

Contents

INTRODUCTION	ix
CHAPTER 1: Historical Imagination I: Interpretation, Narrative, Constructivism	1
CHAPTER 2: Historical Imagination II: Evidence and Intentionality	27
CHAPTER 3: Early Christian Reimaginings	51
CHAPTER 4: Renaissance Reimaginings	75
CHAPTER 5: Enlightenment Reimaginings	97
CHAPTER 6: Historical Imagination and Cultural Studies	121
CONCLUSION	137
Notes	145
Index	155
About the Author	159

INTRODUCTION
Changing the Record

While exploring a virtual archive, I happened upon the following document, presented here without context and in English translation.

BEAUCHAMP, Jean	240239
Status	Married
Date of baptism	08-05-1644
Place of origin	La Rochelle (Ste-Marguerite) (Charente-Maritime) 17300
Current location	La Rochelle
Parents	Michel and Marie Roullet
Father's occupation	Gardener, then carpenter
Parents' wedding date	12-05-1630
Parents' wedding place	La Rochelle (Ste-Marguerite) (Charente-Maritime) (17300)
First mention of the country	1666
Occupation upon arrival	Migrant
Date of marriage	23-11-1666
Wedding place	Montreal (Notre Dame)
Spouse	Jeanne Loiselle
Death or burial	Pointe-aux-Trembles (Montreal), 04–05–1700

Remarks	His brothers and sisters are baptized in La Rochelle (Ste-Marguerite): Pierre, 14–03–1633; James (pioneer), 08–07–1635; Mary, 21–02–1638; Guillaume, born in 1646, buried at age 6 on 25–12–1652 (Notre-Dame). His father Michel Deschamps/Beauchamp was born in Nanteuil-Auriac-de-Bourzac (Dordogne, 24303). His paternal grandparents are Jean Deschamps, who died before 1630, and Louise de Lanterna. His maternal grandparents are Elie Roullet, who died before 1630, and Marie Bardonneau, married on 17–06–1607 in La Rochelle (Protestant Temple).
Identification	DGFQ, p. 60; DGFC, vol. 1, p. 33
Reference	AG-LAR, p. 17
Act copy	AD-17 scanned

What are we to make of this? Is this document "historical"? History itself, whatever we take this ponderous word to mean, knows almost nothing of Jean Beauchamp. This man held no political, ecclesiastical, or military office and was to all appearances an ordinary man of his time. The document itself is over three hundred years old and to my knowledge has been cited by no historian. Regarded as a bare particular, it carries minimal significance and likely none of it "historical."

Let us add a bit of context, for without this the document sheds little light. This text is what in the seventeenth century was called a *fichier origine*, a government document containing information regarding migrants to New France. The French were scrupulous recordkeepers, and the historical authenticity of texts of this kind is easily confirmed. What is in question is its significance, and if we are speaking historically then we are likely to say that both it and likely the man himself have none, but on what basis? This man was no Louis XIV; he played no major role in events that would later draw the attention of professional historians. Scholars who have researched this particular period and location have found no reason to speak of him but for the curious fact that shortly after arriving in Ville Marie (later renamed Montreal) he married a woman who had the distinction of being the first person born in the young colony to survive to adulthood and who for many years was also a student of Saint Marguerite Bourgeoys. Our Monsieur Beauchamp now warrants perhaps a footnote in historical accounts of this city or this saint, but likely not more. He is not a historical figure.

Or is he? Suppose now that the reader happens to possess the surname Beauchamp and discovers that this man is one's ancestor. Genealogy (not in Nietzsche's sense) is also history—an unassuming history, no doubt, and of probable interest to no one outside a particular family line. Be that as it may, the document, hitherto mute, now comes alive for us and assumes a meaning that may be small or large, depending most likely on the relation he bears to other persons of this line. There is the rudiment of a trail here that may be followed or indeed that demands to be, some thread of narrative which if tracked in the right way might issue in a story. The document is now historically significant, at least for the limited purpose of creating a genealogy. Monsieur Beauchamp was no Adam, but he did beget X, who begat Y, who begat Z, and so on. His place of origin and family relations are listed here, and many other items of information may be inferred from the general circumstances of the era and from other records of this kind. This is taking on the complexion of a narrative, and as it takes form it becomes possible to glimpse some meaning. As the story unfolds, from its roots in the old country to the trials and tribulations of the new, additional characters enter the stage, conflicts ensue, themes emerge, and time passes. It becomes possible by degrees for an interpreter to establish some meeting of minds with this individual and if not to see the world through his eyes then to know something of his story and to imagine, however impressionistically, what that existence might have been like, what he likely cared about and what he was up against.

Let us linger upon that moment when this ordinary document, or any of the countless artifacts that historians routinely deal with, comes alive and begins to speak to us. What transformation is this? What has happened might be compared to the transformation from a chronicle to a narrative in that some isolated fact or object begins to be regarded within a larger universality. Establishing relations is crucial here: seeing a text or a person in relation to other texts and persons, a time period, place, culture, institution, theme, conflict, or series of events affords a context in terms of which the particular may be interpreted. The bare particular defies understanding. It is neither significant, historical, nor even a source until it is regarded as an answer to a question, "significant for" its contribution to a larger series of events, a "source of" information about a matter into which we are inquiring, and historical insofar as it is seen as an episode in an *histoire*. The concept of evidence is similarly relational: a smoking gun is evidence not "in itself" but relative to a particular crime, and the same can be said of the various sources and evidence with which historians concern themselves. The transformation in our case consists in the realization that an authenticated document affords information that is subsumable within a larger configuration such as a temporal series. It is a link in a chain, and if we subtract this and all other possible chains then the document falls mute but for the nascent narrative that it already contains.

Some familiar hermeneutical themes are at work here. Temporality and narrative, the contextual nature of historical and indeed all interpretation, the doctrine of the hermeneutical circle and the reciprocity of universal and particular are a few. Historians are interpreters who in the course of their research deal at once with straightforward factual statements along with more debatable analytical claims, arguments, hypotheses, critiques, interrogations, relations, and syntheses that are simultaneously empirically rigorous and richly imaginative. They are detectives of a kind, but perhaps most ultimately they are storytellers whose business is to gather and arrange the myriad elements that hold some degree of historical relevance into a structure that contains at least the semblance of a beginning, middle, and end. The work is never complete and reinterpretation is always possible, but at some point when the historian has followed a trail for about as long and as thoroughly as the evidence seems to call for then the account reaches an end that is never more than a resting place. No historian has the last word, for any event into which they inquire has an inexhaustibility about it if we are speaking of its meaning. The human past can be compared to a text that is ancient, lengthy, written in a foreign language, frequently obscure, and in which many pages are missing or have been written over in ways that will sometimes arouse our suspicion.[1] Its interpretation is far from straightforward and any light that it sheds also casts a shadow. Historical knowledge is elusive under the best of conditions and the historiographer's task is no less so for the latter must comprehend at once what historians do and what happens to them, as Hans-Georg Gadamer put it, in the course of their doing, behind their back as it were.[2] The historian is interpreting a past that is living and to which the historian also belongs. The interpretive standpoint that historians bring with them is partial, interested, and theory-laden, and the text that they are endeavoring to understand has been preunderstood in ways of which they may or may not be aware. Some hermeneutic schema is already in play, and the resulting circularity is one upon which historiography must endeavor to shed light. One belongs or has been constituted by that which calls for interpretation and must configure or at times reconfigure what has already been prefigured, as Paul Ricoeur articulated this point.

Our historian of New France, to take an example chosen at random, wishes to know "what happened," also how and why. We want to "know the facts" undoubtedly, but the difficulty with facts is that there are simply too many of them, and until they are arranged into some intelligible order they do not speak. On a given day in 1666 Jean married Jeanne: so what? Who are they, what led up to this and what followed? Until we know the story as it unfolds through time, we have understood nothing, or nothing that bears a meaning that may be described as historical. Numerous philosophers of history in recent decades have described the centrality of narrative in this field of knowledge, and the account that follows takes this as our point of departure. Much, likely most, of this work does not acknowledge much indebtedness to philosophical hermeneutics, as the following account does, but whether one chooses to pay one's debts here or not it remains that many themes and hypotheses that centrally factor in a good deal of contemporary philosophy of history stem directly or indirectly from a trajectory of thought that runs approximately from Hegel through Nietzsche, Dilthey, Husserl, and Heidegger, to Gadamer, Ricoeur, and Foucault, among others, subsequently branching in different directions. The narrative hypothesis that is often associated with Hayden White and Frank Ankersmit has assumed a number of forms, and we shall take it up here as well. Historians, whatever else they do, are storytellers—of a different kind that novelists, undoubtedly, and in a way that bears upon what scholars in this discipline call "sources and evidence." They are beholden to facts, and many in this field have a long habit of emphasizing this point. We have no wish to deny this important theme but to ask what it means to be beholden in this way. Novelists are also beholden, as are artists in general. Not to "sources and evidence" but to something, for to say that they make it up out of nothing is a misconception. Thinkers in general are beholden in some way, free and yet on a trail that must be followed and in ways that are often demanding. There is something that one needs to "get right," and where the meaning of this is not captured by the correspondence theory of truth but involves the work of the imagination. Historical inquiry is detective work, and where the meaning of detection is not immediately evident. We are on a trail, following along, seeing how one fact or piece of evidence relates to another, grasping connections, regarding X in light of Y, interrogating and refuting, and doing a good deal more than piling up facts. We are arranging them—one might say composing them or, if this is too fanciful, ordering them, not according to an agenda conceived in advance but as "the facts" themselves seem to indicate or require. One tells the story that needs to be told, as it needs to be told. If it is an exaggeration to say that it tells itself, it remains that historians do not simply unearth fully constituted truths which they have merely to clean off and present to their readers in the form in which they find them. They appear to occupy something of an intermediate zone between discovery and invention; the facts, truths, and meanings about which they write are neither fully constituted prior to the historian's arrival upon the scene nor the opposite: constructions of the historian's own consciousness. This kind of intermediate zone is ambiguous to the core, and it is the kind of space in which hermeneutical philosophers spend a good deal of our time.

If our point of departure is the narrative hypothesis, let us begin with a preliminary statement of what this means. The texts that historians write and the knowledge that they produce both centrally bear upon the relating of events from the human past which they must arrange into an intelligible temporal sequence that includes a beginning, middle, and end, all of which are contingencies rather than absolutes and which the historian selects for the purpose of shedding light upon a particular topic or theme. We wish to know what happened, how and why, and something of its larger significance, and in pursuing this we are doing a great deal of selecting, arranging, and imagining. Knowing encompasses all of this and includes while also transcending straightforward factual statements of the "Michel begat Jean" variety. History and historical knowledge are likewise complicated, and the narrative configurations that emerge must be faithful to this while including a good deal of analysis, argumentation, and criticism which on the face of things appear more empirical than literary. Historians are not poets but researchers, one may say empiricists of a kind, although any empiricism will need to be squared with what can look like its opposite, an interpretive artfulness more readily associated with hermeneutics and postmodernism. The temptation to opt for one narrow theoretical camp or the other at this point can be strong but ought to be resisted for the reason that choosing either an empiricist realism or postmodern constructivism will bring to light at best half of a complex picture. A phenomenologically sound historiography must take seriously what historians have long reported about the authority of sources and evidence or a position that we might call common sense empiricism while also thematizing the art of narrative configuration to which any empiricism will appear to stand opposed and which, upon closer inspection, likely does not. What historians do, what they say they do, and what happens to them in the doing are all in question if what we are seeking to understand is the nature of historical knowledge.

The account that follows may be described as hermeneutical for a couple of reasons. It follows a broadly similar trajectory of thought as that alluded to above and owes perhaps a special debt to Paul Ricoeur and Richard Kearney, two hermeneutical writers who have done much to advance our understanding of the imagination in particular. We shall also be speaking of some familiar hermeneutical themes that are central to an account of historiography that strives to do justice at once to the historian's longstanding accent on empirical rigor as well as the narrative hypothesis. Historians are interpreters of meaning at the same time that they are discoverers of "what happened"; their knowledge is a synthesis of a myriad cognitive acts—storytelling, questioning, gathering, sifting, abbreviating, assessing, authenticating, hypothesizing, demonstrating, critiquing—and narrative elements from particular characters and events to documents and artifacts, conflicts and themes, reasons and motivations, all of which are in play and must be held together in composing texts that exhibit the basic structure of a narrative. Humanly understandable events possess an interpretability and an inexhaustibility that historians often have an eye for, a meaningful dimension to which the old empiricist language of representation and causation does not do justice and which a more aesthetic vocabulary may.

Ricoeur's analysis in his three-volume *Time and Narrative* continues to employ a vocabulary of representation and Aristotelian mimesis, and of particular importance for us is where he parts company with White in maintaining that the human past is not chronicle-like but has a "prenarrative quality" that readily lends itself to narrative form. Whether we are speaking of history or fiction, the storytelling art is intermediate between imposition and discovery; the order or structure that every narrative contains is neither wholly invented and projected onto experiences that hitherto were without it nor strictly found within them. Instead, we must speak of narrative as a reinterpretation of what has already been understood or preunderstood, a creative redescription that can modify and enrich an understanding that had been not absent but inchoate. In analyzing mimesis, Ricoeur introduces a triad of prefiguration, configuration, and refiguration which carries a good deal of importance for historiography. Human action and experience are temporally structured and symbolically mediated from the outset. The historian's task is not to create these out of nothing but to raise them to a higher order of interpretive clarity. In speaking of the "prenarrative quality of experience" Ricoeur holds that "there is no human experience that is not already mediated by symbolic systems and, among them, by narratives," while time itself "becomes human time to the extent that it is organized after the manner of a narrative."[3] Historians, like other storytellers, configure or refine material that is not raw data but a bearer of meaning to which the configurative act strives to remain faithful and which the reader will later refigure in the act of reading.

Ricoeur builds upon Clifford Geertz's anthropological insights according to which, as the former put it, "we might speak of an implicit or immanent symbolism, in opposition to an explicit or autonomous one," a symbolism that is public and "not in the mind, not a psychological operation destined to guide action, but a meaning incorporated into action and decipherable from it by other actors in the social interplay." This order of meaning is culturally operative, prereflective, and symbolically mediated: "Geertz speaks in this sense of 'systems of interacting symbols,' of 'patterns of interworking meanings.' Before being a text, symbolic mediation has a texture. To understand a ritual act is to situate it within a ritual, set within a cultic system, and by degrees within the whole set of conventions, beliefs, and institutions that make up the symbolic framework of a culture." The imagination works on material that is preunderstood by virtue of the culture in which the storyteller stands, and if it can be said that "plot is an imitation of action" it must be kept in mind that actions themselves are always already both temporal and intelligible, albeit in a preliminary way. The poetic act of "emplotment" is no pure invention but "is grounded in a preunderstanding of the world of action, its meaningful structures, its symbolic resources, and its temporal character. These features are described rather than deduced." Imaginative descriptions of the past are not pure constructions but reconstructions which supplement or transform meaning, thus neither creating nor representing in the traditional empiricist sense of copying it. The "semantic innovation" that imaginative activity introduces

> lies in the inventing of another work of synthesis—a plot. By means of the plot, goals, causes, and chance are brought together within the temporal unity of a whole and complete action. It is this synthesis of the heterogeneous that brings together narrative close to metaphor . . .. In both cases the semantic innovation can be carried back to the productive imagination and, more precisely, to the schematism that is its signifying matrix. In new metaphors the birth of a new semantic pertinence marvelously demonstrates what an imagination can be that produces things according to rules: "being good at making metaphors," said Aristotle, "is equivalent to being perceptive of resemblances." But what is it to be perceptive of resemblance if not to inaugurate the similarity by bringing together terms that at first seem "distant," then suddenly "close"? (Ricoeur, 74, 3) Any such "change of distance in logical space," as he puts it, "is the work of the productive imagination."[4]

The imagination "sees as," "grasps together," and reinterprets what it sees, by means of metaphor and narrative in particular but also within a larger schema that is at once conceptual and preconceptual, cultural and linguistic. While mindful that "[h]istorians do argue in a formal, explicit, discursive way," Ricoeur holds, to cite him once more, "that their field of argumentation is considerably vaster than that of general laws" while "their own modes of arguing . . . belong to the narrative domain."[5] Kearney has provided further elucidation of this theme, arguing that no chasm separates the imaginary from the real and that, echoing Ricoeur, "Every society participates in a socio-political *imaginaire*. This represents the ensemble of mythic or symbolic discourses which serve to motivate and guide its citizens. The 'social imaginary' can function as an *ideology* to the extent that it reaffirms a society in its identity by recollecting its 'foundational symbols.'"[6] Cultural self-understanding is largely a function of the stories that the members of a historical community tell themselves about a shared past. Thus, in the ancient world, "[m]yths were stories people told themselves in order to explain themselves to themselves and to others. But it was Aristotle who first developed this insight into a philosophical position when he argued, in his *Poetics*, that the art of storytelling—defined as the dramatic imitating and plotting of human action—is what gives us a *shareable world*." History and life itself are "always *on the way* to narrative," neither existing at any moment in a pre-storied condition nor culminating in an unrevisable account, while all storytelling is "a kind of creative retelling" of an existence that is inherently storied, "a nascent plot in search of a midwife," as Kearney puts it.[7]

While I draw upon aspects of Ricoeur's and Kearney's work in what follows, I shall not be following either account closely and will be drawing upon a number of thinkers, not all of whom could be characterized as hermeneutical. The account that I articulate can be so described, if a hermeneutical account of the imagination is one that holds that this activity of mind, as the latter has expressed it, "lies at the very heart of our existence," and indeed "[s]o much so . . . that we would not be human without it."[8] It far transcends the capacity to reckon with quasi-visual images or faded representations and goes to the root of what minds do. This basic position, traces of which can be found in an array of philosophers from Nietzsche and Dilthey to Heidegger and Merleau-Ponty, Gadamer and Geertz, among numerous others, will constitute our point of departure in what follows, and while narrative plays a central role in the argument of this study, it remains that storytelling is not all that the imagination or historians themselves do. We are speaking of a capacity of mind that supplies all of us with a synthetic, prereflective, and affectively charged hold upon our world, a fundamental orientation that is historically inherited and perspectival while opening onto a past and a future where uncertainty and possibilities abound.

There are periods, most notably in intellectual history, in which the workings of historical imagination become especially visible. These are what we might call imagination's active or creative phases, during which relatively major alterations are introduced into a culture's self-understanding through a re-envisioning of its future and a re-narrating of its past. A given society lives and moves and has its being in a network of relations, artifacts, beliefs, values, practices, institutions, and so on, in a lifeworld that is never without socially shared narratives and narrative threads in terms of which its members come to know what they are about. Becoming what we are crucially involves a self-understanding that is an appropriation of tradition, as Gadamer in particular taught us to see, and it is an appropriation that is sometimes also a departure. Early Christian thinkers adopted not only a new divinity and institution but also a new way of imagining time. Who they themselves were, or understood themselves to be, was thoroughly bound up with where they stood in historical time, and this was a radical departure from the cyclical view of history that the Romans had appropriated from the Greeks. These imitators of Christ no longer looked back to a heroic age but forward to a coming kingdom, and it was no small modification but a transformation some centuries in the making in understanding and self-understanding. Time itself now had a teleological structure that was nonsense to the Greeks and their Roman intellectual heirs. Not only the divinities had changed but also the historical record, both its narration of the past and its conception of the future, and a similar observation applies to the later transitional periods that were the renaissance and the enlightenment. Here again it is not only scientific or philosophical doctrines that changed but also larger cultural narratives and imaginative schemas, and again not overnight but in ways that exhibited profound continuity with what had come before. Historically minded intellectuals were changing the conversation in ways that bear recalling not only since the consequences remain with us but because if our topic is the nature of historical knowledge it profits us to reexamine what happened during these relatively creative phases in intellectual history, when past and future alike were imaginatively reconfigured as part of a larger movement of ideas. When what Michael Oakeshott called the conversation of humanity takes a turn, worldviews are revised, stories retold, and history reconfigured in a process that is more overt than what transpires during less eventful eras. Some creative modification occurs, and the dynamics that underlie this must be thematized. Shining a spotlight on the times—what was happening, who did what, who wrote what, and so on—and the manner in which the terms of the conversation were altered sheds light on the historical imagination itself. We shall speak of this as a certain kind of activity or set of activities, and to understand an activity it is best to see it in operation rather than as a static object.

The following inquiry focuses on the imagination in the context of historiography. Our hypothesis is that an expansive conception of historical imagination may be articulated through a combination of phenomenological-hermeneutical analysis and historical inquiry into particular time periods in which the past or major elements of it were significantly reconceived by historians and other intellectuals. While its relatively active phases find the imagination engaging in no qualitatively different activity than what historians carry out in the more usual course of their investigations, analysis of a few such eras brings into sharper relief themes that are operative in historical interpretation in general. We begin in the first chapter with an account of what we might call the subject side of historical imagination, or what the historian brings to bear upon evidentiary material in fashioning narratives that are at once well-grounded in historical sources and richly disclosive. This part of the analysis focuses on the manner in which historians deploy an interpretive and imaginative schema (*imaginaire*) in arranging relevant material into narrative form, a theme that lies at the heart of the contemporary debate in philosophy of history between empiricist conceptions of historical knowledge and postmodern accounts that defend various conceptions of narrative constructivism. Chapter 1 analyzes some familiar themes at stake in this debate, including constructivism, narrative, universality and particularity, and a few related topics. A relatively encompassing view of historical imagination and cognition, I maintain, helps us avoid the pitfalls of idealism and to advance a few steps beyond an empiricism/postmodernism opposition that may be getting old.

The second chapter continues with this general theme, this time focusing on the object side of historical imagination and continuing the effort begun in chapter 1 to overcome the difficulties of the constructivist model. Post-empiricist and postmodern philosophers of history have well demonstrated that historians are storytellers yet have paid too little attention to the nature of storytelling itself and the way in which good stories, as many novelists tell us, in an important sense tell themselves. Our phenomenological-hermeneutical approach draws in part upon Jeff Mitscherling's non-idealist reformulation of intentionality and the cognitive activity of what he describes as "tracking intentionality," a phenomenological hypothesis that Mitscherling has applied within the field of aesthetics but that is capable of shedding important light as well upon some fundamental issues in historiography. Historians do not construct the past so much as follow a trail that they do not invent but that has being in a sense to which neither empiricism nor constructivism has done justice and that calls for phenomenological analysis. In the process we shall revisit the question of the relation between subjectivity and the historical object and also the notion of historical empathy.

The next three chapters analyze how historical *imaginaires* change and some of the factors that are at work in the transition from one historical era to the next as well as the play of continuity and discontinuity that is visible in what are later regarded as historical turning points. The philosophical argument of chapters 1 and 2 may be illustrated by looking at how historically minded writers during a few important transitional periods—late antiquity, the renaissance, and early modernity—imagined and especially reimagined their respective pasts, with a focus on their different recountings of Greco-Roman civilization. Chapter 3 looks at how a number of early Christian thinkers were reimagining their classical predecessors, the emergence of the notion of "paganism," and some related themes. The historical focus continues through chapters 4 and 5 where the topic shifts first to renaissance reimaginings of the same Greco-Roman civilization and late antiquity and, second, to enlightenment recountings of their ancient and medieval forebears.

The account of historical imagination that I develop in theoretical terms in chapters 1 and 2 and illustrate historically in chapters 3 through 5 carries implications for cultural and area studies, some of which I shall explore in the final chapter. Scholars in cultural studies are far from agreeing upon a definition of culture, a methodology, or any higher universality with reference to which they may interpret cultural phenomena. As with historical research, there is a need for universality in these disciplines and the notions of imagination and imaginative schemas, and of culture as crucially involving these, goes some way toward providing this. An era, also a culture, is or has a particular cultural-historical orientation that is conceptual but also more than this. Many of the same factors that come into play in historiography and the historical imagination have clear counterparts in cultural and area studies.

Developing these themes may go some way toward clarifying the methodological basis of these disciplines.

The dubious reputation that "revisionist history" has long held owes largely to its association with ideologies that have so often motivated their adherents to amend our understanding of the past for motives that are merely political. The worry is justified, of course, but this should not lead us to overlook the many ways in which historians are sometimes legitimately compelled to reimagine a past that is nothing absolute but a legacy that continues to claim us even as it is the task of historical interpretation to overcome alienation and to make contact with a past that is other in the fashion of an ancestor—different and also not different but of a piece with what we are. It is a living past into which historians inquire, and as is invariably the case when our objects of interpretation are human actions and sufferings, matters become more complicated the more closely we examine them and no neat separation of subject and object or past and present are to be found. All four are relata; the relation between values in both of these pairings is internal and dialectical, as the study that follows attempts to show, and the same can be said of the relation between particular activities of the historical imagination and the imaginative schemas in or from which they operate. If historians are a certain kind of storyteller, the narratives that they fashion are neither inventions nor discoveries but something intermediate in which we find a relentless back-and-forth between the activity of the subject and the *imaginaire* that largely defines the historian's perspective. Since neither pole in a dialectic has primacy, we shall be defending neither an objectivist nor an idealist historiography but one that endeavors to avoid the pitfalls of both. A hermeneutical account encompasses the interpretive as well as the pre- and re-interpretive dimensions of historical inquiry, all of which call into play an imagination that is on a trail it did not devise.

CHAPTER 1

Historical Imagination I: Interpretation, Narrative, Constructivism

Might one not say of historians what could equally be said of philosophers: they work on the border, such as it is, between art and science or partake of both in their investigations into human affairs and its myriad complexities? Both work with methods and disciplinary conventions at the same time that they are storytellers, and argue and demonstrate in roughly equal proportion that they speculate and metaphorize. One may emphasize one side of this division or the other, on the basis of some theoretical commitment perhaps, but there is little point in doing so if historical inquiry pays no heed to such a border, even as we might wish that it did. Accounts we have long heard from the epistemologically—especially empirically—minded still need to be taken seriously even while more current trends lean hard in an antithetical direction. Our questions bear upon the nature of historical inquiry and historical knowledge, and to answer them we shall need to move beyond an art-science distinction which has become problematic if not altogether obsolete. Historians are simultaneously empiricists of a kind and storytellers, among other things, but in view of the ancient and still extant tension between *logos* and *mythos* this synthesis continues to appear counterintuitive and in need of elucidation. Exactly what is it that historians do, how do they go about it, and how does all of this compare to what philosophers, scientists, or artists do? These are questions of historiography, and where the distinction between this discipline and history itself approaches the vanishing point. What historians do, what they say they do, and what philosophers of history have said about what they say is our topic, and our hypothesis will be that the concept of imagination, in a particular and expansive connotation of the term, sheds a good deal of light on this line of questioning.

Why imagination? Why not knowledge, inquiry, investigation, or some similar term that would bring what historians do into closer association with truth or accentuate its cognitive dimension? Our intent will be to dispense with none of these terms—cognition, truth, knowledge, inquiry—but to understand what scholars in this field are up to and something about the texts that they produce, to get to the root of a form of knowledge that is as old as our tradition and as relevant to the present as any knowledge could be. There is no understanding the historical present but by the reflected light that is afforded by a knowledge of the past, just as individual self-understanding is made possible by an account of how one came to be who one is. We are how we have come to be and what we are on the way to becoming, not a being that is frozen in time. Historical epistemology and ontology are brought together—historical hermeneutics is a preferable term, and the account that follows may be characterized as hermeneutical for a few reasons. First, we shall be drawing upon themes that have been previously articulated by some of the principal representatives of hermeneutics including Wilhelm Dilthey, Friedrich Nietzsche, Martin Heidegger, Hans-Georg Gadamer, Paul Ricoeur, Richard Kearney, and some others, and also the account that follows regards the practice of historical investigation as fundamentally interpretive and imaginative in a sense of these terms that will require clarification. We shall speak of historical imagination as fundamental and as comprehending at once what the historian brings to a given line of inquiry as well as everything that falls on the object side of the division between subjectivity and objectivity. This division itself, of course, is notoriously vague and the notions of imagination and imaginative schemas will also go some way toward clarifying this matter, as will the phenomenological concept of intentionality which we shall discuss at greater length in chapter 2.

The focus of the present chapter is what we might call the subject side of historical imagination, or what the historian brings to bear upon evidentiary material in fashioning accounts that are at once well-grounded in the sources and richly imaginative. Our analysis focuses on the manner in which historians deploy an interpretive and imaginative schema of one kind or another—either wittingly, behind their back, or some combination—in arranging relevant material into narrative form, a theme that lies at the heart of the contemporary debate between empiricist notions of historical knowledge and postmodern accounts that defend various conceptions of narrative constructivism. This chapter analyzes some themes that are at stake in this debate, including constructivism, narrative, imagination and imaginaries, universality and particularity, and a few related topics. I shall argue that a more encompassing view of historical imagination and cognition than we find in the literature helps us to avoid the pitfalls of idealism and to advance a few steps beyond the empiricism/postmodernism opposition.

The concept of imagination will do a good deal of labor in the account that follows. By this term we shall mean a capacity of mind that far transcends the production of quasi-visual images to one that is verbal, as Ricoeur has shown, but also more than this. I shall speak of historical imagination as nothing separate and apart from historical reality but a capacity and activity that brings us into working touch with the past, that opens onto lifeworlds that are distant in time and place but not wholly other to our times or fully beyond reach, and that strives for comprehensiveness and "a sense of the whole."[1] Dilthey, as one scholar notes, "saw that our lived experience of the human world gives us a sense of being a part of it," a sense that is unquestionably vague but fundamental to our experience of history. "Given this pre-given relatedness to the world, the task of the imagination is not to produce connections where none were visible, but to specify an indeterminately felt connectedness and deepen it to bring it into focus."[2] Let us think of imagination as a term encompassing at once the "images" with which it has been associated since Plato along with stories and story fragments, various kinds of metaphors and ciphers, rhetorical tropes and affectively charged interpretations, none of which clashes either necessarily or in the usual course of inquiry with truth, argument, or evidence. Imagination incorporates them all and aims for a synoptic view of the past that is less a construction than an elucidation, an allowing something that was hidden to be seen with some relative clarity and verisimilitude. I shall suggest we conceive of imagination not narrowly as a subjective inventing of something that stands at some remove from reality but more fundamentally as a mental activity that underlies a good many specific cognitive acts from questioning to remembering, selecting, abbreviating, evaluating, hypothesizing, doubting, and some others. When historians imagine particular episodes from the past, they are doing nothing that is less cognitively sophisticated than what empiricists will speak of—"fictionalizing" or otherwise dressing up into aesthetically pleasing form a truth that has already been grasped. They are grasping it for the first time, not cooking raw data for the data as they always already are for us are already cooked, preunderstood, or prefigured as phenomenologists, hermeneuticists, pragmatists, and postmodernists have variously brought to our attention for some time now. It is not only the artistic imagination that gives rise to meaning, transforms, glimpses possibilities, configures and reconfigures, notices connections and tendencies, sees-as and synthesizes, and subsumes particulars under universals. Historians and knowers in general do this, sometimes in conformity with methods and sometimes not, depending on the object of knowledge and the discipline. Historians, or so I shall argue, work in the space between objective discovery and subjective creation, neither unearthing then representing wholly determinate happenings from the past nor conjuring them out of thin air but engaging in an activity akin to conversing or participating in a dialectic in which subjectivity and objectivity are mutually constituted and past and present are understood together. They bring a system of prejudices, an imaginative schema, and a disciplinary perspective to bear on the past, not to speak for it but to make it possible for it to speak at all, and where the distinction itself is problematic. Imagination is there from the beginning—taking in what is there to be seen and going to work on it in a single gesture. The model is not a judge "hearing" evidence in the sense of taking it in without prejudice at time T1 and at T2 retiring to chambers to imagine what took place and deliberate upon a verdict; indeed it is implausible that judges themselves do this. We need to thematize the "pre-"—prejudice, preunderstanding, prefiguring—for it is here that historical and all interpretation receives its fundamental orientation and anticipatory trajectory.

Central to a conception of the historical imagination is the role played by narrative, as historiographers and philosophers of history have pointed out for a few decades now. Historians, among the various other things that they do, are storytellers, as a great many scholars have brought to our attention. The more noteworthy early proponents of this view include R. G. Collingwood, Arthur Danto, Louis Mink, W. B. Gallie, Morton White, and Paul Ricoeur while Hayden White and Frank Ankersmit have become its best-known contemporary defenders. The basic hypothesis is that when reporting upon the past historians configure what they see in a way roughly analogous with the novelist, and that it is in narrative form that the history of any period or event is understood and communicated. W. H. Walsh makes the point this way: "What every historian seeks for is not a bare recital of unconnected facts, but a smooth narrative in which every event falls as it were into its natural place and belongs to an intelligible whole. In this respect the ideal of the historian is in principle identical with that of the novelist or the dramatist. Just as a good novel or a good play appears to consist not in a series of unrelated episodes, but in the orderly development of the complex situation from which it starts, so a good history possesses a certain unity of plot or theme. And where we fail to find such a unity we experience a feeling of dissatisfaction: we believe we have not understood the facts we set out to investigate as well as we should."[3] Hayden White, in his seminal *Metahistory*, speaks of the historical text as "a verbal structure in the form of a narrative prose discourse. Histories (and philosophies of history as well) combine a certain amount of 'data,' theoretical concepts for 'explaining' these data, and a narrative structure for their presentation as an icon of sets of events presumed to have occurred in times past. In addition, I maintain, they contain a deep structural content which is generally poetic, and specifically linguistic, in nature, and which serves as the precritically accepted paradigm of what a distinctively 'historical' explanation should be. This paradigm functions as the 'metahistorical' element in all historical works that are more comprehensive in scope than the monograph or archival report."[4]

White's *Metahistory* runs well over four hundred pages, but its main argument can be summarized briefly. Historical accounts in their basic structure assume the form of a usually complex narrative which the historian does not strictly speaking find in the events themselves but rather invents and imposes, again in analogous (not identical) fashion to the novelist who is free to create a story as he or she pleases. Historians are not quite so free, for they are beholden to sources and evidence, but the central point is that they are not naive empiricists but poets of a kind. The narratives they craft are constructed, not discovered, and where the distinction is rather categorical. Human beings do not enact stories in the present; events themselves of which historians will later speak are not experienced in narrative form but simply happen. Here is how White formulates this important point: "It is sometimes said that the aim of the historian is to explain the past by 'finding,' 'identifying,' or 'uncovering' the 'stories' that lie buried in chronicles; and that the difference between 'history' and 'fiction' resides in the fact that the historian 'finds' his stories, whereas the fiction writer 'invents' his. This conception of the historian's task, however, obscures the extent to which 'invention' also plays a part in the historian's operations. The same event can serve as a different kind of element of many different historical stories, depending on the role it is assigned in a specific motific characterization of the set to which it belongs. The death of the king may be a beginning, an ending, or simply a transitional event in three different stories. In the chronicle, this event is simply 'there' as an element of a series; it does not 'function' as a story element."[5] Events happen in the manner of a chronicle or in a "one thing after another" kind of way, and it is only the historian's poetic retrospection that gives them narrative form, for instance, by placing them at the beginning or end of a particular sequence. Another sequence might have been chosen; this is a free decision that a historian will later make while the event itself is dumb. Mink formulates the point succinctly: "stories are not lived but told" at a later time, sometimes by historians.[6] An event's narrative quality is nothing implicit or inherent to the event but a transference from aesthetics, and where an historian's options, according to White, include four "prefigurative (tropological) strategies"—metaphor, synecdoche, metonymy, and irony—as well as four genres—romance, comedy, tragedy, and satire or some combination thereof—and also four ideological preferences—liberalism, radicalism, conservatism, anarchism (White exhibits a curious fascination with the number four).[7] The choice of narrative strategy is in no way bound by the events themselves but is free, again as a novelist is at liberty to take a storyline wherever they choose.

Through the art of what Ricoeur termed "emplotment," the historian "integrates into a meaningful unity components as heterogeneous as circumstances, calculations, actions, aids and obstacles, and, lastly, results" of human action both intended and unintended.[8] Ricoeur, White, and other narrativists differ on particulars, but the basic hypothesis has become widely accepted among philosophers of history not limited to postmodernists and hermeneuticists. Historians do more than report facts; they interpret them in the sense of imposing a meaning that is afforded by the narrative form and not discovered. Patterns, relations, tendencies, and causes are similarly invented, and if they are often spoken of as if they belong to events themselves this is an illusion. Invention can happen behind the historian's back and often does, but it remains that the narratives they relate are not real but quasi-fictional representations constructed after the fact. The transformation from sequence to story is in every case an imaginative construction, and while this may be well or poorly carried out, any qualitative judgment we form will rest on aesthetic, not factual, considerations. It is a reading of the past in which, as White and many other postmodernists hold, "anything goes." Citing White with approval, Keith Jenkins writes:

> For we could only presume the "the facts of the matter" set limits to the sorts of stories/narratives we can tell if we believe that the events themselves have in them a latent story form and a definitive, knowable plot structure. In which case—*if they did*—then we could indeed dismiss, say, a comic or pastoral story "from the ranks of competing narratives as manifestly false to the facts—or at least to the facts that matter—of the Nazi era." But of course they don't. For as White says elsewhere "one must face the fact that when it comes to apprehending the historical record, there are no grounds to be found in the historical record itself for preferring one way of construing meanings over another."

The concept of historical truth does little work here when it is not denied outright, a factor that has led many historians to take a suspicious view of this now popular thesis, particularly its bolder formulations such as that defended by Jenkins. As he formulates this view, "historians are not only able to impose any narrative (substance) they like on 'the past' but they *have* to do so given that the past, however construed, has no narrative substance of its own."[9]

The conception of historical consciousness and imagination that I propose to defend accepts a form of the narrative hypothesis that departs in significant ways from White, Jenkins, and many of their fellow postmodernists. Jean-François Lyotard pointed out that "[s]cience"—and scientific conceptions of historiography no less—"has always been in conflict with narratives," while postmodern and many other thinkers endeavor either to play down the conflict or to eliminate it.[10] I wish to eliminate it, and without jettisoning truth, reason, evidence, or imperatives of disciplinary rigor which have traditionally gone under the name of objectivity. If historical objectivism—positivism, naive empiricism—no longer seem like tenable options, we need not regard postmodern constructivism or idealism as the only alternative, as many are currently quick to do. The course I wish to chart is intermediate between the two while being somewhat more sympathetic to the postmodern position than the empiricist.

Let us focus on the constructivist thesis which White, Jenkins, and other postmodern philosophers of history typically propose. Different writers formulate this view differently, of course, but let us characterize the thesis roughly this way: human beings dwell in a world of our own invention, less a natural world than a cultural one where culture is spoken of more or less in accordance with Clifford Geertz's view "that man is an animal suspended in webs of significance he himself has spun, I take culture to be those webs, and the analysis of it to be therefore not an experimental science in search of law but an interpretive one in search of meaning."[11] The analysis Geertz was speaking of is anthropological, but the same can be said of the historical: we are not seeking laws but interpretive meanings. Meanings themselves are not discovered but imagined, where this means produced, invented, imposed, projected, constituted, or constructed, all of which are rough synonyms. "Because," as Jouni-Matti Kuukkanen expresses it, "there is no narrative structure or any other 'untold story' in the past, there is nothing to tell and nothing to discover, even if we had the 'access.' The past only becomes narratively structured through the imagination and the hand of the historian, who imposes order and meaning there."[12] It is not only narrative structure that does not exist prior to the historian happening upon the scene but any order, meaning, cause, relationship, event, and indeed "the past" itself. According to White, "The historical past is a theoretically motivated construction, existing only in the books and articles published by professional histories,"[13] while Willie Thompson articulates the constructivist's point still more succinctly: "the past *is* essentially nothing other than what historians write."[14] The past, for Jenkins, is "a blank canvas or screen onto which historians can paint or project any history to suit."[15] It is constituted, not found, and an ontological Rubicon separates the two.

This is of course an extension to historiography of the same constructivist thesis that postmodernists and many others apply quite generally to the world of human experience, and the issues it raises echo those in cognate fields. Postmodernists typically prefer the strong version of this thesis, that "historical interpretations," as White puts it, "are little more than projections," although his choice of "little" rather than "nothing" in this passage is curious.[16] What is this little? It would appear to be events as recorded in a chronicle: now this, now that, leading nowhere, coming from nowhere, bearing no relation to other events, and devoid of significance. All of that comes later and is created by the pen of the historian in no way that admits of what one might call grounds. Talk of grounds or justification embroils us in pointless epistemological and metaphysical debates, although White qualifies this by asserting that "the best [only?] grounds for choosing one perspective on history rather than another are ultimately aesthetic and moral rather than epistemological."[17] Historians are poet-moralists if not complete relativists. Jenkins may be overstating it when he writes, "We're all relativists now," and adds "that's fine," but not by much.[18] Any narrative form, order, or meaning of which a historian speaks has no counterpart in historical reality, and their construction cannot be justified in the ways that traditionally minded historians believe but at most on an aesthetic or moral-political basis.

Interpretation itself in every case involves a certain act of violence on the part of the historian, and it is a violence to which "history itself" does not object. Events of the past not being inherently tragic, romantic, or anything else, they raise no protest in being differently emplotted. Indeed, how could "the past" raise objections when it does not exist until historians take up their pens? "The given" or "the real" being a myth of objectivist epistemology, there is nothing outside of or prior to linguistic description, or not after the linguistic turn which has exercised a similar effect upon historiography as other branches of contemporary philosophy. The only matter to which language refers is itself, all being—including the historical past—is for us and according to us, and any "data" are only previous constructions which we have forgotten are constructions. Historians are no different than the rest of us, suspended in webs of our own linguistic and cultural creation which we mistakenly project onto the world. There is either no knowable reality or no reality that is prior to language, and therefore nothing for historians to get right or wrong. The intellectual debt to Michel Foucault and Jacques Derrida is especially noteworthy, although the philosophical sources of this view within much recent philosophy of history are many.

Whether we are speaking of the historical past or the cultural present, the real and the imaginary are indivisible, and narrative is the preferred form of interpretation by which to speak of them. The vocabulary of narrative, imagination, and imaginaries has made the rounds in recent decades, from philosophy and historiography to disciplines of the humanities and social sciences quite generally as well as a good deal of popular discourse beyond the academy. Within philosophy it was brought about by the linguistic turn in analytic thought and by a variety of phenomenological, hermeneutical, and postmodern writers in the continental tradition, and while I am broadly sympathetic to the narrative-imaginative turn in philosophy of history of which White has been the principal spokesman I also suspect that a course has been overcorrected. Standing ideas on their heads and swinging pendulums, in my view, are a recipe for error when the better move is to reject what Nietzsche called "the faith in opposite values" for a neither-nor position.[19] Neither historical objectivism nor idealism (constructivism, subjectivism) is the better route provided such a viewpoint can be articulated, and this is always a tall order when a dichotomy is as old and deeply rooted as this one.

Let us turn more directly to the notions of imagination and imaginative schemas (*imaginaires*), both of which have received a good deal of attention in the recent literature. Both concepts have received varying interpretations and at the heart of all of them is a basic hypothesis which applied to the philosophy of history might be formulated this way: any knowledge of the human past is conditioned by a finite and historically specific point of view which can be understood as a broad framework of language, beliefs, values, tradition, practical knowledge, stories, symbols, and other cultural artifacts, all of which afford a perspective from which the past becomes accessible for us and in such a way that any distinction between real and imagined is difficult and perhaps impossible to sustain. Thus formulated, I am prepared to endorse this hypothesis as well, but the details will be important. A little more specifically, I shall speak of an imaginative schema as a framework of interpretation that is historically emergent, largely (not wholly) presupposed and prereflective, encompassing and sometimes totalizing, highly variable, cerebral but also (and especially) embodied, self-justifying and self-serving, affords self-understanding and a range of possibilities, and includes a conception of the good along with stories, metaphors, and characters that illustrate this conception. Like Hegel's *Sittlichkeit*, a schema of this kind emerges from the soil of a given culture or it is the soil, and it is highly valued by those who see and navigate their way through the world from within it. Having a self-evident appearance, it often does not take kindly to critical questioning by those who do not share its worldview and can become a fighting creed. When they do not see one another as rivals, different imaginative schemas tend to regard each other with mutual incomprehension, rather as different species occupying the same barnyard. Examples include the different forms of monotheism, polytheism, modern science-technology, nationalism, democracy, capitalism, individualism, Marxism, feminism, progressivism, and romanticism. George H. Taylor mentions "capitalist, constitutional, cosmopolitan, democratic, ecological, economic, feminist, global, historical, hyper-modern, humanitarian, nationalist, political, politico-juridical, populist and religious" social imaginaries, and one could undoubtedly add to the list. Every society has one and often more than one. Indeed, it is little exaggeration to say that social reality itself is constituted by a social imaginary and that reasoning itself is conditioned by it. As Taylor points out, reason itself has its conditions of possibility, and "It is a mistake to attempt to convince others of the errors of their social imaginary by appeal simply to 'reason'; that appeal will usually not reach the deeper values that a social imaginary may protect."[20] The practice of reasoning has already been prefigured by a schema which, as Saulius Geniusas expresses it, "form[s] the contours of action, intuition, knowledge, and understanding" and "predelineates the general outlines of human experience and of the human world."[21]

I suggest we think of the historical imagination as a capacity or activity that operates from within one or another such framework and not, as the imagination has often been conceived, as either radically unconditioned or removed from the order of truth. The way that events from the past show up in our consciousness invariably has a "for us" quality that typically escapes our notice and that needs to be made explicit. Their appearance is simultaneously constituted and receptive—these two at once or in a single gesture which is difficult to conceptualize but that a variety of especially phenomenological and hermeneutical thinkers have been endeavoring to think for a long time now. Let us consider a couple of ordinary examples. An event such as a large-scale natural disaster might be regarded by a monotheist as an act of divine intervention or punishment for sin. From the standpoint of this imaginative schema, this may be an entirely logical inference while within a modern scientific framework it is not on the radar of possibilities. Any inquiry into this event will not consist in any paradigm-neutral marshalling of reasons as to why we should see it one way or another but presupposes a worldview that is taken as given and that informs what will count as a reason. Much of the work of interpretation has been done in advance, and any resulting conversation between the monotheist and scientist is ill fated. The same happens in politics: the nationalist will regard the decline of a traditional language as a cause for lament or a call to action while the individualist may see it as a personal choice and an object of indifference. Any debate between the two will quickly lead to an impasse and mutual recrimination. What appears as a reason for action within one schema appears as a reason for inaction in the other, and the issue is this appearing. Its showing up that way is nothing given but is made possible by a framework of narratives, symbols, values, beliefs, and meanings that are affectively charged and largely tacit. Our sense of what matters again cannot be separated from the "for us"; for our individualist, the disappearance of a tradition simply does not matter—not unless some number of persons prefer it, in which case it would not be disappearing. For our nationalist, it is a disaster, and for reasons of which the individualist will not feel the weight.

We shall look at historical examples in chapters 3 through 5, but briefly for now: consider an event such as the fall of the (western) Roman empire in the fifth century. For the lover of classical antiquity this event represented the end of an era and a fall from greatness, even wholesale civilizational collapse and a transition into medieval barbarism. This old story still has its proponents, but within a Christian worldview it not only does not ring true but also represents almost the opposite of the truth. For the latter, this event coincided with the development of Christian institutions; it was no cause for lament but a transition into a different and altogether preferable form of spirituality. Historians can and do debate the collapse hypothesis, but at some point one suspects that some are beginning to speak past one another, as happens when two parties narrate the past from within different imaginative frameworks. The frameworks themselves, being largely presupposed, are not up for debate. The empire's end appears now as a collapse and now as something decidedly benign. Again, let us think about this appearing: is consciousness here inventing something or is its posture receptive? If we wish to say it is both at the same time, how can we understand this both? It "is" this way, "for us." Is this a contradiction, a facile compatibilism between two positions between which we are in principle compelled to choose? I am with Nietzsche when he advised suspicion whenever a philosopher presents us with a dichotomy and insists that we choose between options that number precisely two. There may be a way to move beneath this opposition by further thinking through the concepts of imagination and imaginative schemas that we are discussing.

Imagine a wattle fence. If properly constructed this piece of ancient technology exhibits remarkable strength, yet what is the source of its strength? A building rests on a foundation. How is it with the fence? It has none. Instead, one lengthy strand, not particularly strong unto itself, is weaved together with a second, a third, and so on, and all are woven around posts which themselves may also not be especially strong on their own. The posts should be strong but often are not, and in either case the fence itself as it rises from the ground becomes progressively stronger in basket-like fashion. One may secure the wattle to the posts with wire but need not, and the wire itself need not be especially strong. But the result is a fence that is unmovable and that will stand for decades with minimal maintenance. The whole rests upon itself, as one might say of a rope. We do not have two things—a ground floor and an underlying foundation, where the latter has a kind of primacy—but one that is interwoven and where the primary–secondary distinction makes no sense. This, I suggest, is how it is with imagination (an activity) and the schemas (more activities) within which it operates. Constructivism awards primacy to the latter, often to language in particular, but the judgment of primacy must be questioned. For the constructivist, language, a social imaginary, or a standpoint of some kind constructs, invents, or imposes intelligibility on past events, where the events themselves are dumb. Events do not speak for themselves; this much is clear, but the inference that they are constructed by the historian's narrative involves a leap and a one-sidedness. At the time of its occurrence the dissolution of the western empire and its replacement with various smaller kingdoms was neither mute nor devoid of significance.

The parties involved understood what was happening, who was doing what and what meaning it carried, even while its meaning for them (likely different meanings for different groups) is not its meaning for later generations of monotheists or for us. Its meaning changes, depending on how it is emplotted and the larger framework that gives the narrative a certain orientation and trajectory. But there is a reversibility here: the imaginative schema is nothing separate and apart from narratives and meanings like this one. Indeed, it just is these narratives and meanings, arranged together in a certain way. To sustain the judgment of primacy, we must have two ontologically distinct beings or realms of being—one constructed, one constructing—and we would appear to have one: a particular bearer of meaning (an event) constituted by a consciousness that is already constituted by an encompassing framework of meanings in a process of mutual constitution. Meanings give rise to meanings as sentences give rise to sentences and organisms give rise to organisms.

Appearing is at once an inventing and a receiving. I know of no word that adequately encompasses both activities. John Dewey suggested "transacting," and this is not a bad approximation. As he expressed this point in *Knowing and the Known*, "What has been completely divided in philosophical discourse into man *and* the world, inner *and* outer, self *and* not-self, subject *and* object, individual *and* social, private *and* public, etc., are in actuality parties in life-transactions. The philosophical 'problem' of how to get them together is artificial. On the basis of fact, it needs to be replaced by consideration of the conditions under which they occur as *distinctions*, and of the special uses served by the distinctions."[22] We shall return to this, but for now let us conceive of the imagination and the schema from which it operates as ultimately if ambiguously one, "parties in life-transactions" or in historical consciousness that are as poles in a dialectic. One does not construct or have primacy over the other, and while a schema or a language may be described as a perspective, it is a perspective on the world.

"We are imagining beings," as John W. M. Krummel aptly remarks. "We imagine the past as well as the future to make sense of the present," and our doing so is one with the art of storytelling.[23] "There is," as Kearney puts it, "a whole set of collective stories and histories which need not bear the signature of any individual author, and which exercise a formative influence on our modes of action and behaviour in society."[24] What he elsewhere calls "the narrative imperative" comes in many forms: "myth, epic, sacred history, legend, saga, folktale, romance, allegory, confession, chronicle, satire, novel. And within each genre there are multiple sub-genres: oral and written, poetic and prosaic, historical and fictional. But no matter how distinct in style, voice or plot, every story shares the common function of *someone telling something to someone about something*."[25] Indeed, "about something." Historical narratives are not about themselves but what happened, and we are not altogether

Historical Imagination I: Interpretation, Narrative, Constructivism   13

free in the telling. We are not making it up—in a connotation that we shall attempt to clarify in the next chapter—or in a sense we are and are not. The narrative hypothesis is also applicable to the person: one understands oneself precisely by configuring and relating to others a personal history in terms of which one acquires a sense of oneself and by which others may also know us. The identity of the self is nothing thing-like but dynamic, ongoing, and bound up with actions and decisions that constitute episodes in the story that one is. It is something imagined by oneself and others, and not a priori but out there in the world of experience and the transactions of social life.

    The opposition between historical empiricism and postmodernism turns in significant part upon the question of narrative and whether these are imposed upon or found within the events of which historians speak. I have suggested the neither/nor (or both/and) option if such a position is capable of being articulated. Recall Fyodor Dostoevsky's famous pronouncement, through the character of Dmitri, in *The Brothers Karamazov*: "Without God and the future life? It means everything is permitted now, one can do anything?"[26] What moral philosopher would presently maintain this—that we must choose between a particular monotheistic worldview and a happy-go-lucky relativism, with no possibility of an alternative ethical vocabulary? Some committed monotheists perhaps, but not many others. This is a simplified analogy to how arguments have often been couched in modern historiography. On one hand, we have some version of empiricism which speaks of truth—specifically the correspondence theory—representation, facts, evidence, sources, causes, common sense, and so on. The language is epistemological, and if any concessions to aesthetics or politics must be made then these are after the fact, embellishments which a historian may add in order to spice things up but for no other reason. On this set of views, either historians are not storytellers at all or the stories they relate are window dressing to real knowledge, or there is a true story to be told about the past but the historian's job is to find and represent, not create, it. In any event, the lines separating knowledge from imagination, truth from fiction, what happened from stories later told, and real from revisionist history may be clearly drawn. On the other hand, we find a categorical rejection of the former and a pendulum swing to an antithetical extreme: from the one to the many, truth to aesthetics, reasoning to fictionalizing, explanation to political struggle, and if not a frank relativism then something approaching it. There being no historical epistemology, the alternative is a conception of narrative interpretation that is incapable of anything that an empiricist would recognize as a justification. Interpretations refer to other interpretations, not historical reality, so if objectivity is out the window then subjectivity reigns.

    Where these two sets of views agree is where Dostoevsky's theist and atheist agree: it is one or the other and any refusal to choose is either a failure of nerve or bad faith. The case for any strong objectivism, in my view, is untenable for reasons I shall discuss in the next chapter. The case for radical constructivism or subjectivism is about equally untenable. The narrative hypothesis in some form is phenomenologically compelling, but a distinction does need to be retained between interpretations that are illuminating, compelling, or reasonable and those that are not. Historians, after all, do know how to distinguish better from worse accounts. Doing so is an ordinary aspect of professional practice just as it is in any field of inquiry, and it is not only carried out on the basis of aesthetic or political considerations. There are truths that from the historian's point of view are inconvenient, unflattering, or disturbing, matters that are the case no matter how anyone feels about it, and we can say this without falling back into talk of correspondence, "the mirror of nature," or epistemological and metaphysical debates of the kind that do need to be left behind. Things happened, and historians are not wholly free to craft the story as they wish. The difficult part is in explaining exactly how this is so. One needs to "take account of" and "do justice to" the sources and evidence, but what is this "taking account"? Might this "doing justice" already be doing something behind our back? Are historians representing something that is already there, or there in part perhaps? Something pushes back when the historian says, "Julius Caesar died of heart failure in the year 452." No, he did not. What, then, is this "pushing back"? Here we need a dose of what I am tempted to call reality, some break on the constructivist's free-for-all, but what dose is this and do empiricists and closet empiricists alone have access to it?

Our account of the "pushing back" will center around the phenomenological concept of intentionality which we shall discuss in chapter 2. Our aim is to approach historical inquiry from two directions: the side of the subject, which we have been discussing, and the side of the object which is the theme of the following chapter. What we seek is to transcend the empiricism/postmodernism opposition and to give an account of narratives and narrativizing that refuses the dichotomy of imposition versus discovery. We require a phenomenologically sound description of our mode of engagement with a history that is in some respects over and done with and in others that is living and which historians not only know about but also participate in along with the rest of us. For now, let us say broadly that from the side of the subject the historian knowingly or unknowingly imports into any inquiry not only a personal point of view but also an imaginative schema that fundamentally orients interpretation, and that the schema itself is nothing apart from or prior to the activity of narrative interpretation itself. To craft and to tell a story, historical and fictional as well, is not to make it up—or not exactly, and not in any way one likes. Something pushes back, as historians themselves are well aware. One does not jump into a river from the dry land of a standpoint, language, or social imaginary but finds oneself always already in the midst of it, and the swimming one does is not the deploying of a strategy worked out in advance but a participating in the same imaginary.

One way that historians do this is by negotiating their way through the hermeneutical circle. This old theme in philosophical hermeneutics goes back to Friedrich Schleiermacher who in the nineteenth century proposed that interpretation operates by the same principles whether we are interpreting religious texts, literary works, laws, historical events, or anything else, and that all of it is done by means of the hermeneutical circle. Understanding has a circular or, better, spiral structure such that we grasp the meaning of the text as a whole by relating it to the individual parts and we understand a part in terms of the whole or by relating the particular to a larger universality. What matters here is context: a word or sentence is a particular segment of a larger structure such as a paragraph or a chapter, and it is the larger structure that affords the context with respect to which the sentence can be understood. An event in the past may be seen as a culmination, a prelude, as foreshadowing later happenings or a dead end. The meaning of any particular is nothing in itself but lies in its contribution to a larger story. There is no starting point for interpretation; rather it comes about in a non-linear, circular way. Heidegger noted that we do not enter the circle from some place outside it but find ourselves already thinking within it; there is no interpretation that is outside of or prior to it, and thinking itself is invariably a looking back and forth between text and context. "What is decisive," as Heidegger stated, "is not to get out of the circle, but to get into it in the right way."[27]

The historian must identify the larger context in which any particular is to be known, as the example of the "life and times" account illustrates. Why should "and times" be tacked on if what the reader is interested in is the life of a historical figure? It is not there merely to make the book longer but to illuminate an individual life, which as Heidegger also pointed out is, or was, a being-in-the-world or a being that is what it is through participation in a network of relations, practices, tradition, and meanings. A good deal of a historian's work involves tracing the myriad relations that link a subject to its times, and where tracing is not the same as constructing. A historical actor does not act in a vacuum of culture, politics, or whatever the larger context is that sheds light on the individual; they were responding to X, reacting against Y, imitating Z, trying to bring about S, following in a tradition of T, and so on and so forth, and as the web of relations grows larger and more complex our sense of the individual becomes progressively enriched. All of it needs to be composed into a narrative, the explanatory power of which is a function of where the subject stood in relation to their time and what was happening within it. The historian may also suggest a possible relation to the present; perhaps the person or event that is the subject of the analysis foreshadowed or in some way stands in relation to our own era. The past can be a teacher, an exemplar, or a warning, and showing this is well within the historian's means.

This raises the question of the historian as rhetorician. It is no exaggeration to characterize the field itself as rhetorical on the grounds that scholars do not (ought not and likely could not) restrict themselves to the mode of utterance one finds in chronicles, nor a combination of this with some creative window dressing, but seek to persuade, argue, criticize and defend hypotheses, offer reasons and theoretical explanations, and advocate views of both a historical and extra-historical kind. Like many philosophers, historians have often been inclined to understate or deny the rhetorical dimension of their practice and to present their accounts as straightforward reports on what happened and why, but there is a disingenuousness about this. Nietzsche's description of philosophers as "advocates who resent that name" applies equally to historians, many of whom have jettisoned the resentment.[28] The author of a biography of a Roman emperor, for instance, need not be an apologist for that figure but often approaches this. Recent accounts of Nero suggest that he may not have been quite the madman he has been described as for two thousand years, or there may have been a method in it. Perhaps Marcus Aurelius was not exactly the sainted figure that has come down to us but a more complex individual embroiled in circumstances he did not perfectly navigate. Perhaps any figure later designated "the Great" (there are many of them) was not quite as great as we had imagined but someone whose contribution to humanity involved a generous admixture of cruelty. These hypotheses are the ordinary stuff of historical interpretation, and they involve argument and criticism of competing analyses.

Then there is advocacy of a more ideological kind, most of which is not overt but by the end of the book the reader will more than occasionally get the point, and it is not seldom political. As Allan Megill has noted and lamented, a view "has come to center stage in recent years . . . that the true function of history is *to support the good cause in the present*. In this view, history is politics—and even war—by other means." His lament stems from "a remarkable inattentiveness to questions of evidence [which] often accompanies the notion that history ought to serve the good cause."[29] Truly apolitical and value-neutral historical analysis was never a real possibility since part of the baggage any thinker brings with them includes values of one kind or another, although there is a leap from this basic hermeneutical statement to the kind of overt politicizing of which Megill is speaking. Many a postmodern historian and historiographer have enthusiastically embraced Nietzsche's and Foucault's demonstrations of the vital connection of knowledge and power while turning them to ideological purposes of their own, where the idea is that if ideological neutrality is impossible then once again we must fly to the opposite extreme and pursue historical investigation for our own partisan purposes. This is an extreme form of a plausible hypothesis, which is that this form of knowledge serves us and has always done so, as Nietzsche said of knowledge in general. It serves particular interests and cannot be separated from power or the will to power. "Ever since historical study became professional," as Geoffrey Elton remarks, "it has time and again destroyed just those interpretations that served particular interests, more especially national self-esteem and self-confidence."[30] At the same time, however, it has promoted other interests, from the narrowly sectarian to the various "good causes" that Megill noted. History is not, we may safely say, an apolitical profession and never has been. Interests of some kind are promoted while others are not, and it is not unheard of for such interests, whatever they may be, to become hegemonic within the field and the larger academy. We shall have occasion to revisit this point.

The claim that historians are rhetoricians and advocates includes connotations that are not limited to the political. Justifying assertions, drawing inferences, persuading readers, and critiquing competing interpretations is a large part of what historians do, and all of it factors into the narratives that they relate and refine. The many interests that come into play include debunking myths, setting the record straight, advancing a theory, participating in a movement, following or challenging trends, changing perceptions of a historical occurrence or personage, correcting omissions, filling a hole in the literature, indulging personal curiosities and affinities, and let us not forget professional advancement, among many others. Also fundamental to such inquiry in general is its relevance to our own historical self-understanding since it is in seeing how some present state of affairs came to pass that we gain an informed and often critical view of it. The present historical moment is comprehended only, once again, contextually or in its coming to be and its anticipations of a possible future. Historical investigation, in short, is at once rational, rhetorical, interested, and about as agonistic as other disciplines of the humanities and social sciences. It is doubtful that any history is altogether "for its own sake"; it serves purposes that may be tacit, subtle, or several in number, but investigators bring these with them in discerning the relevance and significance of the past—which always means its relevance for us given the questions of the present or a particular standpoint within it.

The rational persuasiveness of an interpretation is bound up with the historian's hermeneutic skill not only in building narratives but also in setting out context and establishing a fit between universals and particulars. A particular battle is "seen-as" a turning point in a war, a decisive episode in a relationship between states, the end of this or a prelude to that, or otherwise in relational terms and in light of a larger universality in terms of which that battle can be understood. It is not a bare particular; indeed, the bare particular, in being unspoken, remains unknown, existing in no relation to a knower.

Approaching it involves placing it in relation to a concept, viewing it as a possible instance of X or Y, seeing-as, discerning, and emplotting.

Part of what is involved in getting into the hermeneutical circle "in the right way" is that any fit we establish between concept and event must not deteriorate into an exercise in apriorism. Interpretation is not inherently "violent," but it becomes so when the historian projects and imposes universals onto particulars rather than discerns them already at work there, and it is a distinction that can be razor-thin. Seeing a historical particular in light of a universal—a given conflict as a democratic revolution, let us say—is not violent in the event that it bears more than a passing resemblance to another revolution of this kind, and where the resemblance is not pure construction. Judging what fits in this sense is more readily described in negative terms: it is not hermeneutically violent, an act of legislation or reading-in of what is not there, an ideologically motivated imposition, a case of making it fit, and so on. Many a bad interpretation commits this error, and it is often a difficult matter to separate from a more careful reading which is at once creative and receptive, active and passive as it were, in equal measure and in one gesture. Remaining with our conflict, suppose we now characterize this as an act of terrorism. More than aesthetic invention or politicizing is involved in discerning democratic uprisings from terrorist acts. When our narrative of the protests in Tiananmen Square in 1989 characterizes the actions of the protesters as a threat to public order or national security and the government's response as a simple matter of law enforcement, a failing has occurred that any competent historian can be expected to see: a sectarian interest has imposed a category that does not fit the case. It is an instance not of seeing or even constructing a resemblance but of ideological distortion. The kind of fit of which we are speaking is not pure invention. If it were, we should be free to say things like, "What happened in Tiananmen Square was a measured response to a terrorist incident." No, it was not. This is a clear instance of interpretive violence for the reason that a universal has been imposed on the particulars rather than found in them. Imposing and finding, projecting and discerning—again, no chasm separates these two, but competent historians can usually be counted upon to know the difference. Some interpretive judgment is involved, and it is the kind of judgment that is the normal business of historical inquiry.

One cannot make it up, or if one makes the attempt then something pushes back. An example from intellectual history: the spread of Christianity in the centuries of late antiquity spelled the end of Greek and Roman philosophy until its eventual rebirth during the renaissance. Again, no. Very little died, as we shall see in chapter 3. Ideas were transformed and reinterpreted, some texts were lost and others were preserved, philosophy relocated into institutions of the church, and various other things happened, but classical philosophy did not go into the full eclipse that has often been imagined. What pushes back against the false narrative is what we must continue to call evidence—the many instances of Greek and Roman ideas being translated, reconceived, turned to a new set of purposes, and integrated into a new imaginative schema but not abolished. The concept of renaissance itself served the interests of certain fifteenth- and sixteenth-century intellectuals while overlooking much in the centuries they began to call medieval. The "dark ages" was more than a misnomer; it was a self-serving distortion. We shall revisit this as well.

The way to think about universals is as existing dialectically with particulars and only this way, not as anything that stands apart from them, as Gadamer taught us to see.[31] Concepts do not first exist in fully constituted form, perhaps in a mental box called the mind, and are then deployed onto an equally determinate set of individuals as a general deploys strategies and soldiers. Instead, we should think of both as coming to be only in their mutuality, as two poles of a single dialectic. If anything has primacy here, it is the dialectic itself, not the relata that comprise it. We "deploy"—if what is meant by this word first to have in advance and then to employ for a purpose also conceived in advance—neither concepts, a conceptual scheme, a language, nor an imaginary but again find ourselves already in the thick of it, in a world of particulars that it is too late to regard in the conceptual nude. What is a revolution apart from what happened in America in 1765–1783, France in 1789–1799, and so on? It is a castle in the air. A universal is not this but a relatum the other aspect of which is the relatum that is a particular, both of whose being consists only in their mutuality.

Historians illuminate events, then, by painting a larger picture in the sense of placing them in a living context and in the larger structure of a narrative and in no case by regarding them in isolation. The task of imagination is to discern and show the universality that is implicit in the particulars—to exhibit, for instance, how the death of Julius Caesar must be regarded as an assassination that came about for reasons arising from the tangled web of Roman politics. How did it come to pass, what players and political factions were involved, why did the assassins do what they did, and what consequences, intended and unintended, followed are the kind of questions that are asked. The facts contained in a chronicle entry must be brought to life, and not in the manner of a bad Hollywood movie but in a way that is faithful to the evidence as we know it. Where historical fiction often strives to maximize entertainment value and sensationalism, the historical consciousness of which we are speaking is beholden to the phenomena in a much more rigorous sense. Its being evidentially sound and richly imaginative are two sides of a single coin.

Much of the art of history, as we saw briefly above, involves gathering the myriad phenomena that bear a relation of some kind to the historian's subject and arranging them into an intelligible form. We are not holding a mirror to the past or passively taking in what is there. As Marc Bloch noted, "Mere passive observation, even supposing such a thing were possible, has never contributed anything productive to any science." He went on to say, "There is no worse advice for a beginner than that he should simply sit patiently waiting for the inspiration of a document," although this founding member of the Annales school did not recognize the full complexity and artistry involved in this activity.[32] Kearney comes much closer: "History-telling," he writes, "is never literal . . . . It is always at least in part *figurative* to the extent that it involves telling according to a certain selection, sequencing, emplotment and perspective." He immediately adds "But it does try to be *truthful*."[33] There are several points here to unpack.

First, no matter how long a book becomes, no historian could or would attempt to include everything that is in any way germane to their subject. There is simply too much to encompass, even when the topic one is investigating is relatively specific. One must be selective, and where the criteria governing the selection are a matter for the historian's judgment. One selects what is relevant to the topic, but the judgment of relevance itself is not self-evident. Something is relevant if it bears a non-trivial relation to a significant theme or episode in the narrative, but relations themselves are far too numerous to incorporate indiscriminately. One opts for what matters, what carries a level of importance to the account one is offering, and judges which aspects warrant emphasis, which carry secondary importance, and which may be alluded to or left out entirely, and no rule governs how this is done. This is true of interpretation in general and goes some way toward explaining the inevitable diversity of historical accounts. Judgments of importance, relevance, and significance are not subjective in the sense of arbitrary or a reflection of the scholar's idiosyncrasies alone, but they are underdetermined by the evidence and are part of the art of historical narration. So is what Kearney calls "sequencing"—arranging or weaving together events to form episodes in a larger temporal configuration, viewing X in relation to Y, and so on. Events lead toward, foreshadow, motivate, and respond to other events, and this is a large part of their historical significance. The sequence is not always linear, but there is an organic quality in the organization of events that the historian attempts to track and exhibit. An action is regarded not in isolation but as part of a larger configuration, as an organ of the body is grasped in terms of its relation to other organs and its larger functioning within the body. How it contributes to a sequence and fits into the whole must come into view, where again we are grasping the particular by relating it to a larger universality.

The larger universality is indeed a narrative, as so many philosophers of history have pointed out in recent years. In larger terms, we understand a historical event in seeing how it came to pass, what led up to it, who did what and for what reasons, what followed from it and what it meant, or in short by knowing the story. A good part of the labor and the artistry lies in "emplotting" a great many particulars—persons, actions, conflicts, motivations, consequences, circumstances, difficulties, chance—or showing how each of these relates to the others and leads in a certain direction. A narrative contains a plot which is capable of being followed by the reader and which exhibits a kind of progression that is more akin to musical progression than linear progress. We are not marching a straight line but seeing how one thing led to another in the way that human actions typically unfold: in circumstances A, person B saw fit to respond to C, with much help from person D and overcoming opposition from E, which motivated action F, with the result that G and also the unintended consequence that H, which generated new circumstances I, which led person J—and on and on it goes. Complexity abounds, but the historian's task is to follow along and compose a narrative that does justice to the details without getting lost in them. Which details should be included, how many of the nearly infinite particulars and their interrelations warrant attention, what should be emphasized, what themes emerge, how long should the book be—how questions of this sort are answered determines in significant part how the narrative will unfold. No little creativity goes into the synthesizing or weaving together of story elements, and it is in this respect that the historian's art most resembles the novelist's. Both involve weighing relative importance, a value that is contingent simultaneously on an element's contribution in advancing the narrative, its significance to the people and time period of which we are speaking and to a contemporary audience no less, and on the historian's own perspective and values, none of which can be encapsulated in a rule. All such factors comprise what Ricoeur called "the configurational dimension" of narrative composition, in which "the plot transforms the events into a story. This configurational act consists of 'grasping together' the detailed actions or what I have called the story's incidents. It draws from this manifold of events the unity of one temporal whole" in a manner that he likened to Kant's notion of reflective judgment. "The act of emplotment has a similar function inasmuch as it extracts a configuration from a succession."[34] The "manifold" to be configured includes the who, what, why, and when of the story, everything that is capable of being taken into account and none of which arranges itself. When Thompson remarks that "It is possible to imagine a piece of historical writing which was an aesthetic disaster and wretchedly composed, yet yielded new knowledge and interpretations of the utmost importance," he may be drawing too simple a distinction between aesthetics and knowledge or analytical interpretation.[35] The configurative art underlies both, albeit not in identical ways. Historical narratives need not be beautiful, but they do need to hang together, paint a coherent picture, take account of everything that is relevant, and make sense—and we can say much the same of fiction.

Kearney's point that historical interpretation "does try to be *truthful*" is surely accurate, although introducing the little word "truth"—even the less epistemological "truthful"—into this discussion is fraught with issues. Truth as correspondence does need to go; no historical account corresponds to a fully objective state of affairs in the human past, or demonstrating that it does would be an impossible task. Not correspondence but truth in a different connotation—truthful, faithful to the phenomena, evidentially rigorous, coherent, illuminating—does have a place here, and it is a concept that we should not understand in categorical opposition with falsehood. Here I am inclined toward Nietzsche's view that knowing invariably requires a certain act of "falsifying" in a sense of both a simplifying of our object and an appropriation which grasps not the thing in itself but the aspect that serves us. Knowledge is an arrangement that is artificial, interested, and rigorous at the same time that it involves a sizeable element of "forcing, adjusting, abbreviating, omitting, padding, investing, falsifying, and whatever else is of the *essence* of interpreting."[36] We are not simply taking in and representing what is there but compressing the manifold into an expedient classification. Nietzsche's general account of interpretation emphasized a distortion and falsification that is not a failure to correspond but a perspectival and aspectival revealing of our object. One Nietzsche scholar speaks of interpretation as not constituting but "participat[ing] in Being," as "neither the cause, principle, nor measure of reality." "Each appearance," Jean Granier continues, "is an *apparition*—that is, a *real manifestation*—and there is nothing to look for beyond these manifestations. To be is to appear—not in the sense that appearing is the equivalent of Being, but in that every apparition is a revelation of Being." Historical interpretation strives to be true to its object while involving what Granier calls "some *creative initiative* on the part of the interpreter."[37] Instead of truth or falsehood in the traditional sense of this opposition we would do better to speak of historical narratives as striving for a coherence, strictness, and revelatory power that is never complete but that is often compelling.

At bottom, historical consciousness is an imaginative engagement with the past which from the side of the subject involves the following cognitive acts (among others no doubt), many of which overlap and all of which involve the move from chronology to history. The historian, first of all, must judge what is worth preserving in our shared memory of the human past. Not everything warrants remembering and no formula determines the selection from among the nearly infinite set of characters and incidents in the long history of our species. This is a judgment the historian must make on the basis of criteria that are also a matter of judgment. One selects a topic of inquiry and a beginning and end point, and goes to work sifting among the myriad events, persons, and details that may factor into one's account. All such selecting and discriminating depends upon a discernment of some particular's historical value and relevance to the topic.

Much of the labor involves posing questions, formulating hypotheses, and inquiring in something like Dewey's sense of the term, where one sets out from a "problematic situation" and goes in search of answers to specific questions and attempts to verify or falsify an hypothesis based on the best available evidence. Much trial and error is involved, a confirming and refuting of hypotheses each of which is a possible answer to a question the aim of which is to resolve the problematic situation that occasioned the inquiry. Historians are investigators or detectives of a kind, working with information that is often either incomplete or overabundant, and must sift through and track down evidence before inferring what must have happened and why. A good deal of inductive reasoning must be carried out, reckoning with probabilities in much the way that a judge, lacking complete information, must estimate what is likely to have occurred, and seeing probable connections. There are gaps to fill in, relations to establish, sources to find, and many stones to overturn before any coherent account can emerge.

Nietzsche's point about "falsifying" interpretation also warrants emphasis. The historian is not making it up, but they are exercising a great deal of creativity in selecting among the evidence, highlighting what is salient, abbreviating or omitting what one deems secondary, and compressing the manifold into a form of the historian's choosing. Creativity extends to the questioning act—everything that is understood about history (and about everything else, according to Gadamer) should be seen as an answer to a question—where the act itself establishes the parameters for what will come into view. Like scholars in any field, the better historians have a sense of which questions are worth pursuing and which are ill conceived for one reason or another. They may also have a sense of when to call an old account or source into question, when to be trusting or suspicious, for one doubts not indiscriminately but when it is indicated by the evidence. Of course, historical evidence does not literally indicate anything or speak for itself; this is something the historian must discern, and again a good deal of creativity is in play here. Nietzsche himself demonstrated the point as well as any; the art of questioning, suspecting, doubting, genealogizing, and reckoning with possibilities is practically unmatched in his works, both philosophical and historical. The art of historical interpretation as he practiced it in his genealogical writings had an attitude and a partisanship that was not merely political in the usual sense but worked with an agenda of his own devising. A century later much the same could be said of Foucault.

Whether historical analysis ought to be overtly political is a question to which we shall return, but for now let us take note of a point that has become obvious, that no chasm separates the historical from the political. Historians bring with them if not a fully elaborated and partisan agenda then at minimum some tacit assumptions and values that bring some matters to light and leave others in shadow. The rhetorical art is not limited to politicizing but includes efforts of various kinds to persuade an audience of the truth of this or that assertion. Kuukkanen's analysis contrasts "the narrativist" for whom "the historian is a kind of descriptivist storyteller" with his own "postnarrativist" view in which "the historian is a *critical reasoner*," and where a fair amount of space separates these two conceptions of what historians do; "historiography is a form of rational practice" that is not limited to "creat[ing] products akin to artistic artefacts" but centrally bears upon arguments, theses, and reasoned inferences, he states.[38] One may claim, for instance, that the French colonization of New France in the seventeenth century was in large part a consequence of religious fervor. A good deal of evidence supports this claim, even while there is much room for debate about the degree of weight this carried in comparison to several other motivations. Historians clearly do try to persuade their readers by presenting arguments and evidence in support of any number of claims, but the opposition that Kuukkanen draws seems overstated for claims of this kind, while undoubtedly a prominent feature of historical inquiry, are also elements in a larger configuration. Scholarly debate about the early history of New France surely includes arguments about motivations and the presentation of evidence to back up the kind of assertions that historians routinely make—but granting this does not take us to a "postnarrativist" position but provides some elaboration upon what persuasive storytelling involves. "[P]roducts akin to artistic artefacts" can also contain truth and more than a little analysis and critical reasoning. Historians suggest hypotheses about what occurred and why, and listen to the sources for a kind of feedback, either by way of confirmation or contradiction. As Walsh expresses this important point, "historians are not content with the simple discovery of past facts: they aspire, at least, not only to say what happened, but also to show why it happened. History is not just a plain record of past events, but . . . a 'significant' record—an account in which events are connected together."[39] The "why" question is less a matter of causal explanation than an elucidation of the reasons, motivations, influences, and contingencies that led up to a given happening, and a good deal of hypothesizing and listening for a response is involved.

All of this factors into the art of storytelling: arranging particulars into a followable sequence, finding the story that fits the evidence, following a trail, questioning and interpreting, evaluating sources, looking beneath surfaces, and identifying meanings in light of a narrative configuration, whether it be heroic, tragic, comedic, romantic, or something else. These acts which are distinct in principle and overlapping in practice contribute to the more comprehensive account that historical texts typically provide and which make possible an authentic encounter with the past. When successful, there is a meeting of minds, what Gadamer called a "fusion of horizons," that takes place between the inquirer, and subsequently the reader, and the time period of which we are speaking. We are not transported into the past but placed on speaking terms with it, not "in" but "with" it in a deep sense of this word. The past is known in relation to the present—also the reverse—as the process of inquiry strives for a larger universality that comprehends not only what happened but also what significance it held at the time and for our time no less. The historical imagination looks up from the particulars for larger patterns and tendencies, themes and lessons from the past that are capable of speaking to the present. It makes possible what we may call a sense of history—some more comprehensive understanding, a familiarity with the larger landscape and a sensibility, a sense of how things stood and what was possible for them, who they were and how they lived and thought, what they achieved and what they were up against, and who we are by the reflected light that all of this sheds.

CHAPTER 2

Historical Imagination II: Evidence and Intentionality

May we speak of a historical rationality, or does the rejection of empiricist and foundationalist epistemology in general and an endorsement of the narrative hypothesis commit us to abandoning any and all notions of rationality, truth, objectivity, and so on in our analysis of historical inquiry and historical imagination in particular? The tradition stemming from Plato has us conceive of imaginative expression as at the farthest remove from knowledge, and our intention in these chapters is to depart not only from this separation but also from the image-centered and visual orientation that the concept of imagination has long presupposed and to replace it, following Ricoeur's lead, with a conception that is primarily verbal and also more expansive than narrative and metaphor and which encompasses the lion's share of the labor that historians undertake. More specifically, we need to square two claims: first is what we have referred to as the narrative hypothesis, and second is the evident fact that historians do not make things up. Historical narratives are artful but not fictional, but exactly how so? What sense can be made of the distinction between fictional and historical narrative, and from the storyteller's point of view? Any answer will crucially bear upon notions of evidence, sources, and empirical or quasi-empirical justification for the kind of descriptive and analytical claims that scholars in this field routinely make—notions that postmodernists are quick to trace back to epistemological theories that have fallen on hard times and to replace with some formulation of constructivism. Kearney has suggested that "we can acknowledge that history is invariably mediated through narrative and *at the same time* affirm that there is something irreducible which, willy-nilly, we 'still call reality.' Without some referential claim to 'reality,' however indirect, it would seem that we would have no justification at all for distinguishing between history and fiction."[1] I shall second Kearney's suggestion here, but the difficult part will be to demonstrate how we can maintain these two claims simultaneously. This will be the task of the present chapter.

Otherwise stated, how might the classical divide between *mythos* and *logos* be bridged in the specific case of historiography, for it is difficult to deny that this branch of humanistic investigation partakes in some manner of both and that while different schools of thought have accentuated one side or the other any satisfactory account will need to do justice to both—but how? Chapter 1 looked at what we called the subject side of imagination in the sense of what historians wittingly or unwittingly bring to bear upon the material they work with, which includes a wealth of cultural baggage and a schema of largely prereflective and affectively charged interpretation. What appears to us has been made possible by a fundamental orientation that largely escapes our notice, as a great many phenomenological, hermeneutical, and postmodern writers have well demonstrated, although we have resisted the language of constructivism. Our task now is to approach the same matter from the object side: something pushes back when historians proffer descriptions or analyses that fail, as rather often they do, but what is this "something" which historians themselves are so well acquainted with yet find so difficult to describe? "Evidence" is the one-word answer we often hear, although I suspect there is more to it than this and that the word itself is far more ambiguous than many believe. These concepts—evidence, sources, historical reality, the past, what really happened—are elusive. The historian is on a trail, and is like a detective in this way, but what trail is this? Is it a construction? It does not appear that way, for if it were then it should be subject to the will, and clearly it is not. There are things that historians not only do not say but also cannot. There is a trail there that they need to discern and follow, and that trail has every appearance of being real, to have being in one sense or another.

What is this object side of historical imagination? We began to answer this question in chapter 1 but must now do so in a more complete way and also introduce a line of argument that centers around the phenomenological concept of intentionality. Historical consciousness does not stand at a radical remove from its object of investigation, including when the latter is distant in time and place, but bears a relation that is often unseen and which has often gone by the name of constitution: such awareness, as with consciousness in general, is always already situated within a network of historical and cultural relations and indeed has been constituted by them, largely behind our back, or so many maintain. An imaginative schema makes possible, forms, and also limits the art of historical configuration in general, although the schema itself is nothing frozen in time but is the sedimented product of countless activities of illuminating and mystifying our world. To speak of these activities as imaginative is not to say that they are private acts of subjectivity occurring at some distance from reality, for these activities and we ourselves are already out there in the midst of historical reality. The past is no alien planet but something on which we are already on speaking terms, and if historians have long been the principal custodians of this we ought to begin with what so many practitioners have long said about what passes for rationality in this field.

What has long been called rationality here is nothing as theoretically elaborate as an epistemology but more like a general way of thinking that we might loosely call common sense empiricism and also realism. We are speaking of a set of presuppositions, conventions, and disciplinary standards that is used in adjudicating disagreements among professional historians and which also tends to distinguish this group from their amateur counterparts. Words like truth and justification, facts and data, sources and evidence, reality and objectivity, causality and explanation feature prominently here, even if their meanings typically remain opaque. Rationality encompasses all of this and is sharply distinguished from a few things: relativism, subjectivism, myth-making, propaganda, ideological activism, and a few others. The fundamental idea is that historical inquiry is research, distinguishable in some important particulars from other forms of empirical investigation but methodologically akin to the others while also sharing their spirit. It is methodologically rigorous, painstaking, and constantly beholden to sources which exercise a kind of authority over everything that historians write. In exhibiting what phenomenologists call the natural attitude, historians typically trust in the reality of the past and accept that while the characters and events themselves no longer have being (the past in this sense is not) their traces remain (the past in this sense is) and are there to be investigated in a basically empirical way. Rationality is both procedural and attitudinal: a fundamental imperative to which these notions give expression can be described as a kind of intellectual seriousness and a determination not to perpetuate the kind of errors that many a premodern historian appear to have committed, from flattering the king to self-serving propaganda and a host of related tendencies with which we are all too familiar. When in the nineteenth century historical scholarship became a branch of the academic profession it needed to partake of the ethos of universities that increasingly saw themselves as research institutions and to comport itself with a new responsibility that was consistent with other disciplines of the humanities and social sciences.

Currently, while the historical profession is nowhere close to having a universally agreed upon methodology, epistemology, ontology, or philosophy of history, many of the notions just mentioned retain a certain hold on this discipline even after the linguistic and postmodern turns sent many back to the drawing board. Rationality, objectivity, and so on, remain robust but also chastened notions that work on the level of working assumptions which most historians, occupied with the minutiae of their research, are not concerned to render philosophically explicit. Many now grant the narrative hypothesis while insisting that the stories they tell are true, if not in the sense of "corresponding with reality" then in a weaker sense of being intellectually honest, rigorous, and indeed accurate representations of what occurred. Novelists, according to a common view, need have nothing to do with reality unless they wish to, while historians have no choice. Alun Munslow writes, "Surely, [most historians] say, poets, dramatists and novelists [imaginatively emplot events] and, while they can also make appeals to rational argument, they don't have to. There is also no necessary impulse toward factual truth in novels and poems."[2] That impulse belongs to the researcher along with an imperative to be objective, at least in a benign sense. Few contemporary historians would reject the need to be objective in the sense of bracketing insofar as possible any merely personal preferences and attitudes that a historian might import into their work that do not meet with a certain amount of consensus in the field. What is rationally acceptable must be based on rigorously vetted evidence and plausibly configured, although the connotation of these terms will lack the kind of clarity that an epistemologist might desire. Allan Megill makes the point this way: "The true historian is not a propagandist or cheerleader . . .. Attentiveness to historical evidence helps keep the historian honest, and hence less likely to impose her own prejudices and good wishes on the past. Conversely, too great an interest in the uses of history in the present is likely to make the would-be historian inattentive to historical evidence."[3] Without speaking for all contemporary historians, of course, Megill's point does capture the kind of common sense empiricism to which we have referred. Sources and evidence are authoritative over everything that falls under the headings of the aesthetic and the political, even as the latter belong in a fundamental way to the data themselves and the ways in which any historian reckons with them. If there is no eliminating interpretation and narration, these notions can at least be given a relatively tough-minded rendering. Speaking phenomenologically, we might say with Maurice Merleau-Ponty that "we give history its sense, but not without history offering us that sense. . . . [O]ur assessment of the past—even if it never reaches absolute objectivity—is never entitled to be arbitrary."[4] We might recall Nietzsche as well: an interpretation, while "an *apparition*" is at the same time "a *real manifestation*" which involves "some *creative initiative on the part of the interpreter.*"[5] It is both at once: creative and rigorous, an appearing that is also a being.

Many historians are understandably reluctant to engage in philosophical disputes about their discipline, and if their skepticism often does them credit it remains that preconceptions abound and that many pertain to the issues of which we are speaking. Determining "what happened" in the past is no straightforward undertaking, and reference to reality, empirical evidence, primary sources, archival research, and so on only takes us so far. Two centuries ago, Leopold von Ranke famously stated that historical research "wants only to say what actually happened," and while the sentiment can be given a strong or weak reading it generally captures a view that remains commonplace among working historians today and which we may well hold onto provided we do not turn it into a false idealization.[6] This mistake was committed in spectacular fashion by nineteenth-century positivists whom postmodernists in particular never tire of castigating and for good reason. Subjectivity, the positivists held, could be removed altogether from historical and all rational inquiry with the strict application of procedures which themselves bore no traces of the unscientific. In an age of science, any form of cognition that did not fit this description needed to be expelled as the discipline of history itself became modeled as closely as possible on the sciences, with the notion of causal explanation at its center. As scientists are not poets, narrative was either eliminated or downplayed along with anything that had a historical or logical association with *mythos*: literature, meaning, subjectivity, interpretation, rhetoric, metaphysics, metaphor, imagination. History is governed by laws, the positivists held, and the work of researchers is to describe their detailed workings, if not quite in the manner of the physicist then in something approximating it.

This incarnation of modern rationalism died a slow death over the course of the last century and its vestiges in a great many disciplines remain, prompting postmodern and various other critics to place many a nail in a coffin that has proven difficult to close, for an age of science it remains. This has not changed, and if one finds few thoroughgoing positivists in the university of today, their descendants are many and vibrant. As postmodernists fly to the opposite extreme, *mythos* triumphs over *logos*, narrative over explanation, and construction over reality in a strategy about which we have expressed some skepticism. Nietzschean perspectivism has won the day, or a one-sided version of it. That thinker's nuanced accent on balancing the Apollonian and Dionysian is often left aside together with his accent on intellectual honesty and rigor, leaving us with a subjectivism that is no improvement over the objectivism it replaced.

What is needed is a more reasonable conception of historical rationality—neither rationalism nor anti-rationalism but an alternative that avoids the excesses of each, and it begins with something like common sense empiricism. I say "something like," first, because that view itself is nebulous and does not constitute the fully explicated epistemology of Hobbes, Locke, and company, and also because the view I shall put forward is better described as phenomenological. Historiography does not need an epistemology. What it needs is a conception of rationality that accords with the actual practice of inquiry while also raising it to a higher order of explicitness. The practice itself is always already rational in a sense that needs to be clarified, and a starting point is to express some reservation about the familiar notions of explanation and representation. A historical explanation, on the old positivist view, is an account that purports to identify the cause(s) that produced a particular event and also to afford a basis for prediction. It answers the why question: what caused the fall of the Roman empire; why did the Axis powers lose World War II, and so on. A satisfactory explanation should conform to the model of natural science and identify the general law or concept that is to a given historical event what gravity is to falling objects. The positivist's strong position has been largely rejected or diluted to a view that continues to speak of causes and effects but now in a less quasi-mechanistic and somewhat ill-defined connotation. "The laws of history" are not what they were; it would be better to say they do not exist, with the possible exception of contingency (which is not a law).

While we are being skeptical, we would do well to throw some cold water on the notion of causal explanation itself. While this vestige of nineteenth-century positivism continues to hold on, it would be better replaced with non-scientific notions such as reasons, motives, purposes, influences, meanings, and circumstances. There are assignable reasons (quite a few of them) why the Roman imperial state in the west came to an end and was replaced by various smaller structures, neither one big cause nor a number of smaller ones in any sense of the word that a natural scientist would recognize, and nothing resembling a law—such as "All empires fall," maybe even (since laws have the character of necessity) "must fall," a statement that is empirically unfalsifiable. Human events, actions, and persons do respond to reasons; they are motivated this way and that, influenced by any number of factors from ideas to individuals, are often purposive, and exist in the midst of circumstances which themselves can incline developments to unfold in a certain direction. To speak of any of these as causes is careless hyperbole, unless we are willing to presuppose some grand determinism that no amount of empirical evidence could sustain. Historical explanation, causality, and law-like order are survivals of a dead dogma about the unity of knowledge and the totalizing reach of science, and if diluting them lessens their implausibility it also empties them of meaning. When why questions arise, it is better to go in search of reasons than causes and effects. A war is won or lost for identifiable reasons: the relative size and sophistication of different military units, technology, strategy, leadership, money, morale, supply chains, battlefield conditions, the machinations of fortune. To speak of any of these as causes is at best awkward, and if "explanation" is a term with which we cannot bring ourselves to part (for whatever reason) then reasons, motives, purposes, influences, meanings, and circumstances afford a more than adequate analysis of the term. Such explanations are seldom grand of scale. The answer to the historian's question, "What happened?" is most often mundane: it was a tax revolt. "Why did it occur?" translates as what did the participants think they were doing, what were they upset about, and what were they trying to achieve? Light is shed by seeing it as a particular kind of event, analogous in some ways with other events, and one in which the parties involved had reasons, acted with ends in view, enacted particular meanings, and so on, none of which are material or quasi-material causes.

The concept of representation also retains a powerful hold on contemporary historiography, including surprisingly enough within postmodernism itself or the work of a couple of its more noted defenders. So much of contemporary philosophy in general remains deeply rooted in British empiricism, for which the concepts of presentation and representation are indispensable, that it comes as no surprise when even some of its ardent critics allow the concept of representation or indeed "representationalism" through the back door, albeit in new guise. Hayden White and Frank Ankersmit are the most prominent examples of this. A detailed analysis of the particular form of representationalism these writers advocate would take us a bit far afield, but painting in broad strokes the latter author follows White's lead in prioritizing the aesthetic dimension of historiography while focusing on the way in which the historical text represents, in contrast to describes or interprets, events from the past. As Ankersmit expresses this basic thesis, "the vocabulary of representation is better suited to an understanding of historiography than the vocabularies of description and interpretation. What the historian does is essentially more than describing and interpreting the past. In many ways historiography is similar to art, and philosophy of history should therefore take to heart the lessons of aesthetics . . . .. Since both represent the world, art and historiography are closer to science than are criticism and the history of art; the explanation is that the interpretation of meaning is the specialty of the latter two fields." The work of history, he maintains, may be likened to the work of art in that both represent rather than interpret their object: "the historian could meaningfully be compared to the painter representing a landscape, a person, and so on." The historical narrative does not describe events in the sense of interpret what they mean or meant but "represent[s] (historical) reality by giving it a meaning, through the meaning of his text, that reality does not have of itself."[7] The historical event, like the landscape, is meaningless until the historian (or the painter) arrives on the scene and constructs it in the act of representation. This is not the classical empiricist's copy theory of representation, or what Dewey derisively called the "spectator conception of knowledge" for which "knowledge is intrinsically a mere beholding or viewing of reality," where an unconditioned subjectivity grasps an objective and fully determinate reality.[8] For Ankersmit, the historical representation does not copy a preexisting reality, such as a meaning, but again constructs a meaning that the past "does not have of itself." Prior to the historian's inventive work of representation, historical events are without meaning, whereas on what Ankersmit describes (inaccurately) as the hermeneutical view meaning is there from the beginning and the aim of interpretation is to discover it. To cite him once more, "the vocabulary of representation can help us to explain the coming into being of meaning out of what does *not yet* have meaning. Meaning is originally representational and arises from our recognition of how other people (historians, painters, novelists) represent the world."[9]

Empiricists and representationalists work with some dubiously tidy distinctions: discovery versus construction; interpretation versus representation; meaningful versus meaningless; real versus imaginary; subject versus object. It is better to conceive of these as rough and ready distinctions only which in some circumstances accomplish some intellectual labor without opening up a chasm. Some dialectical nuance is needed here, and it is largely phenomenological and hermeneutical thinkers who have taken us beyond the tired old dichotomies that still beset a great deal of contemporary philosophy of history. Is the business of historical inquiry to unearth an objective and fully constituted meaning or does the historian construct meaning in the activity of representation? This is a badly formulated question, and about as poorly as whether artists discover meanings or create them. The answer is both/and or—what comes to the same thing—neither/nor. We need to think about it differently, which means changing the question and still more the vocabulary, for if the latter remains the same then we shall remain in orbit around a planet from which we need to break free. A new empiricism or representationalism is not the way forward, for once the false dichotomies and foundationalist excesses are removed from these doctrines not much is left. Neither view has an answer to Nietzsche's question of from what perspective could we compare a representation to a reality (event, fact, state of affairs), unless the historian is able to step outside of both and see the whole as an omniscient god might. A conception of historical interpretation that is loosely speaking empirical, and more strictly phenomenological, is the better option, and to say this in no way commits us to the dubious proposition that meanings exist (or the reverse) prior to the act of historical configuration or representation. There is an immediacy to the form of contact that the historian has with the past, and if we are looking for analogies between works of history and works of art then it is here that we need to look.

We shall return to this in due course. First, let us reiterate that while common sense empiricism affords a rough starting point for an analysis of the object side of historical imagination, we need to jettison the language of representation, mental pictures, law-like order, and causal explanation. Ankersmit's "No representation, no past"—or "the past depends for its (onto)logical status on its representation"—has a one-sidedness about it.[10]

Historical accounts clearly bring something new to the past, but to say this does not amount to claiming they represent, copy, or otherwise substitute for some ontologically separate object, or that the object itself is dumb before the historian arrives on the scene. The past is not dumb, devoid of significance, or altogether chronicle-like. If it does not (exactly) speak, it indeed must be spoken for by the historian, but this speaking-for is not (exactly) a construction. Any radical separation of the real and the imaginary is belied by the stubborn fact of the "sources and evidence" that historians continually remind us of, particularly when voicing opposition to the postmoderns. They are not making it up; it really did happen that way, and its happening was never meaningless, although those meanings do call for interpretation or reinterpretation, and the historical text also did not write itself. No interpretation, no understanding of the past—which is not synonymous with "no past."

Constructivism and empiricism are about equally prone to excess, and from opposite directions. The former readily becomes a kind of subjective idealism in which any serious talk of sources and evidence is thought tainted by association with some kind of objectivism or foundationalism. This move is often made hastily and without due appreciation of the role that evidence clearly plays in historical research. As Perez Zagorin aptly states, "Historians operate within definite constraints, of which they are fully conscious, arising from the nature and limitations of their evidence. While it is for them to determine that something is evidence and what it is evidence for, when they have done so the evidence exerts a continuous force upon them. They are not free to ignore it or make it whatever they please. Its pressure acts as a major determinant in giving shape to the historical work."[11] Historians must, as another scholar puts it, "do justice to the evidence, and while that is not fixed in the way some would have us believe, it is nonetheless not made up by the historian. There is something 'hard' about it, something which cannot be argued away, but must simply be accepted."[12] This is something of a truism among professional historians and making the point does not commit us to any particular historiographical theory. It is less an epistemological stance than a disciplinary convention to which historians of very different theoretical orientations could agree without much argument. Historians must base their statements about the past upon evidence and sources, and where the latter term can be spoken of, as Robert Stein suggests, as "not strictly an isolated entity, static or frozen in time, but exist[ing] now as a relation and in an act of reading. It is a relation between a present entity (let us get to the heart of the matter instantly and call it a text), a present reader of that text (in this case, the historian) and a disciplinary structure (in this case, history) that supplies the reader with an interpretive context, a purpose for reading and a protocol for interpretation. The source is a social fact, and one fully mediated by language."[13] Sources and evidence are neither absolute nor unconditioned but are in every case relational: a document, let us say, is a source of information about X, evidence for Y, as interpreted by Z, from the point of view of A, and so on. They are not raw data, but nor are they altogether under the historian's power. Sources may be primary or secondary, reliable or suspect, but they do need to be reckoned with in one way or another, and in a way that is not true of fictional narratives. They have an authority about them of which historians are well aware, even while some creative artistry is necessary in making them speak to us.

An example of empiricist excess comes from the *Annales* school of modern French historiography which much like its positivist predecessor wishes to sideline narrative and the aesthetic as much as possible and limit inquiry to explanation and descriptive analysis. The entire realm of the imaginative is once again neatly separated from the empirical and the objective, as historical research is brought decisively under the umbrella of the social sciences. This interdisciplinary and epistemologically ambitious school of thought finds an ally in some recent approaches that speak anew of historical objectivity as a realizable ideal. An important example is Peter Novick whose conception of historical objectivity he describes this way:

> The assumptions on which it rests include a commitment to the reality of the past, and to truth as correspondence to that reality; a sharp separation between knower and known, between fact and value, and, above all, between history and fiction. Historical facts are seen as prior to and independent of interpretation: the value of an interpretation is judged by how well it accounts for the facts; if contradicted by the facts, it must be abandoned. Truth is one, not perspectival. Whatever patterns exist in history are "found," not "made." Though successive generations of historians might, as their perspectives shifted, attribute different significance to events in the past, the meaning of those events was unchanging. The objective historian's role is that of a neutral, or disinterested, judge; it must never degenerate into that of advocate or, even worse, propagandist.[14]

Novick takes this to be a broadly agreed upon definition of objectivity among modern historians, and his allies include writers such as Arthur Marwick and G. R. Elton, all of whom take aim at postmodern and hermeneutical accounts in no uncertain terms. Here is Elton's curt take on hermeneutics, as contrasted with the view he defends: "Hermeneutics is the science which invents meaning; historical study depends on discovering meaning without inventing it. Hermeneutics seeks to reduce variety to cohesiveness, while history accepts the probability of unpredictable variety. Therefore, hermeneutics is a term not only not applicable to the historian's operation but positively hostile to it; its use enables the student to impose meaning on his materials instead of extracting meaning and import from them."[15] Here again we find the usual polarities: invention versus discovery, imposition versus extraction, one meaning versus many, real meaning versus "significance," historical versus fictional narrative, and so on, and also a complete distortion of hermeneutics which we shall need to correct as we proceed. If not some form of objectivism then an intellectually irresponsible subjectivism, while the opposition itself is nothing more than an assumption.

To get out of this morass we need to begin by exercising a bit of hermeneutic charity, for the two sets of positions that we might broadly call empiricist and postmodern both have a point that once suitably qualified enjoys considerable validity. The empiricist's emphasis on the centrality and authority of evidence must surely be retained, but without inflating this into an untenable epistemology. Historical investigation is as fully rational as any other field of knowledge, and its claim to rationality comes down to the traceability of its interpretations to sources and evidence of a kind that fictional narratives might employ but typically do not. I have called this basic point common sense empiricism, and when not transformed into a dogmatic scientism it is a sensible and not particularly controversial description of historical inquiry or an important dimension of it. On the face of it this view does not conflict with the narrative hypothesis, which is at the heart of postmodern historiography. The validity in the latter position centers around the idea that historical knowledge crucially involves interpretation in the specific form of narrative and that such narratives involve some imaginative work on the part of the historian. The postmodern and empiricist positions both become dubiously one-sided when they commit the error of becoming so enamored with their own insights that they lose sight of the truth on the other side and fall into an oppositional stance that is needless. I have suggested that the way out of this impasse is to focus on the historical imagination, and from the side of both the subject and the object. The former was our focus in chapter 1. Regarding the latter, the empiricist's stress upon sources and evidence affords a good starting point, but we shall need to qualify and supplement this while employing the resources of phenomenology, focusing on the concepts of intentionality, temporality, the pre-narrative quality of experience, and the intertwining of subjectivity and objectivity and of the present and the past. We shall look at each of these themes in what follows.

Let us begin with a modest prefix. For over a century now, phenomenological and hermeneutical thinkers have devoted enormous labor to trying to thematize the "pre-" in the sense of a thinking that is operative before any explicit activity of either interpreting, perceiving, reasoning, judging, critiquing, or theorizing, and that makes these activities possible and also limits them. The pre-reflective, pre-thematic, pre-understood, the way the stage is set prior to the drama, is singularly elusive, happening as it does behind our back. Yet it goes on, has "always already" (to use an overused phrase, but one from which there is no getting away here) gone on, prior to what we commonly think of as cognition and experience generally. Locke's *tabula rasa* misses the mark as widely as Descartes' notion of the prejudice-free meditator. The crucial point both thinkers missed is what has happened before all explicit perception and ratiocination, for this "happening before" has given consciousness an orientation and a trajectory that is for the most part taken for granted, more operative than thought. It arises from our embodiment and our embeddedness in history, culture, language, and a network of relations all of which precede our activities of perception and understanding, inference and analysis, and our conscious intellectual operations in general. Historical narration is no exception to this, as Ricoeur in particular attempted to elucidate.

"Stories are not lived but told," Louis Mink asserts. "Life has no beginnings, middles and ends . . . .. Narrative qualities are transferred from art to life."[16] Alasdair MacIntyre replies that "stories are lived before they are told," setting up yet another dichotomy.[17] Whatever impulse it is that has us frame questions of this kind in binary terms should be resisted. Mink's assertion lacks nuance, and if MacIntyre's reply is an improvement, as I believe it is, it does not go far enough or deep enough into our experience, for that experience itself has a pre-narrative quality which Ricoeur sought to articulate and which we need to think through some more. What is this pre-narrative quality? It seems clear enough that life as we encounter it in the present does not transpire in anything like the manner of a novel; the latter exhibits a sense of direction and a plot, it has a coherence that has been artfully fashioned even if it is complex, and is without extraneous elements while our experience of life is shot through with incoherence, the extraneous, dead ends, and many an unrelated episode which may at some later time be retrospectively configured as a story while lacking at the time we are undergoing it the aesthetic elegance of a novel. This much is true, however, our lived experience is commonly not of random or range of the moment happenings but of sequences, relations, directionality, partial continuity, purposiveness, and habitual actions, all of which hang together, however loosely, in an organic way. This will often be more felt than understood, but the things that we do and that happen to us typically have a pre-narrative significance in virtue of which it will become possible to locate them within the form of a story unfolding over time. Let us think of an example from everyday life: if the reader is presently reading these words, that activity would not be describable as a narrative, particularly given a short timeline. One has been reading, let us say, from the beginning of the present chapter and intends to push on through until the end of the chapter before closing the book and doing something else. Regarded in isolation, that activity is not a story, however experiences like this do not happen in isolation but within a larger context. The present action belongs to a larger sequence: it is part of our project of reading the book as a whole, and therefore constitutes the middle part of a sequence that includes a beginning and an ending. This beginning-middle-end structure can be and normally is extended much further: reading this book belongs to a larger project of learning about a particular field of knowledge, which may itself fit into a larger project of pursuing a degree, becoming a philosopher, writing a book of one's own, or any number of others. The action does not stand aloof or have any kind of in-itself quality but exists in relation to a before and after in virtue of which it is understood, that is, if it is capable of being understood at all or if it can be said to have a meaning. The truly isolated action—assuming such a thing is even possible (and one should not assume this)—is without any meaning at all. Such an action would have no end in view, come out of nowhere, lead nowhere, respond or in some other way be related to nothing, and this description does not apply to much at all in our experience. The example just mentioned lacks the depth and complexity of *The Brothers Karamazov*, it is true, but to say that its status as a narrative is "transferred from art" is not accurate. We understand its meaning in the way that we understand anything at all: by relating the particular to a larger universality, such as a story, an undertaking, a habit, or otherwise in relation to a context. MacIntyre's claim that "stories are lived before they are told" is a reference to the pre-narrative quality of experience; they are enacted, for the most part pre-reflectively but not unthinkingly.

We can think of other examples: a person goes to work on an ordinary day, and sets about performing the usual range of tasks, punches out at the appointed hour and goes home. Not much of a story there either until one tries to understand what is going on, why they are doing this, what they are trying to achieve. The answer again takes the form of a story: the tasks performed on this ordinary day fall somewhere in the middle of a beginning-middle-end structure; they are earning a living, taking care of their family, pursuing a career, climbing the ladder, coasting until retirement, or are otherwise engaged in a larger project that began at a particular time and will also come to an end. The workday itself is not isolated from the day, year, or decade that preceded and can be anticipated to follow it. Even so small an action as picking up the bass guitar that hangs on a wall in my office and fumbling through a song for a few minutes is a proto-story which began in an adolescence spent largely listening to rock music and led to a present and undoubtedly future failure to sound like Geddy Lee. It belongs to the project of learning to play an instrument and resonates with a lifetime of aesthetic experiences in light of which it holds a meaning. Actions form sequences; they arise from somewhere, lead toward a goal or purpose, and hold significance for the agent and likely others as well. These sequences are pre- or nascent narratives, and our experience is replete with them. As Kearney expresses it, "existence is inherently storied. Life is pregnant with stories. It is a nascent plot in search of a midwife. For inside every human being there are lots of little narratives trying to get out."[18] The midwifery metaphor is apt for the stories of which we are speaking are characterized by potentiality. They become actual narratives in being configured or transformed in a way that Ricoeur likens to imitation or mimesis.

A narrative, on his view, is an imitation of an action or sequence of actions, an actualization of what already belongs to it, where what belongs to it is a "symbolism" and "an initial *readability*" which is capable of, one may say calls for, a certain form of rendering. The storyteller's art renders explicit—actualizes, makes intelligible, or otherwise brings to life (which is not to say constructs)—a configuration that is nascent within a sequence of actions and experiences. The latter are symbolically mediated from the beginning, as Geertz has shown, and their symbolic value amounts to what Ricoeur calls a "prefiguration" that makes the imaginative activity of storytelling or "configuration" possible and necessary. As with metaphor construction, narrating involves a "seeing-as" and a "grasping together" of various matters which become understood as story elements. As he writes, "every narrative presupposes a familiarity with terms such as agent, goal, means, circumstance, help, hostility, cooperation, conflict, success, failure, etc., on the part of its narrator and any listener. In this sense, the minimal narrative sentence is an action of the form 'X did A in such and such circumstances, taking into account the fact that Y does B in identical or different circumstances.' In the final analysis, narratives have acting and suffering as their theme."[19] A story is comprised of what characters do and what happens to them, as can be said of the self itself. One lives a story which is told retrospectively but which is also enacted in the present, and indeed one is that story. We understand any person by hearing the story of their life and not by beholding them as a being that exhibits a set of qualities and is frozen in time. Lived experience does not have the structure of a chronicle. Indeed, the latter is an abstraction, a selective and ordered configuration of events according to the chronicler's estimation of importance and relevance. Now this, now that, and so on is not our experience of life. Experiences and actions lend themselves to the storyteller's art because they are already in motion, directional, fluid, purposive, meaningful, understood or preunderstood, and interrelated with a myriad elements in a larger configuration that itself is always on the way. As David Carr puts it, "narrative accounts . . . must be regarded not as a departure from the structure of the reality they purport to depict, much less a distortion or radical transformation of its character, but as an extension of its very nature."[20]

Part of the nature of such a reality is a theme that has been at the heart of phenomenology from the beginning, and this is its temporality. "Time and narrative" is both the title of Ricoeur's three-volume treatment of this set of themes as well as a logical pairing if we are speaking of time as it is experienced by human beings. His hypothesis is that "between the activity of narrating a story and the temporal character of human experience there exists a correlation that is not merely accidental but that presents a transcultural form of necessity. To put it another way, *time becomes human to the extent that it is articulated through a narrative mode, and narrative attains its full meaning when it becomes a condition of temporal existence*."[21] The correlation between narrative and our experience of temporality was an important innovation with significant implications for the philosophy of history, although the phenomenology of "human time" was much discussed before Ricoeur. Husserl, Heidegger, Merleau-Ponty, and some others provided notable analyses of this theme which are worth recalling. For the sake of brevity, let us single out Merleau-Ponty's treatment in *Phenomenology of Perception*. Our experience of time, he noted, is not of a being standing outside of us but of something that we are in and indeed that we "are." As he expressed this point, "To consider time as just another object, we would have to say of it what we have said of other objects: that it only has sense for us because we 'are it.' We can only place something under this rubric because we are in the past, in the present, and in the future. Time is literally the sense of our life, and like the world it is only accessible to the one who is situated in it and who joins with its direction." The meaning of "in" here—we are beings "in" time—is not that of a material object that is physically contained in another, like potatoes in a bag, but is suggestive of belonging. We belong to time, are of it, of a piece with it; it is the mode in which we have a world at all, not an object inside of it. We "live" time, or exist temporally: "'In' my present—given that I catch hold of it while it is still living and with all that it implies—there is an ecstasy toward the future and toward the past that makes the dimensions of time appear, not as rivals, but as inseparable: to be in the present is to have always been and to be forever. Subjectivity is not in time because it takes up or lives time and merges with the cohesion of a life."[22]

The bare present does not exist, nor do absolute beginnings or endings. A moment that bears no relation whatever to a before and after, like any bare particular, is foreign to our experience and understanding. This moment is dynamic; it is going somewhere and it is from somewhere, it is on the move, fluid, constantly changing into another, and is understood precisely in its dynamism or its tending this way or that. Merleau-Ponty makes the point this way: "Instant C and instant D—as close together as one wishes to make them—are never indiscernible, for then there would be no time at all; rather, they pass into each other, and C becomes D because it was never anything but the anticipation of D as present, and of its own passage into the past. This amounts to saying that each present reaffirms the presence of the entire past that it drives away, and anticipates the presence of the entire future or the 'to-come' [*l'à-venir*], and that, by definition, the present is not locked within itself but transends itself toward a future and toward a past." Human time is "a network of intentionalities," not a linear "series of nows" strung together like photographs in an album but a network within which we are located and in which the three dimensions of past, present, and future lead into one another and are not discrete. The present is constantly before us even as the future "'is there,' just like the back of the house whose front I am looking at," and the past no less. Neither the future nor the past is a representation; again they "are there" in the sense that they "weigh upon me."[23] The future weighs upon the present as a promise or a threat, while the past is a prelude and a source of pride or guilt. The here and now is nothing "in itself" but a myriad of preparations, means, responses, leadings, foreshadowings, consequences, repetitions, continuities, departures, and transactions with a before and after.

The flowing nature of time and the overlapping of its three aspects had been analyzed by Husserl in terms of retentions and protentions (anticipations) which span the larger horizon of what is behind and before us, as the experience of music illustrates. The present sound belongs to a melody or a larger progression that takes shape over time, as a life becomes what it is over a span of years and is understood as a being with a history and a directionality. It is mistaken, then, as Carr points out, to think of narrative as "imposed upon a human experience intrinsically devoid of it so that such structure is an artifice, something not 'natural' but forced, something which distorts or does violence to the true nature of human reality."[24] The constructivist's view of narrative as an imaginative imposition on a past reality that "of itself" is un-storied, chronicle-like, and devoid of meaning is phenomenologically unsatisfactory because of the way in which human time is experienced. The past is capable of being narrated because it is already a nascent story of which the historian is a midwife rather than a Yahweh-like creator.

This art of midwifery, we have argued, involves a large amount of gathering, sifting, selecting, judging, analyzing, synthesizing, and weaving bits of evidence into a larger configuration that relates a version of what transpired and how we may understand it. We have also argued that the historian does not make it up or conjure something from nothing but tells a story that is based upon the evidence, even as the evidence does not speak for itself, or not exactly. Exactly what, then? Here matters become more than a little ambiguous, for historians—like detectives, doctors, lawyers, scientists, or anyone else who works with evidence—commonly say that the sources and evidence "indicate," "suggest," or "prove" that this or that was the case, but what is the meaning of this? A document, coin, or other artifact, duly vetted for historical authenticity, "indicates" that Michel begat Jean, that Hadrian built his wall in order to ward off the Picts, that a particular battle set the stage for war, or that in some way or other event X occasioned, prompted, or afforded a reason for Y. In a court of law, evidence does not dictate a verdict but must be interpreted, weighed, and judged, and the same happens among historians.

There is a story there, or the makings of one; there is something there that the historian is less constructing than detecting, listening to, and following, or their constructing is itself a mode of following.

What following is this? At this point let us return to the comparison numerous postmodernists in particular have drawn between historiography and art. The historian is not only a storyteller but also, as Ankersmit says, "could meaningfully be compared to the painter representing a landscape, a person, and so on." Such art is representational, on his account—a curious view given how much art is neither representational nor intended to be. Be that as it may, the model we are to imagine is a landscape that simply is what it is before the painter happens on the scene and, on the other side of a divide, the painter's subjectivity and activity of creating a work of art. Such activity is free, and apparently without qualification. They do not paint what is "indicated" in or by the landscape but rather create a work as an act of sovereign subjectivity. The difficulty is that many artists themselves—be they painters, novelists, poets, songwriters, or anything else—report something that will have important implications for historiography. This is that artistic creation is not altogether free. A work of fiction, many novelists tell us, in a sense "tells itself," and we often hear the same from artists working in the different forms. The story is one's own, yet one's freedom to tell it is not unlimited. What happens next in the story is, once again, "indicated" by what happened before and the larger trajectory of the narrative. This is not artistic hyperbole but a description of what happens or has already happened in the process of creating the work. One is following the course of the narrative in the same gesture in which one is composing it, or so many novelists and other artists often report. The work creates itself or takes on a life of its own, or so we hear from those who create such works. What could this mean? The landscape does not cause the painting; this much is clear, but the artist's activity is guided by something that is authoritative, and where this is not a cause.

What, then, is it? Jeff Mitscherling, over the course of several books on phenomenology and aesthetics, has spoken of this as intentionality, and this phenomenological concept must now be brought into focus. By this term Mitscherling is speaking not of a mental state or anything that is controlled by a sovereign consciousness but of a relating and a "tending towards": "all *intentionality*," as he puts it, "consists in such a 'tending towards,' or a *directed movement* that one undergoes prior to the activity of conscious deliberation . . .. Our 'tending towards' or 'directed movement' occurs not as the result of our consciously creating and fully controlling the goal or target of our consciousness, but rather as the result of allowing ourselves to be moved or *guided* in a certain direction." We are still operating here within the world of the "pre-": prior to conscious thinking, which includes configuring and relating a narrative, something is already going on which is not a projection of consciousness but something that gives rise to consciousness itself. There is, as he describes it, a "compelling 'internal logic' of the story that's dragging us all along, writers and readers alike. And this logos is more than merely conceptual (but it's also that): if it were, we could anticipate it, get ahead of it, direct it—but we can't . . . we're at *its* mercy. It's guiding us—author and reader alike, each of us necessarily remaining 'passionate,' because we're not 'mentally' in charge."[25] What, then, is?

Mitscherling calls it an intention, where this is to be understood neither as an intended meaning nor any other mental state nor a construction of consciousness but as something that lies before us in our experience, something we encounter, and that is neither a material object nor an ideal one (such as numbers). The phenomenon of which we are speaking has being, but in neither a material nor an ideal sense but rather intentionally, as a relation:

> What a thing is, it is *in relation* to something else. Everything tends this way or that: it is proximal, changing, in motion, on the way, becoming, passing away, opposing, betwixt and between, in process, transacting, interacting, interrelating, in negotiation, intimating, symbolizing, leading somewhere or other. A *is* A, but it *points to* B . . . . Any A that we encounter . . . is dynamic, pushed around by forces, suspended in webs, or otherwise part of a larger phenomenon. It's no bare particular, raw datum, or thing in itself. The world we live in is permeated with intentionality, not in the sense of an external imposition or projection of the mind but where the intention itself exists dialectically, *between* subject and object, and binds them together.[26]

This is the human world—a lifeworld in which we are suspended and from which we are inseparable, and the historical world is no exception.

Mitscherling offers a metaphor, followed by a couple of important qualifications:

> Imagine a glass globe, within which are radiating lines, like strands of a web, thousands of them, all intersecting and going every which way. Imagine now that you stand somewhere inside this globe. You say, where am I? and where you find yourself is in the midst of all these intentions around you. That's your world. All of us are at different points within that same globe. We're locating ourselves in that world and sharing certain values: space, time, color values, what have you. This is why we can talk together, because we're in that globe together . . . . If the globe metaphor suggests something too static, like a closed system, let's remove the glass. The globe now expands to become a dynamic and infinite universe, but the lines of intentionality remain. Also let's not think of these lines as material or quasi-material entities. They have being, but not in the way that material objects do or even ideal objects. The lines may be thought of as states of affairs and situations that exhibit actual or potential directionality, as an event may be seen to be heading in some direction.[27]

A historical event, let us say the end of the western Roman empire in the fifth century, was no singular happening frozen in time but was at once a cessation and a beginning or turning point which bore a thousand relations to other events, involved a wide array of historical actors, anticipated the Christian middle ages while constituting a kind of ending, and so on and so forth down to the present day, and historians continue to rewrite this story and undoubtedly will continue to do so. The directedness of this event led out of the ancient world and into the medieval, away from empire and administrative centralization and toward decentralization, away from many gods and toward the one. This kind of directedness can be compared to what characterizes a narrative or any work of art: it assumes a life of its own and gets away from its creator, gathers an inner momentum—an intentionality—in the same process by which it is fashioned, and is followed by the storyteller in much the way it will later be followed by the reader. The storyteller, as Mark Twain put it, is not sovereign but "can only find out what [the story] is by listening as it goes along telling itself," and "it is more than apt to go on and on and on till it spreads itself into a book."[28] He was speaking of fictional narrative, but something similar applies to the historical.

Many artists speak of a phenomenon that Mitscherling describes as tracking intentions that are not a creation of subjectivity but something substantial which guides the artist and subsequently an audience. This is a radical revision of Husserl's hypothesis regarding the intentionality of consciousness in that intentions are not, as Husserl maintained, a projection of the mind but something real that consciousness becomes aware of and actively follows. Tracking intentionality is done in many forms and by all of us; it happens when one gets swept up in a conversation or is grabbed by a story, when an athlete gets carried along in the momentum of a game, a musician improvises as the song itself seems to require, a detective follows the trail of evidence, a physician tracks the symptoms to a diagnosis, and a historian follows where the evidence leads, or in general in any experience in which, as we say, "one thing leads to another." This mode of following is imaginative, not servile; it is active and receptive at the same time, rather as a judge formulates a verdict that is indicated by the evidence. In all these cases, we do not make it up but allow ourselves to be guided by something in our experience that is beyond our command.

We find ourselves, then, in the midst of a historical world, not as a Hobbesian individual entering the state of nature from some place outside it but already there, suspended in webs of intentionality—participating in a tradition, appropriating a culture, and belonging to a particular time and place. Each of these verbs—participating, appropriating, belonging—points to an experience that is simultaneously an activity and a passivity or that is, in a word, imaginative. It is a creative responding to what is already going on in the world, finding our way through strands of a web that is encompassing and more or less infinite, trying to see the relatedness of things, to grasp connections, and to understand what is happening, how we got here, and where things may be going. The active gathering, synthesizing, and narrating of historical elements which we have spoken of as belonging to the subject side of the imagination is one aspect of a larger phenomenon or one pole of a dialectic, the other pole of which is both the sources and evidence of which historians have long spoken and the intentionality that is implicit to them. The evidence indicates that X led to Y, not in a sense of cause and effect but X foreshadowed, set the stage, or afforded a rationale for Y. Whether a narrative be fictional or historical, one episode sets up the next and the whole is followable because of the organic relatedness of the various situations, characters, and actions that move things along and that the storyteller brings to light. What has happened when a story "tells itself," as with anything in our experience that takes on a momentum and a life of its own, is that the teller has picked up on an intentionality that belonged to the phenomenon from the outset as a potentiality and rendered it actual, made it explicit, in a way closer to midwifery than construction. It gets away from us, as a conversation or a game goes where it will and is not what we anticipated or planned. The fundamental difference, then, between the fictional and the historical narrative is not that the latter is "constrained by the real" while the former is made up but that "the real" that guides novelist and historian alike does not, in the former case, include material evidence (although it might).[29] Both are beholden, not sovereign.

Subjective idealism, as Merleau-Ponty expressed it, "(like objective thought) misses genuine intentionality, which, rather than positing its object, is *toward* its object." "Man is a knot of relations," he stated, "and relations alone count for man," where relations themselves are intentions.[30] As one Merleau-Ponty scholar writes, "existence is defined by, and in fact is nothing other than, a dialogue with the world, intentionality, transcendence."[31] The larger ontological picture we are offering shares with Merleau-Ponty a rejection of the subject/object opposition that remains deeply rooted in so much of modern thought along with the dichotomy of the imaginary and the real. Moving beyond these stubborn dualities has occasioned enormous philosophical labor for well over a century now, and this phenomenological thinker was as significant as any in the effort within this school of thought in articulating a view of the relation between all that has long fallen under the heading of "subjectivity" or "the mind" and "the world" or "objectivity." The details of his account we cannot go into, but the larger picture is one in which subjectivity and objectivity are neither separated by an abyss nor dissolved into one but stand to each other in their mutuality, as flowing into one another or again as two poles of a single dialectic. The relation between subject and object is internal, in the manner of a system, and on the model of dialogue. To say that we are beings-in-the-world means that we are not only in the world but of it, that an umbilical cord of intentionality or relations binds each of us into a network of intersubjectivity that persists through time.

Gary Madison in his classic book on Merleau-Ponty writes, "Subject and world are no longer two independent substances external to one another, but, precisely because they are now defined as two moments of a single dialectical circularity, there exists but an incessant referring back of one to the other. The 'circularity' of the *Phenomenology* is thus an unsurpassable dialectical opposition. The concept of 'being in the world' expresses this radical duality, and the *Phenomenology* is in this sense the height of relativism," although one might better say relationism.[32] Anything that is a part of the human world—be it a historical event or situation, an individual agent or action, a text or artifact, an idea or expression—is understood only in its dynamic relatedness, whether this be a temporal before and after, a location in space or a culture or place, its being a means or an end, a continuation or departure, a purpose and a destining, or otherwise in its tending this way and that. The philosophical quest for in-itself-ness, for that which simply is what it is in relation to nothing, is like fishing on dry land for nothing in our world has an existence that is outside of a lifeworld, cultural web, or network of meanings. The only "relativism" here would be better spoken of as "on-the-way-ism," were the expression not so artless: "The president was on his way to being a one-term president"; "The emperor was a pale reflection of his predecessor"; "This artistic movement anticipated a later movement"; "This architectural style was an appropriation of a neighboring contemporary or predecessor"; "This philosophical text was a development in a long-standing tradition"—these are the kinds of claims historians make in their more "analytical" moments, when they are ostensibly no longer telling stories but engaged in the serious work of historical analysis. Analyzing, synthesizing, informing, narrating, or any cognition we care to speak of, as Mitscherling has persuasively shown, is an activity in which what we are doing is tracing connections, tracking down leads, seeing X in light of Y, reconciling a particular with a universal, regarding in context, and grasping relations that are organic and not static.

The larger picture is of a tensional circularity of subjectivity and objectivity, no longer regarded as separate orders of being but as a unified system. To cite Mitscherling once more, "human consciousness consists in the *mutual creation* of subject and object, these two poles of awareness. To speak of the 'priority' of one over the other, either of 'ideal' mind (idealism) or of the 'material,' external world (materialism), is mistaken . . . . Both mind and world exist, and they exist independently of each other. What they don't exist independently of is the relation that gives rise to and dialectically maintains them both. This relation is intentionality at work, and we find intentionality at work everywhere."³³ Our experience is replete with an operative intentionality in which we and everything we encounter are suspended, a meshwork of associations that are neither objectively given nor subjectively constituted but pre- or intersubjective, and historical consciousness is no exception.

When Dilthey asserted that "What man is, only his history can tell him," he meant that we belong to history in a fundamental sense and understand ourselves only within it, as anything in the human world is understandable in terms of its coming to be and passing away.³⁴ The past, we may say, is not over and done with but is a living past that haunts the present, or inhabits it as the future does. Past, present, and future are not object-like but relata, dimensions of one unified fabric in virtue of which one finds oneself already oriented and poised for what is to come. History is lived in much the way that the body itself, on Merleau-Ponty's telling, is "lived," again not in the manner of a substance but as a network of intentionality in virtue of which one has a certain hold on the world. The body is not what one "has" but what one "is," and the same is true of history. It is because the historical object and the embodied subject participate in a shared world that the latter is able to engage in a dialogue with the past, and "without having to go through 'representations,' or without being subordinated to a 'symbolic' or 'objectifying function.'"³⁵ We are already historically conditioned, "of" and conversant with the past (the future no less), and the same process that finds us configuring and questioning it finds it interrogating us. Subject and object, mind and body, self and other, past, present, and future are all relational terms, not substances but participations in a system within which we all stand.

Historical imagination encompasses not only the overtly poetic dimension of inquiry into the human past—reckoning with visual and quasi-visual images, filling in gaps, constructing metaphors—but a broader capacity of synthesizing the myriad elements that comprise a narrative in a way that makes it possible to render us conversant with a time and place remote from our own. Kearney speaks of a "power . . . of *vicarious* imagination" and "empathic imagination," "a power capable of intending the unreal *as if* it were real, the absent *as if* it were present, the possible *as if* it were actual."³⁶ We are not transported into the past, but it is as if we were, for by virtue of the historian's labor the reader is able to make vicarious contact with the occupants of a world that is ultimately both theirs and ours. The schema within which the historian works is no closed system but opens onto a past that is extant. Whether we speak of empathy, transcendence, understanding meanings, or what have you, historical imagining is a mode of engagement and a meeting of minds. Gadamer spoke of a "fusion of horizons" in the sense that we are placing on speaking terms perspectives that had been alienated, whether by virtue of culture, place, or time. Of course, in the case of historical imagination such understanding can never be mutual, but again if we are speaking phenomenologically it is as if we are conversing with a past with which we can never return. We are following and unraveling threads of intentionality that reveal to us not only "what happened" but "what it must have been like," letting it speak to us by creating openings in which we can experience something of the flavor of the times.

Let us speak of the imagination in an expansive way as an art of gathering, composing, revealing, making contact, seeing the connectedness of things, and narrating—and not in any way but in the way that the story needs to be told and indeed in a non-fanciful sense tells itself. The historian's freedom is neither unconditioned nor unlimited, and if we may speak of truth here then it is not the whole truth but the dimension of it that a particular mode of access makes visible. We need not hesitate to say things did happen this way, that the telling makes sense, even if the historian never pronounces the final word and their interpretations, however compelling, must be reinterpreted over time. Historians work within an imaginative schema that structures appearances that are nonetheless objects of knowledge and tailors particulars with universals (at the best of times anyway) without interpretive violence. When successful, an imaginative account makes it possible for the reader to "get it," to see how events came to pass and might have been otherwise, how they played out and resonated, how one thing led to another, what it meant to them and what it may entail for us, what they thought they were doing and what we may have to say about it. Imagining involves no little hypothesizing and analyzing, following trails, seeing-as, and creatively synthesizing bits of evidence that never speak for themselves. It encompasses the forest and the trees, plotlines, characters, conflicts, turning points, patterns, tendencies, themes, and most often is affectively charged. It makes it possible to see our historical others in relation to their predecessors, their contemporaries, and to us, and to make possible some meeting of minds. We are trying to bridge the distance, to understand how things stood, what it was like, who these people were, what they believed in and cared about, what things meant to them and might yet mean, what they may yet teach us and what they could have learned from us, what they were up against and what their blind spots were.

Our being-in-the-world, as numerous phenomenological writers have brought to our attention, is a being-in-time. Human existence is a transcendence toward the future at the same time that it reaches back to a shared past, both of which weigh upon the present and make it possible for us to understand both our others and ourselves, for self-understanding never happens in a temporal vacuum. Our historical predecessors are never wholly other for we are of a piece with them, connected by a thousand invisible threads in virtue of which we are who we are. Their struggles are not a spectacle we behold as a god might but are our struggles and belong to the same drama in which we continue to participate. Their time is not ours, and they themselves are not us, but on an imaginative telling it is as if they were.

CHAPTER 3

Early Christian Reimaginings

I have suggested that if we wish to understand the historical imagination we must endeavor to square the kind of philosophical argumentation that I have outlined in chapters 1 and 2 with historical inquiry into those transitional eras during which this capacity of mind is often thought to have entered a relatively active phase, where an old worldview was abandoned and an assortment of religious and political thinkers, historians, artists, philosophers, scientists, and so on are regarded, usually in hindsight, as having effected something of a paradigm shift. What is happening when a conceptual and imaginative schema is replaced by or perhaps transforms into another? What is immediately evident, as this and the following two chapters seek to show, is that any such turning point is brought about not by a handful of individuals but by a larger movement encompassing at once intellectuals and some sizeable portion of the society in a phenomenon that may be described as proceeding simultaneously from the "top down" and the "bottom up." An imaginative schema must answer to the existing needs—psychological, intellectual, spiritual, ethical/political, aesthetic, economic—of a population even as it goes to work on those needs and at times generates new ones. Talk of revolutionary developments in this realm is most often a retrospective illusion, and exhibit A will be the centuries of the common era that run from about the fourth through the sixth and which contemporary historians refer to as "late antiquity." This is the period (one of them) long known as "the dark ages" when, according to an old story, the fall of the Roman Empire in the west was succeeded by wholesale civilizational collapse and a long period of cultural stagnation and religious superstition. This account was most famously defended by Edward Gibbon at the height of the enlightenment while today a preponderance of historians of this general era take a decidedly different view, one that speaks of continuity and transformation over the decline and fall narrative which currently finds few proponents.

What happened over the course of these centuries from the point of view not only of intellectual but also of what we might call imaginative history, if by this we intend the general thought world of a given time and place and the narrative of its transformations and variations? I shall employ this term in a wide connotation that incorporates the network of ideas which spans a culture or cultures and is not narrowly classifiable as "philosophical," "religious," or what have you. It is the *zeitgeist* we are after, that undifferentiated cultural and mental climate that is manifested in everything from various forms of knowledge to works of art, morality, customs, institutions, and societal trends, and the manner in which all of this is sometimes transformed on a relatively large scale or at a quicker pace than what is visible in the more usual course of history. All imagining is a reimagining, but there are periods in which this happens in more dramatic ways or where the consequences for later centuries are more far-reaching. This is clearly true in the case of the early Christian reimaginings that are the topic of the present chapter. How did a conceptual and imaginative schema that for untold centuries had spoken of a plethora of divinities find itself displaced by a worldview that postulated one god? The human condition in its totality was reinterpreted in such monumental fashion as to inspire intellectuals some centuries later to speak of the end of classical civilization and the beginning of the middle ages. How was "paganism" defeated, and what was paganism? What were some of the more salient aspects of the transformation into Christendom? What were historically minded thinkers saying through these centuries about the era that anteceded their own, and what does this suggest about the workings or the activity of historical imagination itself? This capacity of mind does not operate in a vacuum of history and culture but participates in what it reconceives, rather as the artistic imagination does not create works of art *ex nihilo* but within a tradition of art or a social critic judges a democracy within a democratic framework.

Citizens of the "dark ages," it will not surprise us to hear, did not think of themselves as living in a time of decline or backwardness relative to the Roman era or indeed to any prior time. This judgment would not be made until the renaissance, and why they began to take this view is a question we shall address in chapter 4. The judgment of collapse was retrospective and made possible by conditions contemporary to the era in which it was made, and it is an estimation by which late antique intellectuals themselves would have been puzzled. What tower had come crashing down, what golden age left behind? Late antique intellectuals were looking forward—to the return of the messiah and the coming kingdom—and back little further than the time of their savior. Historical consciousness was no longer cyclical but teleological and hopeful. How did this change of perspective come about? Was an entire cultural narrative, stemming from the Greeks and appropriated by the Romans, simply abandoned? To see that it was not and that an altogether different set of dynamics was in play let us recall something of the intellectual landscape of the time period during which early Christianity took root in lands spanning the former empire.

While no highly unified picture emerges of a lifeworld that encompassed the various regions of the Mediterranean and beyond, we may speak of a network of ideas and a tradition of ancient lineage which spoke in myriad ways not only to the upper classes but also to larger populations about gods and heroes, ritual sacrifice and mythic narratives bewildering in variety and complexity, philosophical notions and moral/political values that were shared while also contested. The imaginative schema of the Romans had been hallowed by time and was comprised of ideas and sensibilities which Christendom would reduce with not a little hermeneutic violence to a simple concept. Paganism, in a word, was both the precursor and the great other of the imitators of Christ, while the reality that this word designated was at once manifold and particularistic. The Roman thought world was the opposite of monolithic; its orientation toward Rome coexisted with a localism of gods and customs while also recognizing the imperial divinities. The Roman landscape was teeming with gods and holy men, aristocrats and savants, factions and statesmen, poets and would-be prophets all bent on preeminence and harkening to a past which was a source of authority and legitimacy. In the realm of the spiritual, the practices and poets of old were being rechristened: "The idea of the holy man," Peter Brown writes, "holding the demons at bay and bending the will of God by his prayers came to dominate Late Antique society.... [I]t placed ... a 'man of power' in the centre of people's imagination," where the religious center had been occupied by the temples and other sacred sites that had populated the empire.[1]

The transition from polytheism to monotheism was no simple event brought on by the conversion of Constantine but a process that unfolded over centuries while among monotheists themselves no canon or orthodoxy was quick to emerge. The followers of Jesus were traditionalists with a difference; like the polytheists of old and Jewish monotheists, they were myth-makers who borrowed heavily from both their predecessors and contemporaries against whom they were also in competition, appropriating imaginative elements that were received and arranged into rhetorically pleasing forms. Already in the time of Jesus, as Donald Akenson points out, "scores of versions of the Yahweh-faith battled with each other for primacy.... And in that era, the dozens of major ideational components that were lying around the shop floor were put together into literally hundreds of possible Judaisms.... That Christianity and Rabbinic Judaism eventually became the two surviving systems from the multiplicity of Judaisms was the result of a grand-chance lottery."[2] The shop floor contained many a concept, metaphor, mythic narrative, divinity, heroic figure, or cipher which creative minds could reinterpret and synthesize in ways that might satisfy ancient audiences which generally preferred old ideas to new. The various narratives that comprised Greek and Roman *mythos* were not jettisoned but distilled by early Christian thinkers into a single story with multiple variations and which asked to be believed on faith. What Brown calls an "easy-going unity of heaven and earth" which polytheists had accepted since before Homeric times was being transformed by Christians who "claimed power from heaven but they had made that heaven remote and they kept its power to themselves, to build up new separate institutions among upstart heroes on earth."[3] Gods new and old filled the heavens, and the draw of monotheism had more than a little to do with earthly representatives with a shrewd eye for politics and persuasion alike. The followers of Jesus were on a mission in a way that the old polytheism had never attempted. Converts needed to be won and an institution legitimated using whatever means proved effective, from theological argumentation to force and everything in between.

Exactly why and when growing segments of the population of the empire and the kingdoms that succeeded it came over to the new monotheism is difficult to say. Many factors were involved in a process that took a few centuries to unfold, but one of them was the way in which history was being written and rewritten. History had long been a branch of rhetoric if not indeed *mythos*, the story of some usually heroic past which was expected to abide by the rhetorical conventions of the time while also striving for some manner of truth. Historians needed to be truthful and artful at once, and it helped immensely if they could also flatter political authority. The core of an aristocratic education was the art of persuasion and public speaking, and history was a branch of this art. An account of Rome's past loomed large in the imagination along with a narrative of imperialism that on a common telling brought harmony and peace to the lands it had conquered. How the empire came to be, the glorious fashion in which it triumphed over barbarism, and the blessings that ensued were the central elements in accounts that were propagandistic and faithful to the evidence in roughly equal measure. Historical writing served its audience, and he who paid the piper called the tune in a manner that would not change in the transition to the new religion.

What would change are the piper's patron and the dimension of the past that served the new narrative. Rome's former glories were now beside the point. The past that mattered was the Old Testament, the history not of empire and its heroes but of Genesis and the prophets, all of which needed to be recast as one long prelude to the life of Jesus and his subsequent church. Secular history held little interest; it was sacred history that now reigned supreme, the art of discerning the hand of God through the manifold episodes of history and the anticipation of the savior's return. The Christian imagination had no use for the cyclical conception of history which the Romans had appropriated from the Greeks—an account for which the great model of history is nature with its eternal rhythms of night and day, birth and death, the change of seasons, and so on. A model that spoke of the eternal recurrence of the same had no place for a savior or anything radically new in the continual coming to be and passing away of things, no creation or final culmination, and, for Augustine, no hope. The larger picture of history, for Greek and Roman thinkers quite generally, consisted in an eternal clash of forces playing themselves out repetitively and in endless variation. Any notion of forward movement or teleology would have made no sense to them. Indeed, the historical present was most often regarded as a deterioration from a golden age that always lay in the past.

Augustine may be said to be the first philosopher (or theologian) of history in the sense of having developed a large-scale narrative of historical events which includes a beginning, middle, and end structure, although prior to the bishop of Hippo, Eusebius had already recounted "the reign of Constantine as the culmination of human history. He evokes the Hebrew prophets, the ruin of the Jews, the humble fishermen who converted the world despite persecution, Galerius' confession of failure, the countless monks, dedicated virgins, and other ascetics of his own day, the unification of the Roman Empire under a single monarch, and the Christianity of the northern barbarians. In all things, God displays the hidden power of his mighty right hand. Constantine had legislated the gods and heroes of pagan antiquity out of existence and made the whole world worship the true God together, receiving divine instruction every Sunday."[4] Eusebius had created—and not from scratch—a form of historical writing that featured the Christian deity as the governing force in human affairs and in which events themselves are interpretable in light of a divine plan. God intervenes in the human drama, on this account, for a purpose that is often inscrutable but unfailingly present. This thinker was building upon cosmological and eschatological notions that Origen had formulated and sought to ground in the Old and New Testaments and which would play a decisive role in the legitimation of the Roman church. As Charles Freeman points out, "There is a clear moral dimension to Eusebius' approach that was endorsed by later Christian historians. The destruction of the Temple in AD 70, for instance, is a clear indication of God's rejection of the Jews. God intervened, according to Theodoret, to win the battle of Frigidus for Theodosius. If the will of a Christian God is destined to triumph, then the persecution of pagans is justified." He goes on to write, "It is hard to overestimate the importance of this ideology for the unfolding of medieval Christendom. It justified the authority of the church as the instrument of God's power and so provided an effective cloak for its territorial and political ambitions. It was not until the fifteenth century that the recovery of the Roman historians inspired the renaissance humanists to write histories that were rooted once again in secular values."[5]

Augustine's contribution in *City of God* developed this set of themes into a more fully elaborated Christian account of history or, perhaps better, a historical account of Christianity. This was sacred, not profane, history. The latter mattered little, essentially only insofar as it lent support to a sacred narrative and not at all for its own sake. Historical interpretation still served the interests of political authority and provided it with an important source of legitimation in an era that had long accepted as an axiom that Rome, including the "new Rome" that was Constantinople, was the center of the civilized world. Like the original people of God, Christians under Augustine's influence accepted the notion of sacred time as a narrative running from Adam and Eve through until the Final Judgment. The central episode in this account was of course the coming of the messiah, followed by the onward march of the new chosen people toward the eventual, universal salvation of souls through the intermediary of the church. In the world-historical contest of the cities of God and humanity, hope and redemption on a grand, eschatological scale were now possible but not inevitable. Humanity faced one fundamental, existential choice, and any history that was worth recounting was the story of its consequences through the centuries and culminating in an envisioned future. In Karl Löwith's words, "What really matters in history, according to Augustine, is not the transitory greatness of empires, but salvation or damnation in a world to come."[6]

Salvation history on this account is purposive, its *telos* connoting at once a temporal end and a goal or fulfillment. The past contained no golden age but rather a fall and a loss of innocence, followed by the great battle of earthly and heavenly cities the eventual outcome of which is contingent on human choice. The meaning of history is one, where again we are speaking of sacred, not secular, history. Rome's own past was full of significance but as a preparation rather than the culmination that prior historians had spoken of it as, and a preparation that was anything but glorious. Writing in the early fifth century, Augustine's student Paulus Orosius commented in his *Seven Books of History against the Pagans* (the title itself says much), "but now I have discovered that the days of the past were not only as oppressive as those of the present but that they were the more terribly wretched the further they were removed from the consolation of true religion."[7] The decline of the western empire and advance of the "barbarians" was perhaps nothing to be lamented for the hand of providence was visible here as well. Human happiness was not in decline, he surmised, and many of the conquerors were themselves Romanized Christians no less civilized than the empire's erstwhile rulers. History was on the side of God's people and his church, and documenting this was the task of Christian historians whose imaginations were fired by not only cosmology but also eschatology, teleology, fulfillment, providence, faith, and, above all, hope. History had one big meaning: the realization of a divine purpose which animated particular events in ways invisible to the secular historian.

The ascendant monotheism supplied an orientation that slowly displaced its predecessors and rivals. The process took a few centuries; we are not speaking of a revolution brought on by the first Christian emperor but of piecemeal modifications to a received worldview which over time resulted in a paradigm change visible as such only in hindsight. A mission of proselytizing and conversion had animated the followers of Jesus from the beginning, and by late antiquity the wind was in the sails of Christian authorities who never lost sight of the imperative of legitimation. All socioeconomic classes needed to be sold on an imaginative schema that was indivisible from power, and the Roman state had supplied the model. Since Augustus, an emperor served at once as political and military leader as well as chief priest (*pontifex maximus*) in an order in which religion and power were of a piece, although to describe the pre-Constantinian empire as a theocracy would be a misrepresentation. The imperial cult involved a demonstration of civic participation and a recognition of the emperor's authority (*auctoritas*) more than it was an act of private religiosity, and many divinities enjoyed a following that was primarily or solely regional. The new schema was simultaneously public and private, and also universalistic—one might say totalizing. The theological imagination encompassed everything from politics to art to sports, evidenced in the latter case by the circus teams the Blues and the Greens, both of which by the Christian era were employing religious slogans. "To speak about anything significant," as Matthew Novenson points out, "was to speak in the language of scripture."[8]

No substantial division of religion and politics had existed throughout the Roman era, nor would it for centuries to come in both the eastern empire and the successor kingdoms of Western Europe. No other kind of political order seemed possible in a Christian worldview for which worldly authority required divine sanction. This ancient idea began to serve the monotheists' cause overtly during Constantine's reign in the early decades of the fourth century—beginning, as the story goes, at the location of the Milvian Bridge on the outskirts of Rome on October 28, 312. This was the scene of the first Christian emperor's victory over Maxentius in a civil war that spelled the defeat (not the death) of polytheism. Constantine's battlefield conversion was followed by a systematic policy of Christianization to be carried out by means variously gentle and ungentle through the far-flung regions of the empire. Church doctrine replaced the old polytheism as the religion of state while the institution itself was exempted from taxation and other public duties and became the recipient of the emperor's largesse, a policy that Constantine's successors would continue (with the notable but ill-fated exception of Julian "the Apostate" whose two-year reign from 361 to 363 did nothing to stem the tide of the new religion). Before the end of the fifth century Pope Gelasius I was making the Catholic doctrine of church and state still more explicit: the lone source of secular authority was the divine will—as understood and communicated through the intermediary of the Roman church and its bishop, granting the latter a notional primacy that it would fight long and hard to assert.

Constantine did not limit himself to the role of benefactor, ordering the construction and enrichment of churches at public expense, but intervened in doctrinal disputes in which the possibility of schism was ever present. This would play out in spectacular fashion at the first ecumenical council of Nicaea in 325, a church council convened by the emperor to resolve the Arian controversy which bore upon the theologically thorny matter of the relationship between Jesus and God the father. Arius, an Alexandrian priest, had been making a case for the ontological primacy of the father and the consequent subordination of the son, to which the faction of Athanasius replied that the Arian doctrine effectively denied Christ's divinity. The emperor, to make a long story short, sided with the latter and very much expected Arius and his followers to fall in line. When they did not, the controversy continued in part owing to the emperor's preference for the term *homoousios* (in Latin *consubstantialis*, connoting "of the same essence" or *ousia*) to signify the equality and oneness of the divine father and son. The word was more than slightly ambiguous, but Constantine's concern lay not with establishing theological precision but with unifying factions that were often given to rancorous disputes for which the emperor, no theologian himself, had little patience. The aim was to consolidate the faithful, and if dialogical consensus was not quick to emerge then power politics would do. The authority of the bishops and their secular ruler was what mattered, and if generations of theologians were left to debate the meaning of *homoousios*, this was an academic detail that did not trouble the emperor.

The imaginative schema that was taking form crucially depended upon terminological choices and analyses that were often famously intractable. As Averil Cameron remarks, "The second century, in particular, was a battleground for the struggle of Christians to control their own discourse and define their faith. Indeed, the continuance of that struggle, which has characterized Christianity throughout its history, is demonstration enough of the crucial importance of text in historical growth and the acquisition of power. The history of Christianity could literally depend on one word," and did both at this church council and another in 381, among other instances.[9] The issue in the latter case was once again the Arian controversy, with the emperor Theodosius I summoning bishops to Constantinople and siding with the faction that supported the Nicene formulation while declaring all others heretical. As the emperor declared, "All peoples whom the rule of our gracious benevolence directs shall, as is our will, steadfastly adhere to the confession of faith which the divine apostle Peter delivered to the Romans. . . . [A]nd as we judge all others unreasonable madmen, we brand them with the ignominy of heresy and declare their conventicles shall not bear the name of churches and they shall be punished, first by divine vengeance and thereafter through the chastisement of the judicial proceedings which we, supported by Heaven's judgement, shall institute."[10] Theodosius was the same kind of unifier that Constantine had been and adopted the same means: persuasion when possible and force when necessary, and it was often necessary. Heretical churches were confiscated and a variety of legal measures against heretics and pagans ensued in the campaign to amalgamate the faith and eliminate rivals. The Nicene Creed emerged victorious and condemnation, moral and legal, was the consequence for Arius and his embattled supporters.

By the end of the fourth century, Augustine was formulating a political philosophy that rendered the established practice explicit: the church was the deity's sole representative on earth and it acted with an authority that was incontrovertible. Political legitimacy flowed from God and no other source, and all citizens needed to be brought into conformity with the church's teachings. God had used force in the scriptures (as Paul had been thrown to the ground prior to his conversion), and his institution may and ought to do the same for the salvation of souls. Provided the church was acting from conviction, no principled limit existed upon the power of an institution that was helping to further God's plan for humanity. Toleration of dissenting opinion served no purpose but to enable sin, and a theoretical basis was laid for the persecution of heretics, pagans, and Jews alike. Augustine was not inventing theocracy; the practice was both ancient and contemporary, but the departure it represented from the imperial era was significant. Roman politics had been a complex mélange of aristocracy, autocracy, military dictatorship, theocracy, republicanism, imperialism, and some democratic notions, with one or two elements gaining ascendency for a period followed by one or two others over the course of a few centuries. Augustine's politics was less complex: an uncompromising brand of theocratic institutionalism had won the day, and it was this view that would dominate Christian conceptions of church and state throughout the middle ages.

If polytheism did not die with Maxentius at the Milvian Bridge, it was in full retreat. As a political force it was finished, and if the larger cultural phenomenon hung on in different forms for centuries this was despite all institutional efforts to suppress it. The early Christian imagination had a taste for the absolute, and this was an important point of distinction from its Roman predecessor. The latter had also ruled at the discretion of the gods, but the gods were many and spoke in many voices. The territories over which the central administrative structure had ruled were vast and contained a great many regional differences of culture, language, economy, and so on which a pragmatically minded state needed in some measure to respect. Compromises between centralism and local autonomy were struck, as between the emperor and the senate, the landowning and the lower classes, and the empire itself and its foreign counterparts. Rome could rule with an iron fist and it could also bend, and this combination goes some way toward explaining its longevity. The absolutism of the monotheists had long seemed to the Roman aristocracy both presumptuous and impious, something largely tolerated in the case of the Jews (with important exceptions no doubt) owing to the ancientness of their tradition but irritating in the case of the upstart followers of Jesus. A pluralistic empire required a generous dose of pragmatism, and when the Christians were not having it the two parties were on a collision course which led to the episode at the above-noted bridge at which God stood with the superior army and its commander. History had spoken, or so later generations of Christian thinkers would opine, and any lingering dissent was mere willfulness in the face of God. No good was to be had in tolerating it.

There was an all-or-nothing quality to the new religion, an appetite for the unconditional and the totalizing. As Ernst Cassirer noted, "The absolutist tradition of Christendom leads men to assume that if we don't have absolute standards we can't have any standards, and that if we are not standing on the Rock of Ages we are standing on nothing."[11] The church had a canon that brooked neither nonconformity nor compromise and an intellectual leadership that had inherited the prestige of the poets, philosophers, and rhetoricians, all of which roles were not suppressed but absorbed into the institution and its worldview. Its God being the jealous sort, any divinities of old needed essentially to be hounded out of existence through the missionary zeal of his temporal authorities. Constantine's policy was to elevate Christianity as the new religion of state and, as a corollary to this, to chastise and then eliminate its opposition. Legal measures against heresy followed through the course of the fourth century. Charles Odahl writes, "Constantine issued a constitution to governmental officials which ordered that heretics and schismatics be deprived of the legal privileges granted to Catholics, and that they be subjected to compulsory public services. These measures did not fully eradicate dissident groups, such as the Donatists, Marcionites, Valentinians, and Paulianists, but they did hinder their growth and convert some of their members."[12] Similar actions against polytheists and Jews escalated over the decades. The process could not be completed by a single emperor, even one as long-reigning as Constantine, and it fell to his successors to complete a task the difficulty of which should not be underestimated. Pagan rituals were increasingly prohibited; temples were systematically demolished or repurposed as churches, their wealth and art works absorbed by the state; statues and shrines were destroyed by militant groups often with the tacit blessing of the bishops; nonbelievers were excluded from the military and public offices in a general campaign to eliminate the old ways. Before the century's end, Theodosius I had brought Constantine's vision closer to reality as Nicene Christianity had become the law of the empire, heresy was equated with treason, and paganism in all forms was officially proscribed. All public and private sacrifice was banned in an edict of 391, any remaining temples were closed and often destroyed by groups of zealots, synagogues were burned, traditional holidays were abolished, the Vestal Virgins and other pagan associations were dissolved, and even the Olympic Games did not survive a general purging of polytheist traditionalism.

As mentioned, the general phenomenon that was "paganism" persisted with much tenacity in spite of a systematic and ongoing program of religious and political authority to eradicate it, whatever exactly "it" was. What was paganism? The Latin *paganus* connoted country dweller and became a term of insult comparable to "bumpkin" or "hick," in contrast to ostensibly sophisticated urbanites who had adopted the new religion. A pagan was to Christians what a gentile was to Jews: the nonbelieving outsider, and neither term was value-neutral. In no sense was "paganism" a religion, nor did it refer to a distinct human grouping. It was a polemical term covering a wide assortment of ritual practices (sacrificial offerings in particular), sacred sites, mythical narratives, and divinities—a whole imaginative schema that was of ancient vintage, deeply rooted, pluralistic, and notably less dogmatic than its monotheist competitors. They were not an organized group and lacked both an institutional priesthood, a holy book, and a unifying creed that could be readily compared with the state religion. Despite this, paganism's decline was protracted over a few more centuries. The old gods were not quick to flee, and the new orthodoxy was less inclined to deny their existence than to condemn them as demons and their adherents as idol worshippers.

This was a society or set of societies that was in many ways deeply conservative, and no sudden transformation followed Constantine's conversion and elevation of the new religion. The old practices took a long time to die out, especially in rural areas, and one institution of longstanding that did not change was the class system. The aristocracy did not suffer any dramatic loss in the transition to a new order that professed a love of the poor and downtrodden. The poor remained poor as urban elites gravitated into the church and the clerical profession while retaining their hold on secular power. The collapse of the western empire did not spell the collapse of the Roman governing class; indeed, "members of the Roman Senate and other secular elites continued to dictate much of the cultural and religious life of Rome for centuries to come."[13] Through the centuries of late antiquity the upper classes' hold on power continued both at Rome and Constantinople as well as the various regional centers of the former empire. The usual pattern saw invading groups not displacing local elites so much as joining their ranks, while the meek who were to inherit the earth would have to await their inheritance in the afterlife. Preeminence remained where it had been for centuries, even while the ideology had changed. The notion that the first shall be last and the last first was laudable on a spiritual plane, but it translated awkwardly to the real world of religious politics.

Let us not overstate the violence of the age: a social order in which a network of urban landowning elites held the reigns while a majority of the population worked the land was hardly new in the general era of which we are speaking, and indeed it had been the norm throughout the ancient world and would remain so for centuries to come. Neither during nor following the imperial era was it perpetuated through force alone—a phenomenon that is difficult to measure in any time period and whose constant tendency is also to seek legitimation by partaking of the imaginative schema that prevails in a given time and place. Whether "controlling the narrative" was done in earnest, from cynicism, or some combination, the nobility needed to turn it toward their purposes both to preserve their social position and to further a religious mission which we may presume to have been largely sincere. Power and persuasion were difficult to disentangle and the aristocracy continued the time-honored practice of exercising authority in the accustomed manner, which is by employing a worldview that spoke to the population as a whole and in a manner that they had come to expect. As Brown points out,

> We are dealing with an upper class which accepted that authority, fear, the direct use of force against religious places and even, if less frequently, against religious enemies, should be mobilized to impose truth and to banish error. Yet precisely because it was expected that authority would be used in matters of religion, the manner in which this authority was asserted was subjected to sharp and anxious scrutiny. Correct religion was held to be the glory of the empire; and precisely for this reason, the manner in which uniformity was imposed had to reflect all the more faithfully the overbearing dignity of the imperial power.[14]

Sheer force was one tool in the kit, but it was hardly enough to convince the general society of the legitimacy of political and religious authority over the long term. Worldly predominance had to appear a consequence of the divine will, while within the ranks of the upper classes a sense of loyalty and fraternity remained as imperative as it had been in the days of Augustus.

Authority needed to be won and judiciously exercised, and longstanding norms governed how this was done. Rome itself—less the city than the memory and the idea—retained its hold on the late antique imagination long after it had ceased to function as an administrative center. Constantinople was the new Romania, and the first of many, the place where a notional Romanness persisted along with the sense of superiority that was among its basic ingredients. The center no longer held if we are speaking politically or militarily, but the concept of a cultural center within a divine order was repurposed for a new empire of the spirit. Romanness spelled authority; it signified a tradition and a worldly power which a new order was endeavoring to get in on. The same Rome that had been cast in the role of oppressor in the time of Jesus was being rechristened as the heart of the Christian world and by the fifth century as its institutional center as well. "The Roman primacy," as Joseph Vogt writes, "fortified the unity and moral strength of the Catholic Church during the period which witnessed the eclipse of the western emperor. . . . Now that Rome, as the seat of Peter has become chief pastorate of the world, Rome possesses through religion what she failed to conquer through force of arms."[15] The story, one might say legend, of Peter's travails in Rome after the death of Jesus achieved not a little in lending religious authority to the city itself and its bishop for centuries to come. The location of and factual circumstances surrounding Peter's death are historically far from certain, but the "pious romance" that was being told gained a lasting hold on the faithful.[16]

The doctrine of papal preeminence exemplifies a larger phenomenon. On the face of it, this rhetorical narrative appears either a reverent claim to authority or a power play, and any attempt to apply the surgeon's scalpel will be frustrated. It was both—an act of holy shrewdness which promoted the jurisdictional authority of the Roman bishop while preserving at least a semblance of theological legitimacy. The argument itself ran as follows: Peter had acquired a stature of theological preeminence among the apostles, being the first to recognize Jesus as the son of God and having been granted by the latter the power to bind and loose sin. This grant of worldly power was heritable by Peter's rightful successors, who were the bishops of Rome for the reason that Jesus had conferred upon the apostle the mission of founding a church and it was the imperial capital to which Peter travelled after the death of the savior and was the location of his martyrdom and burial. A synthesis of scriptural, sacred-historical, political, and legal elements reverberated with Roman imperialism in undergirding a claim to papal authority which gained traction with some difficulty and over a considerable period of time. An especially important figure here is Leo I whose papacy ran from 440 until his death in 461. Leo had not invented the doctrine of papal primacy, but he raised the ante at strategic moments in responding to particular circumstances of the time. As George Demacopoulos writes, "the escalation of papal claims that were accompanied by hyperbolic Petrine language in the period 440–600 were, more often than not, precipitated by challenges or insults to the Roman bishop's authority (dogmatic, political, or moral)."[17] Such challenges issued at times from both the west and the east, and Leo's policy was to invoke

Peter as a Christian reiteration of the long-established axiom that Rome was the center of civilization. The earthly authority conferred upon him by Christ naturally extended to his living heir in the eternal city. This was more than a question of prestige. Authority was a seat of truth, buttressed by the doctrine of apostolic succession for which the apostle was an active presence in the life of his church. Leo's preeminence flowed not from himself but from the foremost of the apostles in alliance with the secular legacy of the Roman idea. This hegemony was worldly and otherworldly at the same time and would be asserted as needed. In his words, "[The Lord] desires that his gifts flow into the entire body from Peter himself, as from the head to the body. And any individual who dares to separate from the unity of Peter will come to know that he no longer shares in the divine mystery."[18] Strong words, and highly effective in the atmosphere of the times. This extended beyond symbolism to any matter of legal or ecclesiastical policy on which bishops could disagree. If to many, especially in the east, the claim sounded self-aggrandizing, Leo and his papal successors were careful not to assert it indiscriminately but on an as-needed basis and with assurances that its duly recognized authority would be exercised in the customary manner. When the Roman bishop's will prevailed, they had no need of the Petrine doctrine, but it would prove an effective rhetorical strategy when conflicts arose. Some historical embellishment was involved, but it was an advantage that Leo's peers did not share and in time it developed into a full-blown papal theory with universalist aspirations.

Authority, what one historian of the period describes as "a capacity to get one's own way, a political ascendancy secured by force of personality and excellence of achievement,"[19] was the name of the game, and the Roman see was not lacking competition. It was a value increasingly enjoyed by bishops, a role that was in some ways new to the Roman world, this combination of priest, wise man, rhetorician, and governor who had some predecessor in the Jewish world but lacked a counterpart in other regions of the empire. Polytheist priests lacked a comparable institution and profession; they were largely members of the nobility who gained prominence through part-time service officiating the traditional rites. The bishops' power was theological, moral, cultural, and political all at the same time and disputes over pecking order were not rare. Having come largely from the nobility, they inherited attitudes that included the love of rank and prestige, and as civic life was coming increasingly into the jurisdiction of the church their role combined that of priest, judge, and administrative overseer in matters both legal and ecclesiastical. Their work also included coming to terms with the pagan past in their episcopal see, and on this issue bishops exercised considerable autonomy in determining which among the traditional practices were to be rechristened, tolerated, or proscribed. A conservative society was not about to extirpate its past, and the problem of how to reconcile the ancient inheritance with a new ideological order was a monumental undertaking made still more difficult by a factionalism that often threatened to boil over. The bishop's role was to keep a lid on such matters, and it demanded an art of pious diplomacy. While the social status and wealth of their profession increased over time, bishops faced the twin imperatives of wielding power and gaining an authority that was rightful in the eyes of their peers and, likely to a lesser extent, the general population. Tradition afforded the method by which this was achieved.

For centuries the empire had been governed by a network of urban elites scattered throughout the Mediterranean world and held together by ties of self-interest, class, education, rhetoric, language, and religion, and a similar governing class retained its position in the world of late antiquity. Much had changed, of course, beginning with the ascendant ideology, but the manner of command had not. Church leaders inherited the *paideia* of their predecessors, an education in literature, public speaking, and learned conversation that served as a class marker and created bonds of loyalty, even while the imaginative schema had changed. Authority required a knowledge that included the philosophical, and it was this that imparted a terminology within which the new religion could gain intellectual self-understanding. As Vogt writes, "During the second half of the fourth century Christians made some spectacular advances in the whole field of education, culture and literature. Reconciled to the classics, they branched out in new forms of eloquence and erudition. Study of the Bible entailed exegesis of the Old and New Testaments, the sermon in many respects came to occupy the position once held by public oratory, and theology replaced philosophy."[20] To say that Greek and Roman philosophy was replaced by Christian theology requires some qualification. The question was vexed: how might a narrative first articulated in the language of fishermen gain ascendancy among a Greek- and Latin-speaking urban aristocracy living a considerable period after the time of Jesus? The answer came in the form of a new Christian *paideia*, one that translated scriptural ideas into a philosophical idiom that had been utterly foreign to it. We may speak of this as an educational advance or a retreat into superstition—neither description sheds much light—but in any event, intellectual respectability required placing the new schema on speaking terms with the old, appropriating a received terminology while turning it to new and sometimes antithetical purposes, and it was an art at which various early Christian thinkers excelled.

Thus Origen in the third century was demonstrating how a Platonic sensibility might be incorporated into the new theology. Here was a pagan philosophy with a suitably otherworldly or immaterial turn of mind whose metaphysics afforded some elements of a Christian worldview. Well prior to Augustine, a neoplatonism that began winning favor in the second century was being seen as a kind of hellenistic forerunner and reinforcement of the new ideology. Notions of the One, emanation, *logos*, *nous*, mysticism, and the great ladder of being were serviceable in developing something like a Christian philosophy, a religion not limited to myth and ritual but that could hold its own in the elite circles from which bishops largely came. One should say "something like" a philosophy for the followers of Jesus were typically of two minds about a discourse that was secular, often skeptical, and outside the orbit of Jewish monotheism. Plato and his Roman interpreters remained pagans and the new faith would always remain "nonsense to gentiles" (1 Corinthians 1:23), as Paul had put it. Augustine was hardly the first to undertake a concerted effort to bridge classical with Christian learning and to find inspiration in Plato, yet his emphasis lay decidedly upon faith: the most commendable of hellenistic philosophy could be at most preparatory for the religious life. Christian *paideia* made room for it, but as a training ground of the spirit. Philosophical rationality was useful in resolving some of the many doctrinal and terminological disputes that preoccupied Christian theologians for centuries, but what Augustine called *curiositas* was a sin that he likened to a disease. It was lacking in humility, he believed, to pursue forms of knowledge that are beyond human reach, as the story of Adam and Eve had illustrated. Faith is not rational and does not strive to be. Its source is God and "nonsense" is part of its virtue: "For God's nonsense is wiser than human wisdom, and God's weakness is stronger than human strength" (1 Corinthians 1:25).[21]

There is no separating the conceptual from the imaginative dimensions of Christianity in these early centuries any more than the philosophical from the rhetorical or the discursive from the poetic. It is better to speak of a synthesis of elements variously sacred and profane, historical and mythical, rational and aesthetic, spiritual and political—in whatever combination promoted this improbable movement's mission to win converts in regions remote from the holy land. From the beginning it was like its monotheistic predecessor a religion of the book, and this was important to its success. It required no central temple but an ordinary building that could be constructed anywhere and also books that were transportable and readily available. From the beginning, this movement was focused on books written in the language of the people, and if most of the faithful could not read them they could hear them spoken of by preachers who had mastered the rhetorical art. Writings—in particular the codex—made it possible to form a network of believers spanning the Mediterranean, and the number of such books and letters grew to an extent that soon enough required some creative vetting on the part of church authorities. The fluidity of the early religion would be replaced by a canon and a New Testament which gave the appearance of a unified text thanks to some artful interweaving and not a little textual suppression. The notion of a divinely authored text to which could be affixed the name of an apostle or close relative of the messiah was a variation on the long-established practice of attributing a book or idea to a great man who, as a matter of historical fact, may have had nothing to do with its creation. It satisfied ancient audiences, and so did a myriad illuminated manuscripts, works of art, icons, and relics which all succeeded in firing the imaginations of the faithful. The old book scrolls did not contain pictures and the art of book illumination added a powerful new dimension to the texts that Christian writers were composing, as did religious images depicted in churches, in the homes of the faithful, on jewelry, and so on. Icons generated no little debate, most famously in the iconoclast controversy of the eighth and ninth centuries in the eastern empire. The icons or images that had gained popularity throughout Christendom seemed dangerously reminiscent of polytheist statuary and other items which, iconoclasts feared, were displeasing to God and a violation of the second commandment. Idolatry was serious business, but so was selling the Christian message. In the end, the iconophiles prevailed and forms of religious art and sacred relics, many of which were believed to be invested with supernatural qualities, became a ubiquitous presence throughout the Roman world.

Why the followers of Jesus were able to sell their religion quite as successfully as they did is not easily explained. The factors were numerous and bear upon both the church's activities and qualities of the faith itself: a new historical consciousness and promise of an afterlife, an organized institution with a concerted proselytizing mission, some artful appropriation of received ideas both religious and philosophical, the codex and religious art, and the lack of concerted opposition are a few. The old religion and the new both provided the kind of social cement that made a sense of community and belonging possible, but the latter may have gone about this with greater shrewdness. As Brown notes, "The Christian Church offered a way of living in this world. The skillful elaboration of the ecclesiastical hierarchy, the sense of belonging to a distinctive group with carefully prescribed habits and increasing resources heightened the impression that the Christian Church made on the uncertain generations of the third century. Seldom has a small minority played so successfully on the anxieties of society as did the Christians."[22] During this century of crisis, the movement was advancing in small bands across the empire, particularly in areas of the eastern frontier, in the process creating bonds that included a highly charged sense of identity and mission. It offered a morality that was stringent but forgiving, which all could participate in and which spoke to the lower classes without dislodging the elite. Perhaps above all, they had a uniform and simple story to tell, with a belief system, a book, a terminology, and a church hierarchy that was the same everywhere. There was a sense of mystery about it and a reassurance that one could align oneself with the heavens and one's fellows regardless of one's social position.

There was something deeply Roman about this unlikely religion from Galilee, an almost military resoluteness about its church and an acute sense of who was inside and outside. The outsiders were not only Jews and those whom they insisted on calling pagans but heretics, those fellow travelers who had strayed from the path and required urgent correction. This was no religion for the heterodox, and this was part of its strength. Its spread was reminiscent of an earlier imperialism, and insiders and outsiders alike who were on the wrong side of the divine were barbarians of the spirit who needed to be combated with benevolent coercion. The matter of distinguishing orthodoxy from heresy was a serious business indeed. The Greek word *heiresis* connoted choice, but Christians were using it as a rhetorical term against those within their ranks whose theological formulations were deemed to be both mistaken and criminal: Gnosticism, Arianism, Donatism, Manichaeism, Nestorianism, Monophysitism, Montanism, Marcionism, and Pelagianism were the main culprits. As with the proscription of paganism, anti-heresy measures may be regarded as an exercise in either naked aggression or ancient justice; the two were not cleanly separable in a social order that saw little value in toleration for its own sake. Augustine again provides an example. His was "a harsh age, that thought, only too readily, in terms of military discipline and uniformity," and he himself was no exception.[23] The Catholic bishop was encountering formidable opposition in North Africa from the Donatist church, according to which God's sacraments could only be administered by members of the clergy who were morally faultless. Donatism had become a popular rival to Catholic orthodoxy and Augustine combatted it with an aggressiveness that might strike modern observers as extreme. He provided the rationale not only for rebuking this movement but also abolishing its church and compelling its members to become Catholics, and Honorius' "Edict of Unity" of 405 and a subsequent tariff of 412 did just that. The recalcitrant needed to be brought around to the truth with whatever force was necessary for the purpose, and Jews did not fare much better. An episode during the reign of Theodosius in the late fourth century illustrates the point: an emperor who had carried the fight against pagans and heretics to something of an extreme, he nonetheless intervened when a bishop enjoined the destruction of a synagogue and ordered the bishop to rebuild it and punished the perpetrators. When Ambrose, bishop of Milan, censured the emperor for his action and demanded from the pulpit that he reverse course, Theodosius backed down in this telling showdown with the church.

In the narrative that the church was promoting, of course, it was Christians who had been persecuted, with the Roman state cast in the role of villain. The story that began to prevail is that the followers of Jesus had been thrown to the lions in monstrous numbers and martyred in myriad circumstances before their eventual triumph beginning with Constantine's conversion. An especially important figure in the crafting of this account is Eusebius in the fourth century. It was this bishop-historian, as Candida Moss points out, who "helped to make the history of Christianity the history of persecution. The historical evidence suggests that the majority of texts about martyrs were either written down or heavily edited during this period of relative peace and quiet. These stories were composed because a martyr's opinion, as a holy person prepared to die in defense of Christ, had great authority in the eyes of readers. When it came to matters of truth, there was no better authority than a saint." The best guarantor of legitimacy and truth alike was the much sought after *auctoritas*, a value gained by well-established means which included fashioning a narrative depicting Christians as divinely inspired martyrs bravely bearing their cross in imitation of the savior. The same historian notes, "the traditional history of Christian martyrdom is mistaken. Christians were not constantly persecuted, hounded, or targeted by the Romans. Very few Christians died, and when they did, they were often executed for what we in the modern world would call political reasons."[24] Be that as it may, a good story well and often told spelled truth, be it historical or sacred-historical, and Eusebius' *Church History* was not the only text of its kind which cast the movement for all time in the role of the persecuted.

    Roman audiences had a longstanding penchant for righteous violence. Here again the followers of Jesus were not inventing a motif but making it their own while also upping the ante, adding tantalizing detail to gruesome scenes of torture and horrific death. The son of God himself had suffered an agonizing death, and stories of others heeding his example lent a weight that was more than aesthetic. Violence added sublimity and transcendence to this religion of love and harkened back to the deaths of other great men in the Greco-Roman tradition. Tales of noble death featuring a victim demonstrating heroic forbearance in the face of the unspeakable had long been popular, and Christians were composing these stories by the hundreds. Few of them would satisfy historians of today—this again is sacred history, one might say legend—but martyr stories partook of a tradition while entertaining and inspiring listeners far and wide. "Pious romance" it was, but it was a vital element in the imaginative schema that was becoming predominant at this time. These stories related in vivid detail contained a readily understood moral: one could have confidence in a faith to which such beneficiaries of divine grace had remained true. Similar tales of philosophers and noble individuals dying for their cause had been recounted for centuries in the ancient world, Socrates being the great exemplar but it was hardly the only story of its kind. How one died was testament to one's authority. Christian innovations to this literary form included nothing less than a promise of victory over death itself. The martyrs had taken up their crosses freely, bearing witness to God and as an example for others, and were duly rewarded in heaven. The Christian afterlife was also a crucial element in the worldview they were offering and explains a good part of its success.

Other forms of narrative warrant mention here as well. The early Christian fascination with persecution and noble death was probably not unusual for the time period. Such stories were persuasive to many, and they were "supplemented with descriptions of miracles and visions associated with specific churches and shrines. They drew the Christian faithful to obscure towns and out-of-the-way shrines, and in exchange they offered them the opportunity to commune with the memory of their heroes. Stories were an integral part of this connection. It was said that when martyrdom stories were read aloud, the saints were truly present, sweet smelling fragrances would fill the air, and the world of the martyr and the world of the pilgrim would meet."[25] Grand narratives of good and evil where listeners were cast in the role of soldiers in a cosmic battle inspired the imagination while exemplifying a way of living to which all could in some way aspire. Most were not called to martyrdom, but hearing the stories of their lives and heroic deaths kept ordinary believers on the straight and narrow, these soldiers for Christ in the great war of darkness and light. These stories could teach one how to live while combining action and adventure. Tales of miraculous occurrences and fulfilled prophesies likely also attracted converts to the movement. There was mystery and intrigue here, a synthesis of high drama, magical goings-on, saints and sinners, supernatural forces, elements that could be found elsewhere in ancient literature but here combined in ways that would have persuaded many.

Stories of divine intervention and healing in the name of Jesus were plentiful, as were the lives of the saints. The latter figure was a combination of Old Testament prophet, Greek hero, Roman statesman, philosopher, bishop, and often martyr as well, and the stories of their lives resonated with the life of the savior while often having a down-to-earth quality to which the hearer could relate more personally. Christianity was a personal faith as much as it was a social matter, and if God in heaven was not readily approachable, the saints were—or more so, at any rate, in the manner of a well-connected friend. One's preferred saint was an active presence who could understand one's sorrows and intervene on one's behalf, not unlike the polytheist's divinities which were everywhere and could be appealed to in one's day-to-day struggles. The lives of the saints was a genre that had little to do with profane history. Eusebius' *Life of Constantine* is an example of the form. In its pages one finds no mention of controversy within the church, no political machinations, but instead a Moses figure leading his people out of bondage and into a new promised land of the spirit, a new Rome with all the blessings of the old and none of the baggage. This text was not fictional but aimed for a truth that was more than literal; it was to be edifying and exemplary, written in a style that an aristocratic readership could admire while employing Christian tropes. Cameron notes, "it is clear that Eusebius was deliberately trying to combine typically Christian elements with the technical requirement of high style demanded of imperial panegyric. It is all the more striking in view of his evident stylistic aspirations that he nevertheless draws so extensively and conspicuously on the existing Christian repertoire of sign and image and employs a writing style so full of visual metaphor and imagery drawn from visual art."[26]

Of course, the gospels themselves were by no means restricted to anything so formal as doctrinal pronouncements but told a story ostensibly of universal human significance. The texts and the lives of the saints that were later modeled on them related narratives by which popular audiences could feel moved and inspired. Any truth they contained was more a showing than a telling, a prosaic but still poetic literary form that could satisfy the spiritual needs of their listeners and illustrate the way of life which the new religion was promoting. A good deal of creative history was involved in selling the faith, whether one characterizes this as superstition or popular devotion. None of it was history for its own sake. This was sacred-moral history, and Augustine's *City of God* was a continuation of a tradition stemming from the gospels, the lives of the saints, martyr stories, and other tales that constituted the Christian imagination.

A few final motifs that bear mention are asceticism, pilgrimage, and the crusade. The first of these was, of course, nothing unique to this movement but was taken up by a range of Christian figures and given a certain prominence. Ancient audiences could be impressed by accounts of holy personages withdrawing from common society for a life of self-denial and devotion to their creator. Thomas Sizgorich points out, "It is this tendency, for example, that accounts for the often-repeated trope in which a particularly pious ascetic cuts himself off first from the company of ordinary Roman society and then from Christian society generally, retreating into the desert or into a monastic institution. In such stories, the ascetic then often erects and enforces a line between himself and his fellow ascetics, drawing a boundary around himself within which resides an ever-smaller community."[27] Authority lay here as well, among monks and saintly individuals renouncing the ways of their community and living alone in the sight of God. A related form of religious withdrawal was the familiar practice of pilgrimage. This ancient motif found religious paragons and ordinary people alike travelling to sacred shrines or scenes of a notable occurrence in the life of a given faith. By the fourth century, the church was encouraging Christians to travel to the holy land, and for centuries to come believers would find meaning in visiting the ground that Jesus had traversed or the location of some miraculous event. Constantine's building program had created new sacred sites which were attractive to pilgrims and contributed to the notion of the Christian believer as both spiritual seeker and traveler.

The crusade was a later variation on the pilgrimage theme. The holy land remained the principal destination of this medieval development that was begun in earnest by Pope Urban II at the end of the eleventh century. The first crusade began in 1095 as a military campaign to take back the holy land from Muslim rulers who had conquered the area in the seventh century, and similar armed pilgrimages were undertaken in the middle of the twelfth century and again a few decades later, each with less than dramatic results. Each of these campaigns had a purportedly defensive rationale, as the pilgrims were seeking to reclaim territory—principally Jerusalem—that had been conquered by the infidel and accordingly conformed to the principle of the just cause. Thus Saint Bernard of Clairvaux implored his listeners in the twelfth century, "Go forward then in security, knights, and drive off without fear the enemies of the cross of Christ, certain that neither death nor life can separate you from the love of God which is in Jesus Christ. . . . How glorious are those who return victorious from the battle! How happy are those who die as martyrs in the battle! Rejoice, courageous athlete, if you survive and are victor in the Lord; but rejoice and glory the more if you die and are joined to the Lord."[28] Participation in such a campaign guaranteed the forgiveness of sins and those who perished died a martyr's death. The notion found popular favor through a good part of Europe, even when the term "crusade" was applied to church-sanctioned conflicts against rival Christian groups. Whether the enemy was Muslim, pagan, or Christian heretic, military pilgrimage was conceived as a defense of the faith and a holy confrontation with the enemies of Christ.

There was more than a little politics involved in fashioning a schema that exercised such a powerful hold on the centuries of late antiquity and beyond. This was an age in which secular and ecclesiastical authority were difficult and often impossible to disentangle and the predominant worldview was a tapestry of myths and concepts, narratives and political forces, holy men and fanatics all entwined and which had emerged from a particular cultural heritage. The Christian imagination and historical consciousness was no revolutionary development. It arose from a tradition that was already a meeting ground of Greek and Roman polytheism and philosophy, Jewish monotheism, Roman politics, and an assortment of cultural elements from the various territories of the empire and lands beyond. One schema replaced another with a gradualness that bears no resemblance to a sudden spiritual awakening or collapse into superstition. Later tellings would characterize it as one or the other, but partisanship aside, what happened to the imagination in late antiquity is that some old ideas were repeated and reconfigured in a way that served the spiritual needs of the times and the will to power in about equal measure. History was now a sacred narrative; the golden age was no more and the historical past was reconceived as one long prelude to a hoped-for future. Imaginative history ran parallel with intellectual, political, and military history; indeed it is no exaggeration to describe each of these as organically related to the others. The *zeitgeist* was a synthesis of the religious, aesthetic, political, philosophical, economic, and some other elements, all combined in a manner that would remain remarkably stable for centuries—and for reasons we should not be quick to put down to cultural stagnation or some other negative evaluation as judgments of this order shed virtually no light. An imaginative schema served the needs and the interests that such schemas serve, and for reasons that can be elusive to us.

How it came to pass sheds light upon the capacity of imagination itself, this activity that gathers and composes elements into a configuration that gains predominance in a particular time and place. In retrospect, one cultural narrative succeeded another—to make a long and exceedingly complex story short—as one season passes into the next and not as a revolutionary development. One thing led to another, made sense of another or produced implications that over time transformed the whole, not as effects of causes but for reasons that were particularistic and often responses to whatever else was happening. Historical imagining is a reimagining, sometimes on a modest scale and at others in ways that carry larger implications for what happens next.

CHAPTER 4

Renaissance Reimaginings

We now fast forward from late antiquity to the Italian renaissance. Our reason for doing so is not, as one might suppose, that nothing much happened during the intervening centuries but that from the point of view of imaginative history the period or movement commonly designated by the term "renaissance" again witnessed a transformation in the *zeitgeist* or a relatively active phase in the life of the western historical imagination, and it is this activity that warrants our attention. What transformation was this, what were some of its underlying dynamics, and how in general terms did it come to pass that "classical antiquity" went from being a prelude to Christianization to a pinnacle of cultural achievement, and what light does this shed upon historical consciousness itself? The past was reimagined, not in every particular but relatively and for reasons that must be examined. One cultural narrative in some measure displaced another, and our questions are how, why, and what this entails for our larger theme. I have suggested that wholesale revolution is not the model, and if exhibit A was late antiquity then exhibit B will be the general phenomenon that is encompassed by the Italian word *rinascita*. What had been reborn and where had it been prior to its celebrated rebirth?

Let us begin with some dates and with the word itself. Since the publication in 1860 of Jacob Burckhardt's *The Civilization of the Renaissance in Italy*, many historians have spoken of the renaissance as in some sense the beginning of the modern era. This period, in his words, constituted "not the revival of antiquity alone, but its union with the genius of the Italian people, which achieved the conquest of the Western world" from the time of Petrarch (Francesco Petrarca) in the fourteenth century to about the middle part of the sixteenth (many would extend this to the mid-seventeenth).[1] While employed by sixteenth-century artist Giorgio Vasari, *rinascita* and its French translation did not come into common usage until the eighteenth and (especially) nineteenth centuries. The idea was that the majesty of Greek and Roman civilization or many of its higher attainments had been revivified from an approximately thousand-year slumber and turned to a variety of contemporary purposes in the various city-states of Italy and subsequently through the better part of Western Europe. This reemergence of the classical constituted a monumental transition from the "medieval" to the early modern, a kind of bridge spanning two more or less discrete historical periods and a golden era that followed an agonizingly long period of cultural stagnation. Rebirth was not a value-neutral designation but a decidedly partisan and largely retrospective notion. Citizens of the renaissance commonly referred to themselves and their times as "modern," and not in categorical opposition to what had come before. While some degree of hindsight is a condition of the possibility of historical understanding in general, it should give us pause that the note of idealization so pronounced in Burckhardt's text and century was decidedly less evident through the two or three centuries of which we are speaking. By Burckhardt's time, this "vision of the Renaissance," as Gene Brucker points out, "and more broadly his scheme of periodization, fitted neatly and comfortably into the values and concerns of late nineteenth-century European culture."[2] In this narrative, the fruits of Greco-Roman civilization had gone into eclipse with the collapse of the western empire and remained in this condition until their celebrated rebirth beginning in the time of Petrarch.

Contemporary historians largely reject this picture for reasons we shall examine in due course. First, let us set out in general terms what the renaissance has long been understood to have been and what imaginative schema began to gain ascendancy within elite circles of fourteenth-century Italy. A variety of economic and technological developments bear mention here and become inseparable from the cultural: international trade with various European and eastern markets and in both economic and cultural goods, combined with banking, shipbuilding, and other industries had enriched the urban nobility and led to the creation of universities, port cities, courts, and an expanding network of ideas. By the early sixteenth century Ferdinand Magellan had circumnavigated the globe, contributing to a general broadening of horizons that had counterparts in other areas of knowledge. Technological innovations of obvious note include the nautical compass, gunpowder, and of course the printing press and resultant book trade. The latter market encompassed everything from classical works to bibles and religious texts, popular romances and histories, and whatever else struck the taste of book collectors who were becoming more numerous in the cities of Italy and the various regions of Europe. The western printing press originated in the middle of the fifteenth century in Germany, where Johannes Gutenberg fashioned a technology that was quickly imported into several Italian centers whereupon it initiated a widespread revolution in intellectual culture. Venice itself at this time had in excess of a hundred such presses in operation, dramatically expanding the circulation of information and facilitating book collection and libraries well beyond the monasteries of old. "The new passion for books and book-collecting by the laity," Alison Brown remarks, "encouraged the growth of privately owned libraries, and then, as the humanist movement gathered pace, of 'public libraries' that everyone could use."[3] One historian has estimated that by the beginning of the sixteenth century as many as thirteen million books are likely to have been in circulation throughout Europe while the business of recovering, translating, and publishing books assumed large proportions.[4] Petrarch's passion for ancient texts would become a trend, and while the circulation of books in the middle ages had also been widespread it had depended upon skilled copyists whom the new technology was quickly replacing.

If the *zeitgeist* was changing, it is uncertain in what measure this remained a phenomenon limited to the urban elite. Some four-fifths of the European population through these centuries remained rural agriculturalists who likely were not deeply affected by trends in elite culture. General literacy and mobility into the upper classes do appear to have increased, although no reliable method exists by which to quantify such matters. One historian suggests that in the case of literacy "indirect measures such as the ownership of books and other forms of writing, including accounts, notarial documents, and family chronicles points to a slow but perceptible expansion in the number of craftsmen, peasants, and workers who were able to read and write," although to what extent this suggests any larger participation in a cultural movement is far from certain.[5] It had been possible long before the renaissance for individuals of modest background to rise in social standing in some measure and in certain domains, such as the clergy. Our conclusion must be that while the urban nobility, professional and merchant classes, scholars, artists, and artisans all partook of the changes that were taking place, we do not know to what extent a majority of the population "had" a renaissance in any appreciable measure. One complicating factor is the difficulty in determining whether the renaissance is better spoken of as a historical era or a somewhat more nebulous movement in the realm of ideas. Burckhardt defended the former interpretation, E. H. Gombrich the latter, and though no consensus has emerged among renaissance historians on this matter the more common view currently owes more to Gombrich than Buckhardt, and it is a view with which we may concur. Periodization talk is always dubious, driven as it often is by ideology or historical partisanship of one kind or another. The concept of *rinascita* was evaluatively charged from the beginning, but to get a handle on what it was let us put partisanship aside and speak of a broad cultural movement, the central aim of which was to rehabilitate various forms of ancient knowledge and repurpose them for modern ends. The historical past and present were being reimagined by a wide assortment of artists, scientists, religious thinkers, statesmen, and scholars across the disciplines and on a scale that in time would be characterizable as a change in worldview.

We are speaking of a movement that did not "change everything" but that selectively integrated ancient with current ways of thinking and appropriated a tradition that had not been dormant but partially eclipsed by medieval Christendom. John Jeffries Martin characterizes the renaissance "as a movement—or, perhaps better, a cluster of interrelated movements in architecture, astronomy, botany, cartography, engineering, historical writing, painting, poetry, and so on—the cultural expression both of an expanding and increasingly commercially dynamic continent and of new patterns of consumption and competition for prestige in the courts (from the papacy to the households of dukes and cardinals) and other centers of power (republican governments, guild halls, and churches) whose patronage elevated artists, architects, and astronomers to loftier, more influential perches within society than they had held before."[6] Competition between power centers in Florence, Rome, Naples, and Venice fueled trends that would encompass the larger European network, the major representatives of which included Petrarch, Leonardo da Vinci, Michelangelo, Desiderius Erasmus, Niccolò Machiavelli, Michel de Montaigne, Leon Battista Alberti, Giovanni Boccaccio, Leonardo Bruni, Angelo Poliziano, Giovanni Pico della Mirandola, and various others. As is always the case in trying to characterize movements of this extent, diversity reigns, but insofar as we are dealing with any unified phenomenon it is closer to an imaginative schema and general *zeitgeist* than a specific program of ideas.[7] If a great deal of conscious imitation of Greek and Roman models was in evidence, this was no wholesale replacement of Christian for pagan ways but a relative change of preference and partial elevation of the latter. Fashions were changing, what was old was new again, but notions of revolution and a new historical era should be resisted.

Narrative accounts of the renaissance often begin with the figure of Petrarch, and if we are speaking of the imagination then this seminal poet-scholar-diplomat is a good place to begin. This fourteenth-century Italian had a foot in two worlds and time periods: his own and the Rome of Cicero. "I am alive now yet I would rather have been born at some other time," as he expressed it; "I never liked this present age."[8] From early adulthood what fired his imagination was Italy's classical past, a deep identification with which prompted his travels throughout Europe in search of books that would eventually comprise a personal library of approximately two hundred classical manuscripts, the largest such collection in Europe at the time. Intent on a literary career, he also undertook a variety of diplomatic missions on behalf of Pope Clement VI and patrons in the Italian nobility which involved travel to locations in which copies of ancient books could be recovered principally from monasteries. His passion for books led him to acquire works of poetry, philosophy, and history in particular which he studied with both a scholarly and creative interest in what would become a trend. Convinced of the world-historical centrality and cultural superiority of Italy, the deteriorated condition of Rome during his lifetime and the humiliation of the Avignon papacy weighed heavily upon him and inspired his own efforts to restore the empire both politically and culturally. His writings evince a man who regarded himself as having a foot in two eras, "looking both forwards and backwards," as one historian puts it: "he looks back to the authors of the classical age, and forwards to a possibly ignorant posterity which will care nothing for them." His ambition was to restore the classical past while integrating it with a Christian worldview. Too many medieval writers, he held, had been unduly deferential and unscholarly in their treatment of ancient manuscripts when what was called for was a more critical philological approach and also a creative impulse that transcends imitation. "His aim," the same scholar writes of Petrarch's literary efforts, "is to achieve similarity of style and vision without indulging in identity of expression; the imitator should 'take care that what he writes resembles the original without reproducing it precisely. The resemblance should not be that of a portrait to the sitter ... but of a son to his father, where there is often a great divergence in particular features, and yet a certain suggestion which makes the likeness: what painters call an 'air,' most noticeable about the face and eyes.'"[9] The foremost Roman writers of old had looked back to Greek models without following them slavishly, and the same imperative animated his own compositions. Cicero would become the great exemplar from the pre-Christian period and Augustine from late antiquity. The latter's *City of God* was Petrarch's first known book purchase, and the inspiration it afforded moved him to write poetry that blended Christian with classical Roman sentiment.

If this pioneer of the renaissance imagination did not exactly stand Janus-like on the threshold of a new era, as he himself appears to have believed, he did initiate (not single-handedly) a movement that would lead over the course of a few centuries to a transformation in the self-understanding of the west. In his wake came a humanism that owed much to its ancient predecessor, to rhetoric and grammar, philosophical and poetic expression, and to a stylistic elegance that, as he saw it, had no counterpart from Augustine's time to his own. The intervening centuries were a cultural valley between peaks, one real and one hoped for. "Once the darkness has been broken," in his words, "our descendants will perhaps be able to return to the pure, pristine radiance" that was Italy's noble past.[10] The sentiment would catch on and animate a myriad of undertakings in the disciplines of the humanities and within the arts and sciences generally. The aim was to sweep away the cobwebs of the "middle ages" and to emulate ancient models of Latin language and eloquence which had preceded the technical terminology of the universities. This author's critique of scholasticism—that it represented little more than a tedious obsessing over minutiae—has been echoed through our own time. What was to replace it was a humanism that had about it an attitude that was simultaneously ancient and modern. The cultivated individual embodied *Romanitas*, an aristocratic virtue, knowledge, prestige, connoisseurship, and facility with Latin that far surpassed all medieval backwardness as well as the Germanic "barbarians" of the north.

Petrarch was more than nostalgic. He was a thoroughgoing Romanophile who lamented what he perceived as the failure of his own age to come anywhere close to the pinnacle of achievement that lay in his society's remote past, and it was a sentiment that would be shared by a great many within the urban elite of fourteenth-century Italy and in time much of Europe. If Christian historical consciousness for centuries had fixed its gaze upon a coming kingdom, this wild-eyed enthusiast was focused squarely on the past, standing forlornly in the "cow pasture" (*Campo Vaccino*) that had been the Roman Forum and bemoaning the "dark ages" that stood between the period of Julius Caesar and himself. The imaginative schema of which he was a principal author combined a breadth of vision with a powerful emotional charge that was no youthful infatuation. It could accommodate Christianity while injecting it with a humanistic sensibility that had little patience for a scholasticism and a university curriculum now seen as stultifying. The movement that would take shape saw itself as an avant-garde on a mission to restore ancient glories and indeed to surpass them, and it found a ready audience among the aristocratic and merchant classes of the cities. The affinity for ancient ways applied to everything from the Latin language itself—the refinement of which far exceeded, in their estimation, the barbarism of the empire's invaders—to the various literary and artistic productions that were the fruits of Roman high culture. Classical models needed to be rediscovered and adapted to a worldview that remained Christian but with a difference. The goal was not religious innovation in a doctrinal sense but a cultural revolution that ran alongside doctrine and that humanized it. In the thirteenth century, Dante Alighieri and Thomas Aquinas were already among those seeking a rapprochement of a kind between the Christian and the pagan within poetry and philosophy. The movement for which Petrarch became a spokesman was not his personal creation, but his efforts raised the ante and helped an existing schema to gain a lasting hold on the Italian imagination. An accent on revivalism and tradition combined with a love of novelty, most clearly perhaps in the science of nature or "natural philosophy" for which "the book of nature" was to be studied in a novel manner that would lead by the end of the renaissance into the scientific revolution. Deference to scholastic doctrine would eventually give way to science in a modern connotation of the term, and it was an undertaking that again involved an integration of ancient with contemporary knowledge. Humanists and scientists often being one and the same individuals, the separation between disciplines and between ancient and modern had yet to become an abyss. Everywhere the rule was imitate with a difference or rise to the challenge presented by Greek and Roman models while eschewing all servility. These models could be improved upon, and if the concept of progress was still on the horizon the ground was being prepared. Uncritical and wholesale appropriation of ancient ways was never possible within a Christian conceptual and imaginative scheme. The whole needed to be rendered seamless, and creative minds across the various fields of knowledge were set to blend the old with the new, or the less old, in a way that amounted to a fashionable traditionalism. As Burckhardt stated, "the literary bequests of antiquity, Greek as well as Latin, . . . were held in the most absolute sense to be the springs of all knowledge," but this did not exclude biblical tradition.[11]

The fifteenth-century Florentine humanist Matteo Palmieri articulated a common sentiment regarding the artistic revival of his time as follows: "For some centuries now the noble arts, which were well understood and practised by our ancient forebears, have been so deficient that it is shameful how little they have produced and with what little honour. . . . [A]nyone of intelligence should thank God for being born in these times, in which we enjoy a more splendid flowering of the arts than at any other time in the last thousand years."[12] Condemnation of medieval Latin, literary and artistic production was widespread and issued in a determination to rehabilitate and improve upon Greek and Roman exemplars across the spectrum of aesthetic expression. Latin being the noblest language ever devised—this point was axiomatic—all poetic and prosaic work needed to be written in this language. In prose Cicero was the great paragon while in poetry the models were more numerous and included Virgil, Horace, Juvenal, Ovid, Statius, Lucan, and Seneca. Post-classical writers in general had defiled the Latin language, common opinion had it, culminating in the scholastic idiom which renaissance figures never tired of castigating. The art of imitating these models with an eye to stylistic perfection became a regular feature of renaissance schooling. Latin poetry being the pinnacle of high culture in the opinion of many humanists, this art was to be learned through imitation of the ancient masters, and the other arts were to follow suit. The highest achievements were one and all revivals—not, again, slavish repetitions but novel appropriations, as so much of Roman culture had itself involved wholesale appropriation of the Greek. Painters, sculptors, and architects were all competing for predominance and patrons by the same method that poets and prose writers were doing so: looking forward by looking back, discerningly and creatively, always with an eye to standing on the shoulders of giants. Artworks were produced for a range of ends, from religious devotion to embellishing an array of private and public spaces. Patronizing the finest artists and artisans whom one could afford was a priority for wealthy families who always had an eye out for personal glory. There were many to choose from, many of whom remain household names in the history of art. The achievements of a Leonardo da Vinci, for one, are impossible not to admire, this towering artist-polymath whose genius would be difficult to overstate. A recent biographer writes,

> There have been, of course, many other insatiable polymaths, and even the Renaissance produced other Renaissance Men. But none painted the *Mona Lisa*, much less did so at the same time as producing unsurpassed anatomy drawings based on multiple dissections, coming up with schemes to divert rivers, explaining the reflection of light from the earth to the moon, opening the still-beating heart of a butchered pig to show how ventricles work, designing musical instruments, choreographing pageants, using fossils to dispute the biblical account of the deluge, and then drawing the deluge. Leonardo was a genius, but more: he was the epitome of the universal mind, one who sought to understand all of creation, including how we fit into it.[13]

Such praise is well warranted, although it does not follow that the denigration of medieval art that became popular among renaissance humanists is thereby justified. Medievalists in particular are not about to concede this, even while the heights that many a renaissance artist attained have never ceased to amaze. The judgment of "rebirth" does rather presuppose that something had died, and if this is not the case then something at least had changed.

The ancient standard was new again, and this included Greek language and literature. In the centuries preceding the renaissance, knowledge of both had remained extensive in the Byzantine Empire but was uncommon in Western Europe. Few Greek manuscripts were held in Western libraries and the language itself was seldom taught in schools and universities. This changed in the fourteenth century when a number of Byzantine scholars migrated westward at the same time that Italian scholars were traveling to Constantinople in search of Greek books which they brought back to Italy. To cite Gombrich once more,

> the real systematic study of Greek started when Florentine followers of Petrarch . . . seized on the opportunity that a Byzantine scholar—Manuel Chrysoloras—was coming to Italy and asked him to teach Greek in Florence . . . . In Sicily, Greek *was* known and a Sicilian called Aurispa travelled to Byzantium when the craze for manuscripts had properly started and collected Greek manuscripts. For in Byzantium, of course, the works of Greek literature had never been forgotten and existed in the libraries. We owe it to Aurispa, largely, . . . that we have the Greek authors, for, . . . Constantinople fell under the onslaught of the Turks, in 1453, and that was the end. . . . [I]f you look down a list of Greek authors, Sophocles, Euripides, Aristophanes, or whatever, you are very likely to find that the manuscripts came to the west through Aurispa.[14]

A wide-ranging fashion for antiquity, the migration of Greek scholars into western Europe, a growing knowledge of ancient Latin and Greek, the creation of new translations and sizeable libraries, the recovery of many an ancient text from European monasteries, the Byzantine empire, the Islamic world, and a flourishing book trade combined to produce a sizeable effect upon intellectual culture, not least in the universities where Aristotelian scholasticism still predominated.

On an old version of this story, Aristotelian philosophy had been hegemonic in the universities from their inception and remained so until newly recovered Platonic and other Greek and Roman texts dislodged the orthodoxy. Contemporary historians largely tell a different story, which is that Aristotelian thought continued to make significant gains through the centuries of the renaissance due to new and superior Latin translations and that its hold upon university education remained strong until the seventeenth century. Increased knowledge of Plato within the movement that is under discussion was evident but not revolutionary, and indeed the opposition itself between Platonic and Aristotelian philosophy has long been overstated. It is worth noting that in the eastern Roman empire no such opposition was believed to exist through the centuries in which the texts of both thinkers had never disappeared, and the western migration of Greek scholars did not lend support to any such dichotomy. A great deal of scholarship and commentary on both figures emerged during these centuries, and while Aristotle's works continued to predominate in the universities, the writings of Plato were placed alongside them despite their lack of systematicity. What humanism affected was not the displacement of a monolithic tradition—Aristotelian thought had long been subject to competing interpretations in the works of Averroes, Thomas Aquinas, Duns Scotus, William of Ockham, and others—but a further broadening of it and a more scholarly treatment of the Greek texts. Humanists called upon scholars to read the texts in their original language while also producing better translations. Latin translations of some Aristotelian works had been available in Western Europe since the thirteenth century, but the entire corpus would appear in more adequate form at this time together with other Greek writers, some of whose works had been available prior to the renaissance but very incompletely. If a note of hostility toward medieval scholasticism found expression among the humanists of this time, the result was no paradigm shift but an enriched appreciation of Greek and Roman tradition and improved standards of scholarship. Within Italy itself, scholasticism and humanism emerged at the same time—in the thirteenth century—and developed over ensuing centuries in only partial competition with each other. No tradition was brought to an end. The works of Aristotle, Plato, stoics, skeptics, and epicureans coexisted within and without European universities while some division appeared between "natural philosophy" (biology, psychology, physics, etc.), metaphysics, and logic wherein scholasticism remained dominant and the disciplines in which the humanists were taking primary interest, particularly rhetoric, grammar, poetry, and moral philosophy. Humanist critiques of scholasticism were less philosophical than disciplinary, as the general domain of human expression and action fired the imagination of the avant-garde far more than logic and natural philosophy.

Petrarch's decided preference for the human disciplines and for Plato would become a widespread fashion. Medieval Europe had possessed only two complete Platonic dialogues and by the end of the fifteenth century the entire corpus was available in Latin translation. The longstanding issue of the relation of Platonic and Aristotelian thought received fresh impetus once new translations of both thinkers' works were produced, and without losing ground in the university curriculum or intellectual culture at large, the latter did make way for the former which, many humanists believed, could be more readily integrated within a Christian framework. Augustine had also maintained this, and Petrarch acknowledged a sizeable debt to this fourth to fifth-century theologian. Neither Christianity nor scholasticism was pushed aside by their newly recovered Platonic, hellenistic, and Roman alternatives. The main project was one of synthesis: how to reconcile the foremost among Greek and Roman intellectual currents both with each other and with Christian monotheism and to fashion a worldview that was encompassing, interdisciplinary, modern, and also rooted in tradition. It has often been said that the renaissance produced little or even no philosophical originality, but the claim is overstated. Conceptual creation placed a decided second to synthesis, it is true, but the conclusion that renaissance thought was "merely derivative" should be resisted. An enormous philosophical and artistic heritage needed to be reintegrated and adapted to the times, and if no altogether new system emerged from this movement it did produce a tremendous output of intellectual labor which lay the groundwork for what would follow—the scientific revolution, the reformation, and the enlightenment.

The new humanism was not a hypothesis or philosophical system but a movement of scholars working in the liberal arts or humanities as well as an educational program. The Latin phrase was *studia humanitatis*, and it stood in opposition to Aristotelian scholasticism about as much as the humanities and the sciences do today, which is more a disciplinary rivalry than a philosophical disagreement. The word "humanism" itself did not appear until the nineteenth century, while the phenomenon to which it refers extends back to Greek *paideia* and comes into the fourteenth and fifteenth centuries primarily as an educational program in rhetoric, grammar, poetry, moral philosophy, and history—forms of knowledge that this group judged appropriate to the education of any human being regardless of profession. A humanist (*umanista*), then, was a professor or student in one or more of these fields, and if

Plato often loomed larger than Aristotle in the curriculum this did not amount to a principled difference in viewpoint, nor was such an individual necessarily or even usually at odds with the Roman church. The oppositional stance for which humanism would become known was based primarily on these scholars' discontent with a good deal of medieval literature, but more for its style than its substance. The charges were that scholastic texts had been written in poor Latin style and that their standards of scholarship were insufficiently rigorous and applied too often to pointless lines of questioning. It was rhetorical eloquence that mattered most, and the ancients afforded the models. As Hannah Gray notes,

> By "rhetoric," the humanists did not intend an empty pomposity, a willful mendacity, a love of display for its own sake, an extravagant artificiality, a singular lack of originality, or a necessary subordination of substance to form and ornament . . .. They distinguished carefully between "true eloquence" and "sophistry," perceiving in the latter a perversion, not a consequence, of the former. True eloquence, according to the humanists, could arise only out of a harmonious union between wisdom and style; its aim was to guide men toward virtue and worthwhile goals, not to mislead them for vicious or trivial purposes.[15]

Eloquence was the orator's highest virtue, and where an orator might apply their art in the universities, the church, the civil service, politics, literature, or any other profession. It was a generalized form of knowledge which could apply equally to career and to private pursuits.

If terms like rhetoric, oratory, and eloquence suggest for many modern readers a valorization of form over substance, this is not what was intended by renaissance humanists, whose ambition far exceeded dressing up received ideas into aesthetically pleasing form. Their project involved a selective and creative restoration of the past, and a precondition of this was raising standards of scholarship. A new accent on scholarly rigor, reading ancient Greek texts in the original, and creating Latin translations that were at once more careful and more artful became the fashion. Skepticism enjoyed a new cachet, as exemplified by Lorenzo Valla's philological argument that the "Donation of Constantine," a purportedly fourth-century imperial decree by which Constantine granted political authority over Rome and the western empire to the papacy, was an eighth-century forgery. A new ethos of doubt and scholarly rigor was gaining ascendancy, and by the reformation was urging a new tolerance of religious difference. Humanism was as much an outlook or an attitude as a set of disciplines. It was a posture that looked favorably upon its own time and askance at the several centuries that had preceded it. More than a little historical and cultural chauvinism is visible in the "republic of letters" that this movement saw itself as being. The accent was upon relevance for human life, and many viewed the new standard as a departure from the abstract technicality and irrelevance which they attributed to their recent forebears.

Within the field of history itself, humanists placed this under the general classification of rhetoric and urged at once a critical attitude and a more artful narrative presentation of events than the chronicles that had been the predominant form of historiography in the centuries leading up to the renaissance. As one historian remarks, "throughout much of Europe, the chronicle first lost the privileged position it had enjoyed for several centuries, and soon became the backward, lumbering poor cousin of a slicker, more literary form of historical narrative favoured by the educational elites and their most powerful readers. The models for this new history were to be found in antiquity," principally Livy and Sallust.[16] If the exemplars were ancient, the historical consciousness that was taking shape was modern both in terms of scholarly standards and a new periodization to which we shall return. Medieval historical literature placed an accent upon providence and Christian morality while the humanists, without abandoning moral analysis, were taking a less Augustinian view of the past. Secular history was (partially) displacing the sacred variety, and while the record of human actions and their consequences continued to invite didactic analysis this was combined with learned skepticism and a new emphasis upon evidence and sources. The human past was to be mined for lessons that could be turned to modern, especially political, purposes, as humanistic investigation in general was to serve utilitarian ends. The style, purpose, and method of historical interpretation were all transformed while the field itself was promoted to a higher rung on the ladder of disciplines. At the same time that such works remained dependent on aristocratic patrons, a popular audience was emerging in the age of the printing press for books that could be either read for personal edification or used for political ends. Historical and often political partisanship combined with a new proto-empiricism and -utilitarianism to reform an art the defining mission of which was to impart lessons to a modern readership through an examination of examples of human beings acting variously well and badly.

A good part of the modern fascination with the renaissance is owing to the longstanding association of this culture and time period with the concept of the individual. Humanism is an individualism, on this view, and what the general movement of artists, writers, and scholars was affecting was nothing less than a revolution in the western imagination, from a medieval worldview that defined human beings fundamentally in terms of group affiliations to a new *zeitgeist* in which individual agency came into its own. The great champion of this idea is again Burckhardt, who famously spoke of "the Italian" of this era as "the first-born among the sons of modern Europe." He elaborated:

in the Middle Ages both sides of human consciousness—that which was turned within as that which was turned without—lay dreaming or half awake beneath a common veil. The veil was woven of faith, illusion and childish prepossession, through which the world and history were seen clad in strange hues. Man was conscious of himself only as a member of a race, people, party, family or corporation—only through some general category. In Italy this veil first melted into air; an *objective* treatment and consideration of the state and of all the things of this world became possible. The *subjective* side at the same time asserted itself with corresponding emphasis; man became a spiritual *individual*, and recognized himself as such.

What was Burckhardt's evidence? The medieval individual had something childish about it, an agency that was merely nascent and collectivized while its fourteenth- and fifteenth-century descendants witnessed the "gradual awakening of the soul of a people" and indeed the "discovery of man." He went so far as to claim that the revival of antiquity ultimately placed second to this discovery and that what would come to be called renaissance individualism—this philosophy of "the many-sided men" whose knowledge and talents ranged across a variety of fields—captured the spirit of the age.[17] Evidence was scanty and consisted in the main of autobiographies and self-portraits by notable personages who, in Burckhardt's estimation, represented a new phase in the history of the self. Leonardo da Vinci is again an exemplar; this man was neither specialist nor dilettante but a giant of his time and across a wide range of pursuits, and he was not the only one.

The renaissance individual has come under fire from more recent historians, many of whom regard this notion in the main as a nineteenth-century artifact invented to serve ideological commitments of that time period, and it is an assessment that has much to recommend it. Burckhardt himself told us that he was "treading on the perilous ground of conjecture" in his analysis of the elusive entities that are medieval and renaissance humanity, while medievalists have brought forth their own examples of pre-renaissance figures who appear to have embodied the mode of self-consciousness and agency the Swiss historian claimed was a fourteenth-century discovery.[18] The medieval self, if it is even possible to speak of such a thing, was not a child but a being that understood itself in relation to God and various kinds of kinship and communal associations, and this description appears no less applicable to the centuries of which we are speaking. Individual self-creation was neither unknown prior to the renaissance nor anything like the norm within it, although selective attention to certain notable personages and high-cultural achievements can create this appearance. Religious and collective affiliations were about as evident through both eras. If anything changed during the early modern period in terms of individual self-consciousness, it was nothing so momentous as the "discovery of man" for when had such a being been unknown or known in the manner of a child? False idealization aside, what may be said is that within elite circles during and following Petrarch's time a received imaginative schema was being modified on some difficult-to-measure scale in light of a renewed access and valorization of some ancient texts and ideas. The fashion for Roman ways was beginning to transform the self-image of the fourteenth-century Italian upper classes and in time the better part of Europe—not in a totalizing way but partially, and which a few centuries later could be described retrospectively and through a political lens as revolutionary. A great age of the individual it was not, or not if we mean by this a mode of subjectivity that was either a radical departure from what had preceded it or free of the social ties more readily associated with the middle ages. As Martin writes, "Medievalists have pointed to evidence for an interest in the individual in the eleventh and twelfth centuries," while "[s]ocial historians have made compelling arguments for the decisiveness [throughout the renaissance] of communal, civic, and family structures in shaping notions of identity that they see as rooted in collective rather than individualistic contexts."[19] Selective focus on a limited number of cultural artifacts does not indicate wholesale change, particularly when we are speaking of something as intangible as the self. A novel and relative accent upon individual expression, perspective, and creativity based especially upon Roman models, yes; the world-historical birth of a new metaphysical being, no.

Within this general movement, from patrons to poets, painters, scholars, and so on, the name of the game was prestige. Cultural production, connoisseurship, reputation, and elitism were inseparable while the fundamental goal of upper-class education was to prepare one for membership in the elite. To Italians and sometimes to others, the superiority of Italian culture was self-evident, rooted as it was—and with renewed intensity—upon an ancient tradition which they contrasted sharply with the medieval and the barbaric. Knowledge of proper Latin, classical learning more broadly, aristocratic lineage, and refined taste were all indications of status, the competition for which could be as fierce as the politics of city-states. The refined individual was a gentleman with a keen sense of the superiority of his age and of himself, and the latter needed to be proven through a combination of social connections and class, knowledge and education, wealth and profession, courtly refinement and personal achievement. Preeminence and fame, again on ancient models, were highly valued indeed on the part of persons, courts, and cities alike.

Lordly personages in various European centers throughout the renaissance and the centuries that led up to it maintained courts. This, of course, included various Italian cities wherein aristocratic families competed to fill the void left by the departure of the papacy and its court to Avignon in 1309. The prestige of courts and their patrons rested in good part upon the extent of their largesse and the quality of personages they could attract. As a cultural center, a court drew various elites—artists, scholars, clergy, diplomats, and so forth—to its corridors, and cultural production in general served a few purposes, the foremost of which was invariably the prestige and legitimacy of its lord. The fashion for classical revival dovetailed with an interest in self-aggrandizement on the part of patrons who were commissioning a wide range of public and cultural works which promoted simultaneously the restoration of Roman antiquity and personal fame. Public spiritedness and the drive for predominance were for all intents and purposes one, and the papal court was no exception. Following its return to Rome in 1376, the papacy was a major force behind the program for revival in that city through the fifteenth and sixteenth centuries. Nicholas V "instituted a library . . . and he commissioned translations of rediscovered Greek writings. He also employed Leon Battista Alberti to embellish the city with majestic buildings, counting both among the achievements of his papacy. Sixtus IV used art to reassert the doctrine of papal monarchy in the famous frescoes he commissioned for the Sistine Chapel . . . and he embellished the city with the Sistine Bridge. He also encouraged palace building through his law enabling clerics to bequeath their possessions to relatives. Later popes, Alexander VI and Julius II, built and decorated the Vatican Palace and the new Saint Peter's Basilica."[20] Lesser aristocrats followed suit in patronizing works that honored God while advertising their own magnanimity and the honor of their families, courts, and cities.

At the heart of the renaissance imagination lay a new form of historical consciousness which spoke of the past and the present in a less teleological way than Augustinian Christianity had done. In what would become something of an orthodoxy, Petrarch was interpreting history in more secular and overtly partisan terms as divided into three discrete epochs: the ancient, the medieval, and the modern, where the first and third of these were construed as civilizational peaks between which lay a thousand-year valley which he termed the "dark" or "middle ages" (*medium aevum*). Petrarch's tripartite scheme depicted the mental atmosphere that ostensibly prevailed throughout Western Europe from the fall of the empire until his own time in singularly unflattering ways as one long period of cultural backwardness, superstition, and violence, noteworthy only for constituting in its latter phase a rather bleak prelude to his own era. But for outbreaks of plague and war, the middle ages were essentially static and largely without the noble characters and achievements that we find in ancient Greece and Rome. The general *zeitgeist* was homogeneous and uninspired, or so a story that would last until the present day went, even while the evidence supporting the "damnation of memory" (*damnatio memoriae*) of these centuries was sparse. Petrarch and his heirs were doing to medieval Christendom what early Christian thinkers had done to their Greek and Roman forebears, which is to define themselves and their time in contrast to a despised predecessor while borrowing heavily from them. "Medieval" and "Gothic" became terms of condemnation, the latter denoting the most contemptible of the "barbarian hordes" who had overrun Rome itself. For Petrarch himself, all notional affinities and identifications were with an era that ended with Augustine, and the humanist movement in general would follow him in this.

By the nineteenth century Burckhardt and other historians largely shared the sentiment, regarding the middle ages again as one vast cultural wasteland and childhood of the mind. Contemporary medievalists say otherwise, as one might expect, but the point is that within the historical consciousness of the humanists the grand sweep of time now conformed to a three-stage scheme which was still Christian while also Roman in its accent upon repetition. A case in point is sixteenth-century historian Francesco Guicciardini who was echoing the Greek and Roman cyclical conception as follows: "Everything that has happened in the past or exists in the present will also happen again in the future. But the names and outward appearances of things change, so unless you have a keen eye, you won't recognise them, nor will you be able to formulate rules or make a judgement on the basis of what you see."[21] Rebirth was repetition with a difference; the goal was not merely to conserve but to equal and surpass the achievements of Roman times in imagined contrast with their civilizational and historical inferiors. Emphasis was placed upon the discontinuity between and value connotations of the epochs together with an imperative to reconnect with the ancients while also accentuating the new in a cultural atmosphere that was overtly competitive. New claimants within the elite needed to legitimate their membership by outdoing one another in terms of patronage, social connections, and displays of magnificence, and a similar agonism extended to artists and scholars. The Romans themselves, following the Greek example, had turned more or less everything they saw into an agon and their new heirs were doing the same.

This last point must be kept in mind in understanding such periodizing efforts and designation of eras as high and low, all of which served a purpose. As historian Guido Ruggiero points out, the renaissance

> begins with a conflict in Italy between newer urban merchant-banker elites and older traditional aristocracies, which was soon won by the former. But not content merely to have wrested power and position economically and politically from that traditional aristocracy, these new elites set out to create a social ideology that would confirm them as the true elites of society. A goodly part of the agenda of early humanism and civic culture was concerned with finding in the

ancient world an intellectual rationale for the ideological shift that would put these new urban leaders on top of society, not just because they were powerful, but because they deserved in any case to be on top.[22]

Civic-mindedness and egoism were as two sides of one aristocratic coin, and the trend would spread throughout Europe where princely courts had been operating for centuries. Artists and scholars competed among themselves while keeping a clear eye on what their patrons needed to achieve. He who paid the piper continued to call the tune, and the evaluative division of the epochs itself served both the collective egoism of the times and the personal aggrandizement of the elite, whether new or old, religious or aristocratic. The superiority of the present age, with its venerable accomplishments and personages, had to be demonstrated, and the chauvinism of the present became one with the denigration of the centuries that had led up to it. The celebrated rebirth of the ancient would in time be classified with no little partisanship as "the (Italian) Renaissance" (most often in the upper case), although it is important to bear in mind that contemporaries did not speak of themselves or their times in this way but as "modern" and were hardly the first to do so. Indeed, the term "'modernity' dawns in the sixth century (Cassiodorus is the first Latin writer to use the term *modernus*), but does not begin in earnest until the ninth."[23] "Modern" ("of today") in the hands of renaissance humanists was neither a new nor a value-neutral descriptor but part of an imaginative schema whose membership held themselves in rather high regard.

Upon what criteria and evidence was the notion of a historical rupture based? In chapter 3 we posed this question regarding late antiquity and we pose it here again. Imaginative history—the self-image and mode of historical consciousness that now prevailed within elite networks—had entered a new phase, but had history itself? Nicholas Mann suggests a negative answer: "The more we learn about the period following the decline of Rome, the less dark and uncultured it appears; the more we inquire into what was reborn in the fourteenth and fifteenth centuries, the more we become aware of vital continuities with the past."[24] The evidence for this overall assessment is strong, most obviously in the case of rural agriculturalists who continued to comprise a vast majority of the European population and whose way of life remained notably similar to what it had been for centuries. The economy and general society of renaissance Europe remained primarily rural-agricultural even while larger urban centers which had begun to experience significant growth in the eleventh century were now enjoying a vitality that has often been overemphasized. By the beginning of the sixteenth century, Paris, Rome, Venice, Florence, Naples, and Milan all had populations over 60,000 and were attracting a larger share of immigrants while urban and rural economies remained closely integrated.[25] No wholesale transformation from a rural to an urban economy occurred, while in the world of culture as well the pattern was one of relative and gradual change rather than revolution. This deeply Christian society remained deeply Christian, and this included artists and humanists. Humanism itself, while of ancient vintage, had not died in the intervening centuries but had at most been underemphasized relative to what a group of thinkers in and following Petrarch's time had come to prefer. Roman thinkers including Cicero had used the Latin word *humanitas* to designate the type of knowledge and values that were consistent with the older Greek *paideia*, and the general phenomenon to which it referred did not disappear in the centuries between late antiquity and the renaissance. Throughout this period numerous Roman authors as well as Plato and Aristotle were studied in Italian schools. As Robert Black notes, "The grammar curriculum in twelfth-century Italian schools finished with a study of the poets Vergil, Lucan, Ovid, Juvenal, Persius, Horace, Terence, and Statius, as well as of prose texts by Cicero and Sallust's two histories."[26] The practice of oratory based upon Roman models was not an educational innovation with the renaissance, nor had medieval scholars and clerics ever ceased to engage with a wide variety of classical texts, although the number of such texts and the number of individuals who had access to them undoubtedly increased in the fourteenth and fifteenth centuries. Full access to their Greek and Roman inheritance had remained undiminished in the eastern empire, which never ceased to call itself Romania. As well, the class system in Western Europe did not change in any ostensible transition from the middle ages to the new era. Aristocratic families and patronage networks remained very much in place, even while many of the players changed.

The notion of a historical rupture is based primarily upon two things: the ideology of an elite who were anxious to legitimate their position at the top of the social hierarchy and a lack of knowledge regarding the time period that had preceded their own. The lover of renaissance culture will find much to admire; this much is incontestable, but our admiration of their achievements has too often led historians and others to overlook the achievements of their forebears and not only the ancient ones. Upon what principled basis might we judge that the renaissance constituted an advance in the history of the west, or that the millennium that came before it had been a retreat or a deterioration? This question has no answer, apart from trotting out the many cultural attainments of the two or three centuries of renaissance Europe and comparing them to their counterparts of the centuries immediately preceding—not an exact science, one will say, and aesthetic and similar judgments are not a sufficient basis of judgment. The middle ages also have their aficionados, but apart from cultural appreciation and partisanship no standards exist by which to speak of forward or backward movement. Medievalists have long pointed out that renaissance innovations had medieval roots, as one can say of more or less every culture and time period of which we know, and indeed medieval renaissances, of which there were three.

The first was the "Carolingian renaissance" that was centered around Charlemagne and his successors in the Carolingian family during the latter eighth and ninth centuries. The revival of Roman heritage was not limited to Charlemagne's court but pervaded the Frankish empire and found its leader sponsoring a network of scholars, artists, architects, poets, and others in a concerted endeavor to revivify the past and, inseparable from this, to legitimate his rule. As Rosamond McKitterick notes, "All the scholars who claim to have been personally encouraged by Charlemagne aligned themselves with a particular intellectual tradition that explicitly based itself on an expectation of continuity with the Roman and Merovingian past."[27] Greek and Roman texts that had been preserved in European monasteries were being recovered and studied critically by a group of scholars (the most prominent of whom was Alcuin of York), taught in schools together with Christianity, and transmitted to later generations. The Frankish emperor made it clear what purpose classical knowledge was to serve. Such scholarship remained a subordinate of theology, but it was an important subordinate: "Therefore we exhort you ... to pursue the study of letters ... in order that you may be able more easily and more correctly to penetrate the mysteries of the divine Scriptures."[28] Greek and Latin were fostered, the book trade expanded, libraries were created, old manuscripts were copied in a new script, and a larger ethos took hold that would later characterize the Italian renaissance on a larger scale. A similar description would apply to twelfth-century efforts to return again to classical antiquity, including especially Greek science and philosophy. Increased trade and contact with eastern regions and Arab Spain promoted urban development in the cities of Italy and southern France, which in turn created a need for civil servants, professionals, schools, and scholars on a large scale. Courts and religious schools would play a key role in the conservation of the Roman literary tradition. Some of these schools would become the first universities wherein Aristotelian scholasticism (the Latin *scholasticus* connotes "schoolmen") would come into its own and culminate in Thomas Aquinas. Also worthy of note was the tenth-century "Ottonian renaissance" brought about by another "Holy Roman Emperor," the Saxon king Otto I whose revival effort followed Charlemagne's example while also belonging to a larger project to consolidate power. In all three medieval renaissances, cultural revival on a primarily Roman model and the legitimation of a ruling elite were as indivisible as they would remain in the time following Petrarch.

By the fourteenth century, no rabbit was being pulled from a hat. Three prior renaissances and an eastern Roman empire that had never collapsed pointed the way, while the scale of what would take place in the Italian city-states through these centuries increased. We are speaking not of the crossing of a historical Rubicon but of a continuing conversation the heart of which involved some creative rapprochement between what was known of the Greco-Roman heritage and late medieval Christendom. Achieving some syncretism between classical and modern ideas became the imperative, not for the first time but with a newly enriched access to ancient texts. Greek science and philosophy were not easily reconciled with Christian theology, but the project of articulating a unified conceptual and imaginative framework was far from unprecedented. If many renaissance humanists were inclining in some measure toward secularism, this was not an unchristian knowledge but one that for the most part ran alongside the received religion and scholastic theorists rather than directly opposed them. The notion of the fully secular humanist in this time period abandoning religious and social tradition for a radical individualism is largely a nineteenth-century projection which is belied by a couple of considerations. The first is that while historians have often accentuated the secular and this-worldly interests of many within the humanist movement, this is better regarded as a relative turn than a more fundamental change in orientation. If the balance of Greco-Roman and Christian ideas was shifting toward the former, evidence of any large-scale abandonment of the latter is sparse. The overriding goal was to achieve a new synthesis, and religious piety appears no less evident in renaissance Italy than in the centuries that preceded it. The notion of a historical divide on one side of which was the medieval Christian whose sole interest lay in the afterlife and the otherworldly and on the other the thoroughgoing renaissance secularist is a false idealization. Second, much the same system of courts, patronage, family, class, and professional competition continued to characterize the renaissance world. Burckhardt's rugged individualist of the mind needed a patron and remained part of a network of social connections and obligations in which prestige could be sought. "Whatever their social condition—peasant, laborer, artisan, merchant, scholar—they were not free," or not in any way that could be seen as a break from a prior epoch.[29]

Freedom is always a difficult value to estimate. Whether citizens of the renaissance were any freer than their medieval predecessors is doubtful, depending on what exactly we intend by this elusive word. Measuring freedom across the ages is a lot like comparing grapefruit to pears, and much the same can be said of equality and democracy. Italian city-states of this period have often been characterized as free republics and indeed nascent democracies, yet analyzing the realities of these states within modern political categories does not shed much light. The revival of Roman ways did extend to politics with its myriad complexities. Petrarch had argued that the city-state is best governed by a paragon of aristocratic virtue, and this classical idea touched down to the real world of politics about as imperfectly as one would expect. The reality often reflected the Roman politics of old, complete with its machinations, elite factionalism, and relentless self-seeking, even while terms like commune, freedom, and republicanism enjoyed wide currency. States were dominated by strongmen and oligarchs whose power required legitimation, and cultural production was as imperative to this end as military prowess. The business of consolidating and maintaining power involved gaining the support of urban clerics and nobility much as medieval kings had long done, and this could be an unsavory matter. Robert Davis remarks, "Individual aggression, group contention, and general mayhem were this era's constant and necessary subtext, the background against which both the brilliant artistic and intellectual innovations as well as the most sordid political maneuvering were worked out."[30] Roman republican and imperial politics had also fit this description, as did a sizeable share of the politics of the intervening centuries. There was much about the dynamics of Italian politics throughout the renaissance that was not new, including a kind of conservatism that ensured that ruling elites maintained their social position and that any usurpers would need to play by the same rules. The rules showed some allowance for social criticism; indeed, as James Hankins correctly points out, "to celebrate the past was inevitably to criticize the present," and what some humanists were doing "inevitably brought these (mostly) urban, lay intellectuals into conflict with established guardians of culture and with the monastic and scholastic traditions of learning they represented."[31] A climate of conservatism was not conducive to revolutionaries, but moral reformers speaking at once the languages of Christianity and classical antiquity enjoyed some freedom in calling for reform at the level of personal virtue which had implications for statecraft without fashioning the kind of political philosophies that would later become possible. The political imagination of renaissance Italy continued to dream of empire on the Roman model while self-styled "Roman" and "Holy Roman" emperors were a common feature of both medieval and renaissance politics. Simplifying slightly, every noble dreamed of being king, every king and pope dreamed of being emperor, and every emperor dreamed of being a Roman emperor and the true heir of Augustus. The imperial dream had never died but was hemmed in by too much competition. Individual tyrants were by no means ubiquitous, and important elements of republicanism and democracy did show themselves, however, as was always the case in Roman times, the real world of politics was a hodgepodge of conflicting forces, factions, and ideas whose constant tendency was to boil over.

The centuries of which we have been speaking, as the historian just cited also notes, were "a period when fundamental changes occurred in Western societies across a wide range of beliefs . . . . Christendom disintegrated and sovereign states emerged. The Catholic Church lost much of its authority and new Protestant churches and sects appeared. Religious divisions and wars led to the first tentative expressions of the need for tolerance and freedom of expression. Educational ideals and practice were transformed. Humanists arose to challenge the hegemony of scholastic culture. Christian culture underwent a major reorientation in its attitude to the pagan culture of Graeco-Roman antiquity."[32] What happened was not that a new imaginative schema appeared out of nowhere but that an ancient one had entered a new phase, as a broad movement of thinkers sought to create a novel synthesis of ancient and modern ideas. While the overall configuration of cultural preferences and fashions, viewed in the large, was both original and an important historical development, we ought not exaggerate the scale on which this was happening. Throughout this period the contributions of artists, scientists, and humanists never cease to impress, yet it remains that the renaissance was neither unprecedented nor a monumental stride forward in any linear march through Western history. By the counter-reformation which is often regarded as the terminal point of this movement, the papal hammer came down with force. A church that had supported the movement was reasserting itself and eliminating rivals through notorious means. Stamping out heresy, book burning, and inquisition were the new vogue in a famous case of slamming the door after an unruly guest has already left.

Rome's classical past weighed upon the renaissance imagination and demanded a reintegration which seemed to require an ideological depreciation of the approximately ten centuries that had intervened between a past now viewed with high nostalgia and a present that came to regard itself as an heir to a lost greatness. What from a later viewpoint can look like a paradigm shift or world-historical leap was more like a creative reweaving on the part of an entire movement of thinkers of a plethora of cultural elements both ancient and contemporary in ways that suited the interests of the cultural elites who were doing the reweaving and the lordly patrons on whom they depended. Renaissance historical consciousness imagined time as comprising a three-stage continuum, the twin zeniths of which were a classical Rome that saw itself as the center of the human world and the revitalized city-states that saw themselves in much the same way, and the nadir of which was the centuries that intervened. The larger schema served elements within the aristocracy that were anxiously pursuing their own legitimation atop the social hierarchy at the same time that it illuminated a lifeworld and remained an outgrowth of the lifeworld that had come before it. When the hammer came down and the renaissance was at its ostensible end, not a lot actually ended, and the scientific revolution, the reformation, and in time the enlightenment continued down a road upon which the renaissance had also been a turn and a development.

CHAPTER 5

Enlightenment Reimaginings

If the transformation that the enlightenment represented was somewhat less of a departure from the centuries that led to it than the renaissance had been, there is no doubting the turn that things took from the latter seventeenth century through the eighteenth in the major centers of the west. The constellation of ideas that the renaissance, the reformation, and the scientific revolution brought forth without losing sight of their ancient and medieval predecessors made possible the great synthesis that was the "age of reason," the trajectory of which would not radically change through the present age of science, technology, and instrumental rationality. This episode in the history of the western imagination witnessed once again a new set of variations upon ideas that were received and repurposed for modern audiences, and while it is fully appropriate to speak in the large of a fundamental transformation it must be borne in mind that this relatively active phase in the life of the mind was no creation ex nihilo but something more organic and hermeneutically continuous. A good deal happened, sometimes mixed with fanfare that was overblown, and the manner of its happening again sheds light on the historical imagination itself—what it is, how it goes about doing whatever it is that it does, and, as Gadamer would say, "what happens" behind the doing.

Whenever we are tempted to speak of a paradigm change, it is advisable to examine the phenomenon widely and to regard it not as anything frozen in time but in its manifold coming to be and passing away, as part of a running conversation that exhibits all the fundamental characteristics of the dialogical art. The enlightenment was a new chapter in an old story, as any paradigm shift is, a conversational act that began in the way that winter does. The age of reason no more replaced an age of unreason than the renaissance was a rebirth of something that had died. It was something less dramatic than this, even if some of its principal representatives and later historians would often speak of the enlightenment, as the term itself plainly suggests, as something entirely new under the sun. Metaphors of light and darkness have long abounded when characterizing the transition that was the eighteenth century, most of which was fueled by a partisanship that we must endeavor to get past. An imaginative schema was taking shape and displacing another, and where the schema itself was less a theory than an encompassing narrative comprising affectively charged concepts, metaphors, hypotheses, attitudes, values, and other cultural elements that would form the background against which inquiry in the various disciplines would be conducted. Enlightenment was more *zeitgeist* than worldview, a *mentalité* that was reorienting intellectuals toward an increasingly secular and decidedly optimistic model of knowledge and of history itself, a history now conceived in overtly teleological terms. The story of any intellectual movement must include the central ideas that it promulgated, but before we turn to those let us underscore that when we speak of "the enlightenment" we are designating less a doctrine than an attitude, one that "has to do," as one historian puts it, "with *how* one holds one's views, not *what* views one holds."[1] An intellectual independence was declared, a confident refusal to defer to authority, quite apart from whatever beliefs the individual "knowing subject" would adopt. "Thus the man of the Enlightenment grew up, with his lucid and logical intelligence, his unspectacular courage and his deliberate, carefully calculated mode of action—sober, objective, no longer governed by traditional ideas, by impassioned orthodoxy and baroque enthusiasm. It was as if the Roman stoics had been resurrected."[2]

This change in intellectual climate took a few centuries to occur and followed upon a tradition of ostensibly new beginnings, rebirths, reformations, and revolutions to which the great political revolutions of the late eighteenth century would stand as culminations. Such revolutions require a long period of preparation, and nothing that transpired in the century or so of which we are speaking appeared from out of the blue. Immanuel Kant famously declared that "we do live in an age of *enlightenment*," while denying that "we at present live in an *enlightened* age," if the latter is taken to signify an era in which all obstacles to mental autonomy have been removed. As he put it, "*Enlightenment is man's emergence from his self-incurred immaturity. Immaturity* is the inability to use one's own understanding without the guidance of another. This immaturity is *self-incurred* if its cause is not lack of understanding, but lack of resolution and courage to use it without the guidance of another. The motto of enlightenment is therefore: *Sapere aude!* Have courage to use your *own* understanding!" Kant wrote this in 1784, during the denouement of a movement upon which he was able to look back with some historical perspective. The focus of his analysis was on an attitude of mind and an act of courage that was at once epistemological and ethical; one needed to say no to the "laziness and cowardice" that had defined human immaturity through the centuries of the middle ages, or so he maintained. The enlightened mind, quite apart from the content of one's beliefs, was both rational and self-reliant, and if at the time the phenomenon was limited in his estimation to "only a few" the prospect of "an entire public enlightening itself" was great and "indeed almost inevitable, if only the public concerned is left in freedom."[3] Kant was capturing the spirit of the times in these words, as it pertains to higher culture at least and perhaps not only this. This was an age that thought rather well of itself, if an age is capable of being discerned in the events, the texts, and other cultural artifacts that come to stand as characteristic expressions of a time period or a movement. Enlightenment has long been taken to designate both a century and a loose assortment of thinkers, where both constitute a new adulthood of the mind in ostensible contrast to an immaturity that for centuries had remained in place due to powers both ecclesiastical and secular. While the enlightenment (or enlightenments—French, German, English, Scottish, Italian, American, etc.) is often designated as an era, Kant himself spoke of it as an attitude and a process, more a movement of thinkers than either a philosophy or a time period, and we shall follow his lead in this. The period from about the mid-seventeenth century through the end of the eighteenth roughly encompasses the phenomenon with which we are now concerned, but let us speak of the thing itself as we did of early Christianity and the renaissance as a loose assortment of figures who coalesced around certain ideas which are better characterized as attitudes and ways of thinking than doctrines, more story than theory. Theoretical hypotheses abounded, but in the fashion of an iceberg seen from above; beneath the water line once again was an emerging schema or a relatively novel synthesis of traditionary material and affectively charged metaphors, aspirations, and dispositions which animated a good part of the western world. Not every thinker, text, or work of art of the eighteenth century embodied the enlightenment, and in view of this it is preferable to describe the phenomenon as a configuration of ideas and their proponents who were responding to one another and attempting to make a new beginning in various areas of cultural expression.

No movement includes everyone, and while it is mistaken to classify every cultural expression of roughly a century and a half as a product of the enlightenment we are speaking of an expansive network of philosophers, scientists, artists, political thinkers, historians, and other intellectuals whose overlapping sensibilities were "modern" in a new way. Seventeenth-century thinkers like René Descartes, Francis Bacon, and Thomas Hobbes clearly believed that they were standing at the threshold of a new era in thought and that their own work was affecting a transformation from a medieval civilization at which they looked askance to a new period of scientific rationalism and progress, and in the century that followed the story would gain increasing currency. History was on the march, or so the common sentiment had it, and it was all to the good. This was not, the same sentiment held, a rebirth of the ancient but a revolutionary and unprecedented development. A new beginning called for a resolute rejection of a past now increasingly regarded as a source of blinding prejudices which had cowed minds for centuries if not indeed forever—for the ancients themselves were not authorities so much as lesser forebears. A new historical consciousness characterized this group and it marched under the banner of progress. The present could be favorably compared to the age of Alexander, Augustus, or any other ostensible world-historical high point, for what had the ancients achieved that moderns had not equaled or surpassed? As Jack Lively notes, "Perhaps the most general and striking feature of Enlightenment thought was its self-consciousness, its awareness of itself as a unique, distinctive and important moment in the development of the human mind. In the writings particularly of the French *philosophes*, there is reiterated a constantly expressed confidence in the new-found capacities of humanity and an equally constant desire to trace the genealogy of this liberation."[4] The philosophy of history itself emerged from a general atmosphere of heady self-congratulation, and its original purpose was to chart the past, present, and future along a trajectory that culminated in an idealized future. Greek cyclical and Augustinian sacred history were both at an end amid a wave of optimism which was again more attitudinal than doctrinal. If this new branch of speculation received its basic impetus from Voltaire along with the term "philosophy of history" itself, it was also born of an ethos that was pervading Europe. The celebrated "quarrel of the ancients and the moderns" had tipped in the latter's favor while widespread sentiment had it that the present age was an apex and a coming of age that had followed an agonizingly long tutelage.

The claim that enlightenment figures were advancing to the effect that they knew better than the past was one that the renaissance had not made. Where the latter was a student, the former sought a radical beginning in thought of which Descartes' *Meditations* stood as the great exemplar, although he was hardly alone in the sentiment. The authority of Rome, tradition, custom, institutional power, or indeed anything apart from the intellectual faculties of the knower no longer held. As Max Horkheimer and Theodor Adorno would famously put it in their *Dialectic of Enlightenment* of 1947, "The program of the Enlightenment was the disenchantment of the world; the dissolution of myths and the substitution of knowledge for fancy."[5] The radicality of the claim warrants emphasis; the whole of the human past was to be put aside in a grand gesture of suspension or refusal, including the very tradition of knowledge to which they were making a contribution. Speculative thinking in every field needed to be placed on a new foundation and supplied with a method that was incontrovertible, and if religion itself was to survive, it too required a basis that was independent of Rome and all other ostensible authorities. Skepticism was to be thoroughgoing and apply equally to personages from the past in general as well as any mental faculties, including imagination, that failed to meet the new standard of epistemic certainty. The scientific attitude would become ubiquitous: philosophical, political, religious, moral, and all knowledge was encompassed within a single outlook, on the model of scientific rationality. For the new metaphysical materialism, nature in the connotation of matter in motion is all that there is, with the consequence that all aspects of human existence needed to be accounted for in this vocabulary. The human past in its entirety, as J. B. Bury notes, was being spoken of as a source of superstition and oppression: "Bacon and others had begun the movement to break down this tyranny, but the influence of Descartes was weightier and more decisive, and his attitude was more uncompromising. He had none of Bacon's reverence for classical literature; he was proud of having forgotten the Greek which he had learned as a boy. The inspiration of his work was the idea of breaking sharply and completely with the past, and constructing a system which borrows nothing from the dead."[6] This was a tall order indeed, and its spirit animated enlightenment figures both religious and irreligious, rationalist and empiricist, and all other descriptions in a general movement that caused no little unease on the part of secular and religious authorities. Where "disenchantment" did not signify atheism it did connote a transformation from mythopoetic to scientific, mathematical, and logical thought. Voltaire's strident "*écrasez l'infâme*" applied to institutional Christianity in its entirety while the century's preeminent historian, Edward Gibbon, lamented the role of the church in bringing about the "decline and fall of the Roman empire" and the collapse into medieval darkness. When not hostile to religion across the board, philosophers typically were articulating a religion that was either "within the limits of reason alone," as Kant put it, or otherwise refined into a worldview that was independent of revelation and ecclesiastical authority. Philosophy itself was promising a clean break; the division between premodern philosophy, if it even warranted the name, and what the rationalists, empiricists, and idealists were attempting was categorical, or such was the common belief. Enlightenment philosophy was autonomous where its medieval predecessor had been beholden to theology and thus not the genuine article.

The century-long debate between the ancients and the moderns essentially reversed the Greek myth of a golden age that had existed invariably in the past, as it was the present and a confidently anticipated future that now commanded authority. Where renaissance figures aspired at most to equal and modify a variety of Greek and Roman models, by the seventeenth and eighteenth centuries even Plato and Aristotle were being dislodged by thinkers like Newton, Descartes, Leibniz, and Locke, and by a materialistic and mechanistic view of the world. Mathematics and physics trumped all, including revelation and the Judeo-Christian tradition, pagan speculation, and the institutional power of kings and popes. All such authorities could be surpassed, as mature adulthood is a development over adolescence. Knowledge in any domain, common belief had it, increases over time, and while the foremost of the ancients were indisputably great in their time none of them was of the stature of their modern descendants. Whether in science, the arts, or the humanities, newer is better as it preserves and refines the best of the old, discards the rest, and incorporates discoveries that are unprecedented in intellectual history. The scientific revolution was inspiring an optimism regarding knowledge in general while any sense of finitude or intellectual humility came to seem a priestly virtue that was out of keeping with the times. If obstacles like war, institutional power, and superstition could be held in check, the human race could continue its advance over the past in terms of both knowledge and happiness. Fundamental to such improvement is that the clerical power which had dominated the life of the mind for so many centuries needed to be displaced together with a worldview in which the entire domain of cultural expression stood under the authority of religion. An indispensable condition of intellectual advance was the freedom to follow the method of experimental science wherever it led, without the constraint of Rome, Aristotle, or the tradition in its entirety. This was the meaning of using "one's own understanding"; the crucial matter was that the individual possessed powers of observation and rationality which if unconstrained could be counted upon to discover the truth more surely than any ancient authority. A writer like Hobbes or Locke could formulate a systematic exposition of human nature, knowledge, and political justice in treatises written in plain style and in the English language, and while incorporating modern discoveries and the best of the past without deference to it. No ancient text or figure was sacrosanct.

There was a boldness about the enlightenment that was not limited to the name. It took a certain brashness to judge their own age as equal or, more often, superior to its Greek and Roman predecessors and to dismiss in contempt the millennium of cultural production in the west that followed the Roman period. As Norman Hampson remarks, "However ambivalent their attitude towards Rome, the men of the Enlightenment were virtually unanimous in decrying the Middle Ages. The entire period from the collapse of the Roman Empire in the west to the sixteenth century tended to be dismissed as one of poverty, oppression, ignorance and obscurantism, 'centuries of monkish dullness, when the whole world seems to have fallen asleep,' as [Henry] Fielding put it. 'Gothic' was a term of abuse applied to every conceivable form of ignorance, prejudice, conservatism, or what we still call vandalism."[7] The renaissance schematism of ancient, medieval, and modern was retained and amplified, with the renaissance itself being demoted to a prelude to the present while the middle ages were one long ebb to the flow that were Greece and Rome. The present flow, in their estimation, exceeded its predecessors and rose to a height hitherto unimagined. The evaluation itself was not baseless: the scientific, artistic, and humanistic attainments of the seventeenth and eighteenth centuries were impressive indeed, and documenting these would require a few volumes to do justice to, however what is equally notable is the continuing devaluation through this era of the centuries of the middle ages and most everything that passed for knowledge within them. Premodern science and philosophy were utterly discontinuous with their modern counterparts, or so the common belief had it. Descartes' *Meditations* is again an obvious case in point, where its author announced with great fanfare that every one of the meditator's prior beliefs could be bracketed with seeming ease as a prelude to rational inquiry. Individual reason is sovereign, while in political theory Hobbes was making analogous claims about the individual in the state of nature.

Reason is at work in history as well, and the totality conforms to a scheme that is at last cognizable. If the basic notion had been provided by Augustine, the Christian doctrine of historical teleology which traced the human journey from the fall to the coming kingdom and from the city of man to the city of God needed to be secularized. Some creative reinterpretation transformed providence into progress, ostensibly a theologically neutral model that was governed by empirically and historically discoverable laws. As Bury remarks in his classic study *The Idea of Progress*, "If progress was to be more than the sanguine dream of an optimist it must be shown that man's career on earth had not been a chapter of accidents which might lead anywhere or nowhere, but is subject to discoverable laws which have determined its general route, and will secure his arrival at the desirable place. Hitherto a certain order and unity had been found in history by the Christian theory of providential design and final causes. New principles of order and unity were needed to replace the principles which rationalism had discredited."[8] These principles became sweeping laws of history which were asserted to be observable beneath the surface of historical life taken universally, and if their basis was empirical it required some imaginative discernment to behold their workings in the real world of human doings and sufferings. History is a law-like order proceeding teleologically toward the progressive realization not of salvation but of enlightenment, where this encompasses a number of issues at once scientific and philosophical, economic and technological, moral and political. The set of proponents of this doctrine reads like a who's who list of major thinkers of the seventeenth, eighteenth, and nineteenth centuries and exceptions were few. The notion of progress was as much (likely more) an article of faith than a provable hypothesis, but it emerged from and fired the imagination of a scientific age with or without evidence, the totality of which was unlikely to convince a skeptic. It was among the principal watchwords of the era, and doubting it resembled an apostate questioning the existence of God in an assembly of the faithful. If skepticism was becoming a common feature of early modern thought, it was applied toward the progressive idea somewhat less than might be expected, it being again as much a matter of learned piety than a philosophical hypothesis. When Condorcet spoke of "the progress of the human mind," it was in a prophet's voice: "The history of man from the time when alphabetical writing was known in Greece to the condition of the human race at the present day in the most enlightened countries of Europe is linked by an uninterrupted chain of facts and observations; and so at this point the picture of the march and progress of the human mind becomes truly historical. Philosophy has nothing more to guess, no more hypothetical surmises to make; it is enough to assemble and order the facts and to show the useful truths that can be derived from their connections and from their totality."[9]

A law-like order makes prediction possible, and historical teleology replaced the Greek and Roman cyclical model with a more linear view for which changes in thought, institutions, and whole ways of life when viewed in the large advance steadily, albeit with periods of turbulence and backsliding, from a less to a more perfect state of things. "History shows," as Bury puts it, "that peoples have been moving from isolation to union, from war to peace, from antagonism to association."[10] It can confidently be predicted that a better future awaits us on the basis of principles seen to be operative in the record of the past, according to an outlook that was not limited to educated elites. Optimism abounded and formed a clear contrast with Greek views in which the present was largely a deterioration from a heroic past and hubris was to be avoided at any cost. Something like hubris was now the fashion and history was at once predictable and beneficent. The principles themselves pertained to freedom and equality, justice and toleration, the advance of knowledge and the perfectibility of humanity. A better world was to come, not in the manner Christians had long spoken of but in worldly matters and with an air of inevitability. Social institutions were progressing from tyranny to liberation; intellectual endeavor was advancing from superstition to certainty; economic life was transitioning from backwardness and anticipating an industrial revolution. All areas of human existence were moving in a unified direction and the business of historians was to remark upon the particulars of this while demonstrating their conformity to laws that were abstractable from the whole. Perfectibility had more than a little ambiguity about it, but in general terms it represented the freedom from want, ignorance, and oppression the world over, a new age of reason and illumination which would constitute a culmination of millennia of intellectual and societal development. Condorcet in the text just noted spoke of "the absolute perfection of the human race" as historically inevitable, "as the various kinds of equality come to work in its favour by producing ampler sources of supply, more extensive education, more complete liberty, so equality will be more real and will embrace everything which is really of importance for the happiness of human beings."[11] The human condition in its totality was moving in this direction, and politics was no exception. A variety of liberal, socialist, and other ideological positions would give expression to this idea through this period and beyond, where again the ethos was one of decided optimism that history was on the side of whatever ideology spoke of progress and progressivism in ways that pleased modern audiences. For Kant, it was the reign of Frederick the Great that represented progress in the realm of statecraft and the moral improvement of society, "a prince who does not regard it as beneath him to say that he considers it his duty, in religious matters, not to prescribe anything to his people, but to allow them complete freedom, a prince who thus even declines to accept the presumptuous title of *tolerant*, is himself enlightened. He deserves to be praised by a grateful present and posterity as the man who first liberated mankind from immaturity (as far as government is concerned), and who left all men free to use their own reason in all matters of conscience."[12] Freedom, tolerance, and equality on some interpretation emerged as preeminent political themes through this general period and found diverging articulations in the writings of classical liberals and socialists. The ascent of humanity out of the various forms of despotism that have ruled over human societies through the ages and toward a polity of free and equal citizens was the goal of history in its political dimension and could confidently be expected to materialize at some indefinite future time.

Important exceptions to the progressivists' outlook did exist, beginning with the church of Rome which throughout the enlightenment asserted an opposition that was not unlike its reaction to the later phase of the renaissance. A basically Augustinian view of history continued to find proponents among Catholics and many other Christians and would be difficult to reconcile with the progress doctrine and many other ideas that were emerging from the philosophers and scientists of the time. If we may speak of an enlightenment imaginative schema, it clashed directly with a good many points of Christian orthodoxy—in particular the primacy of revelation over reason and skepticism of tradition and authority—and generated no little hostility between a conservative church and a movement that inclined toward new forms of rationalism and empiricism. Reaction against the progress doctrine found expression also in the writings of Rousseau and members of the romantic movement of the late eighteenth and nineteenth centuries for whom various modern developments amounted to a deterioration from an idealized past which included Rousseau's state of nature. History, on this view, was regressing; it was the "noble savage" who had constituted the apex of humanity while its modern incarnation had become enslaved by institutions promising freedom while delivering its antithesis. Progress was a veneer behind which modern humanity had become subject to conditions that hemmed us in ever more while creating an appearance of liberation. As one historian remarks, "Ownership of property gave birth to competition and exploitation; complex social interaction gave birth to pride and envy. The arts made men soft and effeminate. Human beings became physically weak, unhappy, and highly strung. Worst of all, the progress of civil society brought not political freedom, but its opposite. It [citing Rousseau] 'irretrievably destroyed natural liberty, established for all time the law of property and inequality . . . and for the benefit of a few ambitious men subjected the human race henceforth to labor, servitude, and misery.'"[13] In spite of this, Rousseau and the romantics would remain a part of the enlightenment in the sense that they were critics from within this general movement rather than true outsiders in the manner of the Roman church. To speak of a movement here is not to suggest a doctrinal uniformity but a new constellation of conceptual and imaginative elements that combined in a myriad of ways in the work of different thinkers.

The general schema that this group was formulating sunk deep roots in western culture while drawing in a great many ways upon a tradition that many of their chief spokesmen claimed to be leaving behind. If Descartes and Locke were the foremost representatives of enlightenment through the seventeenth and eighteenth centuries, Kant and Hegel exercised a similar influence upon the nineteenth. The latter two, along with Fichte and Herder, spoke of progress and enlightenment as one with human freedom, the eventual realization of which in the west was foreseeable if not already complete. For Hegel, the attainment of universal freedom was the driving principle of human history writ large, and its actualization through time could be charted on a three-stage model, from the childhood of humanity that was the ancient east, where one was free, to its adolescence through the Greek and Roman era when some were free, through until modern Europe, when all are free. There was an aprioristic quality to Hegel's philosophy of history; this was not empirical history but something more intuitive and rarefied and was consistent in this way with the progressive view which touched down to the real world of human affairs only selectively. Hegel's concentration upon freedom or his conception of it and its onward march through the development of humanity was a refinement of both the progress doctrine and its Augustinian ancestor, and it was a view that Marx's dialectical materialism would take further, as would liberal progressivists, positivists, and others, all of whom regarded their time as a transitional phase into a future that was foreseeable and that approached perfection.

Auguste Comte is an important example of a nineteenth-century thinker who followed this general trajectory a while further and whose interdisciplinary reach and influence would do much to perpetuate an imaginative schema that by his time had the momentum of a couple of centuries behind it. Enlightenment progress remained the driving principle behind Comte's new sociology which promised to surpass even Hegel's speculative flights while speaking the language of science. History was again governed by laws and was classifiable into three stages, the theological, the metaphysical, and the scientific, where the latter culminated in the sociology of the self-same Auguste Comte just as Hegel's developmental account reached its pinnacle in the system of Hegel. History's inveterate habit was to be on the side of whoever was theorizing it, and positivists were no exception. If the latter retained Hegel's apriorism, it assumed a self-image of empirical science as well as political idealism: social life in its totality could be rationally transformed on the story that Comte and the positivists were telling in accordance with the findings of the natural and mathematical sciences and also a philosophically elaborated view of where history is already moving. Marx continued along these lines together with other socialists and progressives, all of whom appropriated the enlightenment narrative while making it fit their own political purposes. Each had their own take on what the laws of history consisted in and entailed politically while speaking with no little assurance of the steady advance of knowledge and justice in the modern world. Progress was an unstoppable force, even while calling upon human efforts to grease the wheels. Meanwhile, Darwin's evolutionary biology was making its own case for the onward and upward development of the species, and in a way that seemed to dovetail with the narrative of which we have been speaking. Progress and evolution were distinct notions while belonging to the same imaginative schema, one that ranged freely across philosophy and politics, economics and morality, sociology and biology, and which appealed to popular audiences no less than academics in virtually all fields.

Any account of this general period in the imaginative history of the west must take special note of the role played by the natural sciences for it would be difficult to overstate the influence they would carry in the formation of the attitudes and general worldview that by the seventeenth century had begun to prevail. The concept of progress had its basis here for it was the achievements of the scientific revolution that created an optimism that would come to pervade the early modern imagination, a central element of which was the aspiration to extend the method and vocabulary of empirical science across the domains of the natural and human worlds. There was no limiting principle to the application of the scientific and technological mode of thinking that was taking radical hold upon matters that had traditionally fallen well beyond its purview. Thinkers across the disciplines were profoundly impressed by what the new sciences were making possible in terms of both positive discoveries and the certainty and methodological rigor of a form of inquiry which was a clear departure from its premodern counterpart. Even renaissance science had drawn no categorical distinction between "natural philosophy"—what enlightenment figures were calling natural science—and "experimental philosophy"—or what would become known as philosophy proper. The Greek term "philosophy" still meant what it had for Aristotle, which is any knowledge that involved demonstration. Philosophy and science were one from this early date through until the eighteenth and nineteenth centuries when the latter became explicitly identified with the method of investigation that was being employed in the natural sciences. The notion of a philosophical psychology was inspired by achievements in physics, astronomy, and chemistry, where the idea was that if the human person is a material being then it may be known in the same manner as any other "system of matter in motion," as Hobbes was referring to the individual in his *Leviathan*. The same method of inquiry can be followed in the human and social realm as in the sciences of nature. As Gadamer would express this important point, "Inquiry into the laws of nature on the basis of mathematical abstraction and its verification by means of measuring, counting, and weighing were present at the birth of the modern sciences of nature. They made possible for the first time the complete application of science to the technical transformation of nature for humanly conceived purposes. And this has marked our civilization on a planetary scale. It was especially the idea of method, or of securing the path of knowledge in accordance with the guiding ideal of certainty, that brought a unified meaning of knowing and knowledge to the fore."[14] As knowledge began to assume a single form, the methodology and ethos of physical science brought all beings under its sovereignty while the paradigm of controlling nature was extended across the full range of intellectual life. All aspects of human reality could be reckoned with in the same manner as atoms and planets as the slide from modern science to scientism became synonymous with progress and, like it, something of an unstoppable force.

The new ideal of knowledge was perhaps best articulated by Descartes, although that thinker was far from alone in formulating an epistemology that sought to provide a new foundation for the sum of human knowledge and which was consonant with the science of his time. In addition to Descartes, thinkers from Galileo to Newton, Francis Bacon, Hobbes, La Mettrie, Locke, Mersenne, and many others were contributing in one fashion or another to the formation of a modern schema the nomenclature for which prominently included metaphysical materialism, mechanism, empiricism, rationalism, and technology. The model of nature as a mechanical system with a mathematical structure was being championed by many and had the advantages of being religiously agnostic while also applicable to the world of social and political life. Hobbes was applying this general framework to the latter in the first systematic modern treatise on human nature and politics and would initiate a movement to which we shall return. Everything under the sun was to be imagined on the model of a watch, a material system characterized by measurable precision, utilitarian functionality, empirical knowability, instrumental reason, efficiency and predictability, and it was a schematism that appealed broadly to intellectual and professional classes for whom the language of scientific rationality carried a distinctively modern allure. Tradition, the increasingly common view had it, had been left behind; modernity itself was an age of science, or such was the self-image with which citizens of the enlightenment began to operate in a trend that would persist through the centuries to follow.

Science itself would become wedded to a distinctive form of technology whose cascading effects would in time become ubiquitous. Modern technology was an order of things, not merely the set of tools and machines upon which human beings were becoming ever more dependent but an encompassing view of the world. On the modern side of the threshold upon which figures like Descartes and Bacon believed themselves to be standing, and with some justification, was what some twentieth-century philosophers would characterize as a technological age, and without the optimism of their enlightenment counterparts. Thus Karl Jaspers, for one, would speak in 1949 of the entire world as having entered "the Age of Technology, which seems to leave nothing standing of what man has acquired in the course of millennia in the way of methods of work, forms of life, modes of thought and symbols."[15] Jacques Ellul, speaking in 1954 of the same phenomenon, would remark upon how over the course of the last few centuries, "Technique has become autonomous; it has fashioned an omnivorous world which obeys its own laws and which has renounced all tradition. Technique no longer rests on tradition, but rather on previous technical procedures; and its evolution is too rapid, too upsetting, to integrate the older traditions." Further to this, "This systematization, unification, and clarification was applied to everything—it resulted not only in the establishment of budgetary rules and in fiscal organization, but in the systematization of weights and measures and the planning of roads. All this represented technique at work. From this point of view, it might be said that technique is the translation into action of man's concern to master things by means of reason, to account for what is subconscious, make quantitative what is qualitative, make clear and precise the outlines of nature, take hold of chaos and put order into it."[16] Having no limiting principle, science and technique moved into the place formerly occupied by the God of Jews and Christians at the center of an imaginative schema. To speak of an age of science and technology animated by a faith in progress is no exaggeration; the central fact of modernity is a technical order that began its career during the seventeenth and eighteenth centuries and in time integrated all aspects of human experience and knowledge into a framework that resembled a closed system. It assimilated nontechnical experience into the technical and enjoined adaptation and compliance while promising order, security, and an entire way of life and of thinking that had been placed on the secure path of science.

The transformation that the enlightenment affected crucially bore upon the concept of knowledge—its content but also, and more radically, its foundation and method. The new schema was a departure from premodern worldviews that had invariably placed a divinity or divinities at the center. On Charles Taylor's telling, "a secular age" was emerging in the sense not that religious faith was disappearing but that it was becoming "one human possibility among others."[17] This is not Nietzsche's "God is dead" but something decidedly less dramatic; over the course of a few centuries the predominant social *imaginaire* of the west found the Judeo-Christian God displaced by science and technique which claimed the same totalizing reach as its monotheist predecessors. Bury calls it the system of Cartesianism, where this means something more diffuse than "the metaphysical system of the master, or any of his particular views such as that of innate ideas. We mean the general principles, which were to leave an abiding impression on the texture of thought: the supremacy of reason over authority, the stability of the laws of Nature, rigorous standards of proof."[18] Cartesianism was not aggressively atheistic but decidedly non-deferential to anything that ran counter to a conception of reason that was mathematical and scientific, that promised certainty and precision so long as its methodological precepts were adhered to, and whose reach throughout modern culture would become unlimited. Aristotelian principles including final causality were cast aside in favor of a mechanistic view of nature in its entirety while natural science would be elevated to a position that had been occupied throughout the middle ages by theology. Human knowledge was a unified edifice erected on the foundation of the cogito and its progress was contingent upon strict adherence to the method of reason. Cartesianism in this sense was a synthesis of rationalist epistemology in a narrower connotation, empiricism, the new science and a mechanistic and technological way of envisioning the world, and progress expressed something of its spirit. Any rising above the "*self-incurred immaturity*" of which Kant spoke required both philosophers and all of educated society to tie the life of the mind in general to the secure post of reason, and while Descartes' *Discourse on Method* and *Meditations* were far from the only texts that pointed the way they managed to reach a broad audience and gain a powerful influence over the movement that would follow. Epistemology would come to occupy a central place in the philosophy of this period and its confluence with science, mathematics, technology, and historical teleology would supplant premodern and overtly religious belief systems. Underlying important disagreements between (especially French) rationalists in a narrower sense and (British) empiricists and (German) idealists was a shared schema with a distinctively modern set of preoccupations and a larger sensibility which manifested itself in a great variety of ways.

An especially important case in point was the thirty-five-volume *Encyclopedia* (subtitled *or a Systematic Dictionary of the Sciences, Arts, and Crafts*), the first edition of which was published in stages between 1751 and 1780 under the editorship of Denis Diderot and Jean le Rond d'Alembert. The latter spoke of the general scope of these works as follows: "From the principles of the secular sciences to the foundations of religious revelation, from metaphysics to matters of taste, from music to morals, from the scholastic disputes of theologians to matters of trade, from the laws of princes to those of peoples, from natural law to the arbitrary laws of nations . . . everything has been discussed and analysed, or at least mentioned. The fruit or consequence of this general effervescence of minds has been to cast new light on some things and new shadows on others, just as the effect of the ebb and flow of the tides is to leave some things on the shore and to wash others away."[19] This extraordinarily ambitious undertaking aimed to gather into a single set of works the sum of human knowledge as formulated by numerous leading figures in this movement as well as some lesser known writers, and for an audience of upper-class intellectuals and professionals. The high price of the volumes put the *Encyclopedia* beyond reach of the lower classes, but the aims of the project included advancing the cause of enlightenment through the general education of a large reading public not limited to the aristocracy. It was to serve as a great treasury of information both useful and speculative for a lay readership and on the premise that the dissemination of up-to-date learning on virtually all subjects would affect a transformation of society. The volumes' authors were tasked with formulating the current state of enlightened knowledge and in pursuing their tasks they exuded a confidence and an optimism that became synonymous with the spirit of progress itself. Their shared self-image was that of an intellectual vanguard whose business was not to debate but to inform, in the process deposing traditional authorities deference to whom had for centuries perpetuated human ignorance and oppression.

If enlightenment was a movement and an ethos—a shared sense of modernity as a radical surpassing of the ancient and medieval and a concerted effort to refashion both a worldview and a good part of society in light of the new Cartesianism—it was not without consequences for political thought. Here again the details are myriad, but painting in broad strokes political progress entailed taking a new view of the *ancien régime*. The centuries of which we are speaking were dominated by absolute monarchs, and a system of rule that appealed to the divine right of kings was profoundly incompatible with the new rationalism that was finding expression in the writings of the leading political thinkers of the time. Absolutism spelled tyranny for a conceptual scheme at the heart of which lay the rational individual which was constituted by an agency at once intellectual and moral. Human nature itself as well as natural law entailed some conception of responsible government or at the very least a despotism that was enlightened and a clear departure from its more conventional forms. While it is overly general to describe enlightenment political theorists as staging an all-out campaign against the power of church and state, the hegemony of the Roman church did come under heavy criticism as well as absolute monarchies that clung to a political and religious ideology that stood in the way of social progress. A scientific outlook required a scientific politics, and thinkers like Hobbes, Locke, Montesquieu, and Rousseau set about to identify the terms of a rational social order which was in keeping with human nature as they understood it. Treatises such as Hobbes' *Leviathan* and Locke's *Two Treatises of Government* ranged across themes both political and metaphysical while the narrative of the state of nature and the social contract came to the fore. Much was preserved from the ancient and medieval natural law tradition even as it was secularized into terms that progressivists could accept. Liberals were calling for individual rights, freedom and equality, toleration and a democratic order that was antithetical to the forms of absolutism with which this era had long and bitter experience. Political and intellectual progress were inseparable, and while considerable disagreement existed with respect to public policy the prevailing sentiment had it that a just social order was a natural consequence of scientific knowledge and rational calculation. Natural law, human nature, and justice were all universal even as nations differed with respect to cultural norms. Nationalism in full-blown form would be a nineteenth-century development, but its roots in seventeenth- and eighteenth-century political thought are plainly visible, as numerous thinkers attempted to identify distinguishing traits of the emerging nation-states of Europe, most of which speculation was more notional than empirical. As for the great revolutions of the period, there is no doubting the influence of numerous political writers within the enlightenment movement. By no means would all have endorsed these developments, but the general logic of their arguments led by a rather straight line to the revolutions in France and America that put an end to governance in the old style.

Similar efforts to turn the page from the intellectual culture of old occurred within the "republic of letters" which would exercise such a profound effect upon common opinion not limited to the elite. This imagined republic was a network of writers from various nations who could communicate with each other and a broad readership with a kind of freedom that surpassed what was possible within the realm of the political. Censorship remained widespread, but within such constraints individual writers could express themselves in relative freedom from both church and state as well as from the system of patronage in which scholars and artists had long worked. For centuries such thinkers had been financially dependent upon commissions from royal, aristocratic, and church patrons, and their autonomy was limited both by a social status that reflected their dependence and by the invariant principle that he who pays the piper calls the tune. While this system did not disappear in the eighteenth century, it had become possible for writers to reach a larger public audience and to gain some relative independence by this means, partly in view of the fact that many in this group were abandoning Latin and opting to publish in their national language. As elite courts and the Latin language both lost ground, a traditional system of cultural production was gradually being replaced by a relatively autonomous group of thinkers writing in the vernacular for a larger audience than their predecessors. French was becoming the new *lingua franca* of high culture while by Kant's time it had become commonplace for philosophers to write in German, French, English, or whatever their language of choice. There was a new freedom as well in the content of such writing; throughout medieval times it had been customary for philosophers and theologians to compose primarily commentaries on either biblical texts or an authoritative figure such as Aristotle or Thomas Aquinas—and commentaries on commentaries on the same—whereas the rising fashion was to create stand-alone treatises such as Descartes' *Meditations*, Spinoza's *Ethics*, or Montesquieu's *The Spirit of the Laws* which while remaining more than a little conversant with tradition was also attempting something relatively new. The treatise itself was not an innovation, but the frequent aspiration of such writing was to transcend the commentary tradition for a more free-spirited exploration of topics that might interest a larger reading public. More accessible than their medieval predecessors, such works disseminated ideas more readily and widely than had been possible in prior centuries and were often translated into other European languages as well.

The republic of letters featured other noteworthy developments including popular writing, the essay, and the rise of the non-academic philosopher. On the first point, as one historian points out,

> the books most widely read in the Enlightenment were often written by men and women whose names are never mentioned in the canon of great Enlightenment thinkers. These authors were professional writers for a commercial market in the written word, turning out to order books and pamphlets on subjects ranging from political scandal to pornography, to newspaper articles, book reviews, children's books, novels, theatrical scripts and opera libretti, to retellings of medieval romances for the rural audiences of cheap publishers, to popular science and travel books. It was these writers, rather than the elite such as Diderot and Voltaire, who produced the bulk of what was actually read in the Enlightenment.[20]

It is best to conceive of the enlightenment not as an exclusively top-down phenomenon of high culture but as a movement that was matched in some part by a more democratic push from below, as information and opinions were circulating somewhat more freely and on a larger scale than in ages past. What Montaigne during the renaissance had called the essay was also making inroads with emerging middle and professional classes while literacy and systems of public education had also gained ground. Concise and elegantly composed texts published in the vernacular appealed to a readership that transcended the aristocracy and the university no less. The latter's hegemony over philosophical ideas through the centuries preceding the enlightenment had ended as most of the leading thinkers of the time (Descartes, Leibniz, Spinoza, Hobbes, Locke, Berkeley, Hume, Voltaire, Rousseau, Diderot) were not university professors but men of letters and would not in the main become so again until the nineteenth century.

"The new intelligentsia," as one historian notes, "had loyalties which were infinitely more varied" than their court and university predecessors. "Sometimes they wrote for patrons, or for paymasters. But often they wrote to please themselves, or with a broad sense of communicating to a general paying 'public' out there. And, as writers freed themselves from the fetters which had constrained the clergy, the world of letters became deeply diversified."[21] Neither church nor state nor the universities were in decline, but their hold on "letters" and ideas had weakened as writers and readers both enjoyed relative autonomy from the authorities of old. This was the era of the freethinker whose newfound independence made it possible to exercise the courage of which Kant spoke. The universities focused narrowly upon training future lawyers, doctors, and clergy, with theological matters always in the forefront of their mission but otherwise leaving the humanities and arts to develop outside of the institution. A secular intelligentsia could emerge who were able and disposed to speak to a broader public about everything from social and practical matters to all manner of speculative issues over which universities held no monopoly, including questions both scientific and philosophical. France was particularly notable in this regard with its *philosophes*, a diverse array of eighteenth-century intellectuals across the disciplines who can be regarded collectively as setting the stage for the revolution without demanding one in any overt way.

Also at some remove from traditional authorities were the numerous academies and learned societies that sprung up all over Europe and America and contributed in no small way to the international republic of letters. France showed the way here as well with its *Académie française* and *Académie des inscriptions et des belles-lettres*, both of which originated in seventeenth-century Paris and created a model that the French provinces would soon follow as well as other European states. Many of these received royal sponsorship after the fashion of the courts of old while still sharing in the enlightenment ethos. The idea of an academy did not follow Plato's model especially closely but was more an association of friendship, learned conversation, and culture. Activities ranged from holding debates to essay competitions, maintaining a library, publishing and corresponding with other such bodies, while membership was mostly limited to elites who could afford the fees. Academies variously pursued scientific, humanistic, and economic aims, essentially any branch of learning in which their members and sponsors showed interest and which could promote some manner of public service. The "learned societies" followed a similar pattern, often in a somewhat less formal manner or on a more modest scale. Smaller urban centers would often seek to imitate what was happening in major cities, not wishing to be in the rearguard of progress and being animated by a similar civic-mindedness to their larger counterparts. Social capital was to be had in organizations that pursued the public good while simultaneously cementing ties of class and maintaining a network of ideas spanning a good part of the western world. In England, the Royal Society of London had its inception in 1660 and again expressed an anti-authoritarian attitude even while receiving royal sponsorship. Its focus was with the natural sciences while other such organizations would often promote more humanistic ventures. Whatever their special interest, academies and learned societies of this kind promoted friendship and cultural education with an invariable aim of improving some aspect of society and promoting a shared vision of progress.

A similar description applies to the countless societies, salons, coffeehouses, clubs, and agricultural organizations that sprang up throughout the western world at this time. The salons were relatively informal conversational societies and social circles organized by urban elites—often women—for the general edification and prestige of their members. Such gatherings bore more than a passing resemblance to aristocratic courts even while it was enlightenment ideas that were being disseminated, and much the same can be said of the English coffeehouses of the period. The salons of Paris were especially well known, but the fashion became widespread throughout France and various western nations and was responsible for a good part of the popularization of philosophical and other current ideas within elite culture, as were the many reading societies that could be found in many a German or French town. Reading material abounded in the form of everything from scholarly treatises to newspapers, journals, and periodicals which such societies published and/or consumed for purposes variously civic-minded, educational, or prudential. Publications of this kind had been made possible by a new freedom of the press which in England had followed upon the Glorious Revolution. Prior to this, Holland had been the lone haven for Europeans seeking to elude the power of the censors, but by the early eighteenth century it was possible for organizations large and small to print and distribute material more or less as they pleased.

Publications and societies of a more utilitarian order also proliferated through this time period and promoted the enlightenment cause within and sometimes beyond aristocratic circles. Economic, industrial, scientific, and educational organizations of many kinds sprang up and devoted themselves to some aspect of the public welfare, an important early example of which was Dublin's Society for the Improvement of Husbandry, Agriculture and other Useful Arts, created in 1731 as a response to the potato famine of 1724. Similar agricultural organizations would form throughout Europe for the purpose of disseminating up-to-date information about methods and technology to a population that remained in large part rural. As farming was becoming more scientific, agriculturalists needed to be knowledgeable of improved forms of crop rotation, animal strains, seeds and tools which served the general purpose of increasing yields to meet the demands of an expanding market. One society that warrants special mention is the Freemasons who combined a utilitarian mission with a more aristocratic bent, and again in general keeping with the ethos of enlightenment. Freemasonry itself became a movement that drew together a wide array of professionals, businessmen, clergy, and scholars into elite circles of conversation and fraternity. As Ulrich Im Hof writes,

> The Freemasons were conscious of standing at a turning point where the middle ages, merging into the period of the baroque, were giving way to the dawn of a new light. They meant to invest the ancient symbols of the building of the Temple with fresh meaning. This entailed a new interpretation of Christian tradition in a humanitarian and enlightened sense. Here we may sense the background of the Glorious Revolution with its reduction of social and confessional differences and its emphasis on the rights of the individual citizen. . . . The Constitutional Articles state that a Freemason should be an individual imbued with goodwill and humane feeling, a "good human being," loyal, guided by honour and decency. He should be a friend to rich and poor alike, in so far as they are virtuous.[22]

A blend of liberal cosmopolitanism and urban elitism, class-blindness and classism, secularism and sectarianism would be a regular feature of a fraternal organization whose general outlook was modern while also bearing clear traces of its medieval origins.

An age of Cartesianism seemed perfectly consistent with the promotion of a wide array of utilitarian ends bearing largely upon overcoming the prejudice of the past and promoting knowledge throughout the society. National public education systems aimed to reduce divisions between the classes and between urban and rural, although in most societies it would not be until the nineteenth century that rich and poor children would largely attend the same schools and receive a similar education. If the *Encyclopedia* volumes were prohibitively priced for the masses, a school reader was not and could encompass for children of all classes reading material that was designed to promote an overall rise in literacy and participation in learned culture. The former value did rise through this general time period, however slowly and variously by region, and public education was the method by which it was achieved together with a modern sensibility more broadly. Moral and religious instruction also required an ability to read the Bible for Protestants in particular as well as the catechism of one's faith. General opinion had it that the spread of literacy belonged to the project of fostering enlightenment on the largest possible scale and bringing populations by hook or by crook into the new era. Knowledge had a vanguard and a rearguard, and if the *philosophes* and other cultural elites were the voices of progress, the latter could in time be brought along through the power of education. Knowledge entailed liberation from both ignorance and the oppression of traditional forms of labor which in time would become outmoded by the new science and technology. The idea of enlightenment since Bacon's time had been that knowledge generally is nothing remote from human life but is to be placed in its service, just as Leibniz would later insist it was science's utilitarian applications that would be the central aim of the Royal Academy at Berlin over which he presided. The goal of speculative activity was not, as it had been for the Greeks, intellectual satisfaction for its own sake but the domination of nature and the amelioration of societal ills.

Such was the early modern viewpoint across various fields of knowledge, and it neither appeared from out of the blue (for when had learned inquiry not in some fashion been placed in the service of human interests, however conceived?) nor disappeared in the couple of centuries that followed the general movement of which we have been speaking. Enlightenment was at once a movement—scientific, technological, metaphysical, epistemological, political, moral, economic, aesthetic—and an intellectual climate, and both exhibited a heady optimism and a progressive self-image which became deeply rooted over the course of the seventeenth and eighteenth centuries. The narrative of history's onward and upward march became a faith that in some measure would unite elites with the middling and lower classes and in a manner that bore striking resemblance to the promulgation of the Christian schema through the centuries of late antiquity. One imaginative schema displaced another, and less suddenly and dramatically than some of its triumphalist defenders maintained. What occurred was not that any floodlights banished the medieval darkness but that over time a novel set of variations on some received cultural elements formed a relatively new constellation of ideas which served their advocates' interests as an older constellation had served theirs. A conversational turn was inseparable from the collective egoism of the urban elites who were its main but not sole proponents.

Whether the transformation that occurred was essentially a high-cultural or a broader societal phenomenon remains a point of debate. Did the common people "have" an enlightenment? To an important extent they did: public education and rising literacy did affect meaningful changes to an old way of life, however gradually; new scientific discoveries and technology produced unmistakable consequences, as did Cartesianism, metaphysical materialism, liberal democracy, some loosening of the class system, and the progressive idea itself. All of it caught on, in the first instance within circles of the genteel and powerful but before long through the lion's share of the population of the west. There is no denying the top-down nature of the enlightenment, but as with any transformation of this kind and on this scale it was matched by a movement from below of which we should not lose sight. In analyzing this phenomenon, as Roy Porter points out, "the spotlight should fall less upon the embattled few than upon the swelling ranks of articulate and cultured men and women throughout Europe, those whom Daniel Roche has dubbed '*gens de culture*'; educated people at large, operating in the 'public sphere' who preened themselves upon their own progressive opinions and 'polite' lifestyles, picking up a smattering or more of Voltaire and Co.—maybe just as a veneer, but sometimes as part of a genuinely new way of living. Such a view would thus mean regarding 'Enlightenment' as a sea-change occurring *within* the *ancien régime*, rather than as the activities of a terrorist brigade bent on destroying it."[23] A good part of that regime remained standing and a golden age of rationality it was not. The great "age of reason" included a fair measure of unreason, will to power, and self-serving prejudice, and the "self-incurred immaturity" that had preceded it was down to sloganeering more than historical fact.

This episode in the imaginative history of the western world involved themes that we have seen before: a new *zeitgeist* that borrowed heavily from the old; a cultural narrative that met the needs and preferences of early modern populations while giving rise to new ones; an old societal elect that remained elect; and a view of history that was an outgrowth of the renaissance and a scientific reiteration of Augustinian teleology. The enlightenment imagination was a reimagining of received cultural elements and a novel integration with the new, a great gathering and reshuffling of ideas in ways that suited the times while keeping one eye on the interests of the powerful. This was a movement and a time period that thought rather highly of itself, as their renaissance and late-antique predecessors had also done but on a new level. The victory that in their eyes they had won over medieval backwardness, ignorance, drudgery, and injustice was of world-historical consequence, and later historians would often repeat this judgment in part from the evidence and in part as a consequence of the continuing progressivist faith. Subtracting the partisanship, what can be said is that while far-reaching changes in knowledge and way of life undoubtedly occurred, the consequences of which remain very much with us, a wholesale revolution it was not and that such changes owed much to earlier movements which included the renaissance and the reformation and to ancient and medieval traditions which were not jettisoned but modified from within and by degrees.

CHAPTER 6

Historical Imagination and Cultural Studies

Implications of the argument we have offered regarding historical imagination extend beyond a single field of knowledge, and our intention in this final chapter is to identify some of these within the discipline of cultural studies. No field holds a monopoly on the concept or the general domain of culture. In addition to the discipline of which we shall speak in what follows, history and its various tributaries (art, intellectual, political, social), anthropology, sociology, psychology, geography, and of course philosophy bear in important ways upon *Homo sapiens* taken not in isolation but in constant relation to a world that is at once social, cultural, political, and historical. The humanities and social sciences broadly conceived all deal with the various and overlapping aspects of a common problem, which is mortal humanity in relation to an environment that is encompassing and that belongs to it in a more fundamental way than many early modern thinkers believed. That culture is always already there, at the center of our being, gives the lie to notions of worldless subjectivity which are not limited to metaphysics and continue to show themselves in the several disciplines of the human sciences. The sense in which this is so and the consequences for cultural studies of this hypothesis and of the larger argument that we have proffered above is the topic to which we now turn.

From their inceptions, the numerous "studies" disciplines (cultural, area, national, gender, racial, indigenous, etc.) which have managed to find a home in the contemporary university have struggled to articulate any sort of unifying methodology or nomenclature that would be capable of distinguishing and legitimating fields which have often come under criticism on a number of grounds including not least epistemological confusion and a certain kind of political partisanship. As Fred Inglis notes, "in the abominable politicization of absolutely everything which has sent the human sciences temporarily insane, there are frequent and contemptuous invectives launched against the lack of method and of content in anything ending in 'studies,'" and it is an observation with which it is difficult to disagree but for the word "temporarily" for the politicization he noted a generation ago presently shows no signs of abating, and the same may be said about epistemological confusion.[1] What manner of knowledge is to be had in a discipline like cultural studies, where the notion of culture itself resists definition, methodological unclarity abounds, and scholarly inquiry is intimately associated with ideological partisanship? Our suggestion will be that an ontological move is needed here, or that the methodological question of how culture is known must be pursued together with the question of what culture itself and *Homo sapiens* as a cultured being may be understood to mean. Here again, the concepts of imagination, imaginative schemas, and cultural narrative will hold center stage. What scholars of cultural studies do may be profitably compared with what historians do in that both endeavor to enter into a particular social-historical world, to place themselves on speaking terms with cultures variously past and present, and to relate a story that is both richly imaginative and evidentially grounded. A culture's underlying being-in-motion, its myriad tendings and dynamics, the forces and undercurrents that animate more surface-level goings-on, the interrelatedness of its innumerable elements and the story of their coming to pass all belong to the cultural interpreter's task no less and likely more than compressing the manifold into ideological categories that are conceived in advance. We are not making it fit but allowing a story to tell itself—critically no doubt, but we shall need to take account of what such critique does and does not amount to. Our argument will issue in a plea for a kind of hermeneutic humility which is not always apparent in the literature of cultural and area studies.

We begin with a few definitional and methodological matters: what is cultural studies and how is it that scholars in this field go about doing whatever it is that they do? It is a self-consciously interdisciplinary field that aims to encompass a variety of humanistic and social-scientific methods all of which are brought to bear upon different aspects of a given culture and with an abiding preoccupation with issues of power and identity and the belief systems with which they are associated. This is not value-neutral inquiry but one organized around a set of themes and key concepts drawn from contemporary social theory and which conceives of itself as advancing the general cause of emancipation. Originating in postwar Britain and America, early figures such as Raymond Williams and Richard Hoggart sought to extend the investigation of culture beyond art and literature to the larger array of social life and popular expression that we find below the plane of high culture. The lived experiences of ordinary human beings were coming into focus, particularly members of the working class and disempowered groups whose perspectives had not been heard in the literature departments in which many of these scholars were employed. As a traditional preoccupation with elite culture was replaced with popular culture and everyday practices, a combination of empirical and social-theoretic methodologies combined with progressivist activism in creating a discipline whose mission was to shed light on cultures by variously explaining and unmasking the contradictions and power dynamics that structure a given culture at a given time. As Elizabeth Long sums it up, "cultural studies has been in large part a theoretically informed, empirically engaged *critical* commentary on contemporary social and cultural life."[2] Especially notable among such theories are Marxism in both its classical and contemporary formulations, Frankfurt School critical theory, structuralism and poststructuralism, psychoanalysis and postmodernism, and feminism and identity politics, where a good part of the literature consists in particularistic analyses of cultural phenomena in which a theoretical-methodological bricolage is brought to bear. Interdisciplinarity and theoretical hybridity being the norm, methodological purity is commonly abandoned in favor of a miscellany which is usually counted as a virtue. If it is not a mystery that, in the words of two recent scholars, "Cultural studies has been criticized for . . . theoretical dilettante-ism, a lack of rigorous scientific method, an ahistorical focus on only contemporary readings of popular mass media texts, and being little more than a fad,"[3] such criticisms may be overstated. We are speaking of an emerging field of very large scope and uncertain relation to several cognate and more established disciplines upon which cultural studies often draws in ways that are not always clear and which continue to inspire some skepticism within the academy. The skepticism might be mitigated were we to take a few steps toward clarifying what culture is and what is involved in interpreting it.

A starting point is the concept of culture and the word itself. The concept is notoriously overabundant with definitions ranging from the more empirical to the semiotic, structural, and political. When this is the case it is generally wise to return to the word's origins, and what we find here is the Latin agricultural term *colere* which means to till or cultivate with a suggestion of reverential or worshipful (*cultus*) protection; the cultural came to signify that which required the careful cultivation of human hands—essentially crops and domestic animals—and in time was broadened to include the totality of artifacts, both material and ideational, that became associated with high culture. A cultivated person was one who had received a particular kind of education or formation which crucially involved an immersion in the kind of artifacts just noted, while by the twentieth century culture had become something of a catch-all term which likely confused more than it clarified and spawned competing theories between which a great many humanists and social scientists felt obliged to choose. The investigation of culture then meant the investigation of these artifacts, and within cultural studies the artifacts belonging to a particular collectivity, in a field that became a kind of "history of the present" or critical analysis of the myriad expressions and experiences that belong to a given location and community. The word has tended to connote not only works of art and literature but also the larger ways of life, worldviews, and social meanings of which such works are commonly regarded as expressions. Distinctions emerged between high and popular culture as well as between the cultures of discrete groups within a given society. As Judy Giles and Tim Middleton remark, "the term culture is often used to mean actual products, such as opera, concerts, literature, drama and paintings; mass culture is often applied to television, Hollywood, magazines, 'pulp' fiction and newspapers. . . . However, as Williams reminds us, from the nineteenth century onwards, with the growth of nation states and the Romantic interest in 'folk art,' it became necessary 'to speak of cultures in the plural' in order to distinguish between the particular cultures of different nations, but also 'the specific and variable cultures of social and economic groups within a nation."[4] While the word remains contested, current usage often suggests a rather nebulous field of meanings, practices, language, texts, aesthetic works, and ideas which hang together in some more or less identifiable configuration, where cultural studies is an investigation, at once empirical and political, of each of these and of their manifold interconnections and contradictions.

The above-noted accent on the political and the critical warrants special attention. Cultural studies is hardly alone among disciplines of the humanities and social sciences to have ventured a few steps leftward over the course of the last half-century, but a phenomenon that broadly characterizes the contemporary academy in general is perhaps especially evident within the studies disciplines wherein the tradition of 1968 and the self-image that it inspired continue to enjoy wide currency. Political avant-gardism is something of the norm in a field that remains deeply indebted to Marx and his heirs, critical theorists, poststructuralists, feminists, and others on the political left and which has often sought to align itself with the "politics of difference" and the "new social movements" which incline in a similar direction. One finds few conservatives in a discipline whose nomenclature in the main is an appropriation from the movements just mentioned and whose animating spirit reflects this fact. If in this literature theoretical speculation is seldom engaged in in any sustained way, the lion's share of the literature is theory-laden in a manner that typically remains below the surface. Something similar may be said of contemporary history as well, as of so many fields, but in cultural studies the indebtedness remains strong to thinkers from Marx to Horkheimer and Adorno, Gramsci and Habermas, Foucault and Derrida, Williams and Hoggart, as well as their recent heirs. One standard text characterizes research in this field as "an engaged form of analysis. (It begins in what was called . . . 'the new left'—a Marxian but not communist movement, working towards forms of socialism outside of trade unions or formal political parties and aimed at emancipating lifestyles and not just at participating in the public world.) Early cultural studies did not flinch from the fact that societies are structured unequally, that individuals are not all born with the same access to education, money, healthcare etc., and it worked in the interests of those who have least resources, namely the working class."[5] Overt Marxism is not ubiquitous within contemporary cultural studies and theoretical heterogeneity remains the norm, but if we are speaking of general tendencies then one or another variant of emancipatory politics remains paramount—not in the manner of political philosophy where overt theory construction might be expected but analyses that are at once theory-laden and particularistic. An accent on specifics is the norm here—demonstrations, for instance, of how particular artifacts or expressions constitute so many commodifications of the culture industry or how inequalities and divisions of class or identity pervade social systems that espouse values of freedom and neutrality. Researchers in this field commonly seek to demonstrate connections between particular cultural elements and corporate or otherwise hegemonic interests, in a general spirit of unmasking and resistance which harks back to Marxian tradition without necessarily displaying this credential. Following upon the division of the left into an assortment of more or less aligned groups, most of whose indebtedness to classical Marxism has become opaque, cultural studies may be regarded as an attempted unification of the academic left into a self-consciously inter- or possibly non-disciplinary approach to social reality which speaks the language of critique and emancipation while retaining an accent on empiricism and particularism.

Long's depiction of "a theoretically informed, empirically engaged *critical commentary*" accurately sums up a mode of scholarship that wishes to retain a claim to scientificity while renouncing value neutrality, a claim reminiscent of the Frankfurt School tradition which remains an important current in contemporary cultural studies. Critics of the discipline have often focused on this point, it not being immediately evident to some how a scientific attitude might be blended with an ethos of left-leaning activism. The crucial premise is that scholarly inquiry is itself a political undertaking and as such a natural ally of either emancipatory movements of the left or their conservative adversaries. The rational investigation of social reality being by its nature ideologically committed, we might as well be honest about this and openly align ourselves with whatever blocs and constituencies have claimed our allegiance. Scholarship and political struggle are unified while "one ample column of Cultural Studies legionnaires has made everything it does into the critique of ideology. Its whole business has been an unmasking. It has unmasked the pretensions of human sciences to understand and value accordingly given human practices, and it has unmasked the presence of coercive political power in even the most harmless-looking details of expressive life."[6]

"Positionality" is a key notion here: scholarship is never neutral or objective but speaks from a perspective which itself is wedded to an ideology of one kind or another. Whatever schema one brings to bear serves either the marginalized or the hegemonic while the business of research becomes essentially a contest of left and right which differs from ordinary politics only in respect of the level on which it operates. The scholar is a public intellectual whose judgments are issued from the standpoint of a theoretical knowledge which itself is one with ideological struggle. Such knowledge is in every case partisan and strategic, and the distinction between theorists and activists all but dissolves.

This mode of inquiry largely concerns itself with contemporary western societies and the myriad power relations and social injustices that are asserted to prevail in a culture at a given time. A pronounced interest in issues of political economy is a regular feature of this literature, from the matter of who owns the culture industry and its various products to the mechanisms and consequences of such production. The entire domain of cultural expression and production must be regarded from a perspective of class power for capitalist interests are typically regarded as driving matters in ways calibrated toward the ends of the moneyed class or the owners of the means of cultural production yet without any strict reductionism. Where Marxists have long regarded economics as the lone driver of basically everything in the human world, scholars of cultural studies today most often adopt a non-reductionist view where, as Chris Barker and Emma Jane put it,

> Culture is seen as having its own specific meanings, rules and practices which are not reducible to . . . another category or level of a social formation. . . . For cultural studies, the processes of political economy do not determine the meanings of texts or their appropriation by audiences. Rather, political economy, social relationships and culture must be understood in terms of their own specific logics and modes of development. Each of these domains is "articulated" or related together in context-specific ways. The non-reductionism of cultural studies insists that questions of class, gender, sexuality, race, ethnicity, nation and age have their own particularities which cannot be reduced either to political economy or to each other.[7]

Simple economic reductionism is typically replaced with a more complex conception in which cultural production and meanings are explained with constant reference to both the corporate entities and profit motive from which they cannot be separated as well as their own imperatives and immanent dynamics. Power and ideology and the critique of the same remain omnipresent considerations in this field of knowledge, and not only among writers who are overtly committed to the Marxist or critical-theoretic traditions. A nomenclature of class and ideology, dominant and subaltern groups, power and resistance continues to inform this discipline along with the close association of cultural narrative and power relations. The former is invariably implicated in the latter, on standard views, and not only in the narrow sense of class interests and economic hegemony. Ideology remains an ubiquitous and hegemonic system of meanings and ideas that dupe powerless groups into a semblance of democratic consent while ensuring their continuing oppression, and where power itself is conceived either in terms of what Michel Foucault termed the juridical or top-down model or, as he preferred, a bottom-up phenomenon which works by constituting subjects and producing fields of knowledge and experience. The influence of this thinker in contemporary cultural studies remains extensive and provides a corrective to the Marxian model in which class power determines everything in the cultural sphere. Power's capacity not only for exploitation but also for producing, constituting, and enabling is a constant theme in this discipline together with its documentation and critique. The impact of French social theory more generally upon cultural studies continues to be profound while ideology critique in its Marxian and Frankfurt school connotations remains a sizeable current within contemporary scholarship.

Upon the division of the left through the latter part of the twentieth century into a loose confederation of groups united around issues of identity—of race, gender, ethnicity, religion, sexual orientation, and so on—these categories emerged as central organizing themes within cultural studies by century's end and remain so at the present time. The politics of difference and identity emerged as a post-Marxian alliance of movements which gained purchase through the social sciences and humanities generally but perhaps especially within the studies disciplines wherein the history and struggles of oppressed groups came to the fore. What to many appeared a grievance-oriented "parade of displeasure and bad temper" represented for its proponents a demystifying exercise in which the constructed nature of cultural meanings and artifacts and their inseparability from hegemonic ideology could be brought to light.[8] Scholarly inquiry is decidedly placed in the service of liberation struggles where the hope is that such knowledge will produce subjects who are capable of resisting their oppression and where scholars are commonly cast in the role of something resembling Foucault's "specific intellectuals" or Gramsci's "organic intellectuals." Neither is a theorist in a conventional sense pursuing knowledge either objectively, disinterestedly, or for its own sake, but a scholar-activist whose local, on-the-ground knowledge of some struggle or injustice positions them to engage in a critique that is informed at once by theoretical knowledge and empirical conditions. Foucault's specific intellectual, for instance, rejects the universal intellectual's large-scale theories and explanatory systems for those local knowledges which had been dismissed for their apparent lack of rigor: "a whole set of knowledges that have been disqualified as inadequate to their task or insufficiently elaborated: naive knowledges, located low down on the hierarchy, beneath the required level of cognition or scientificity."[9] Many a scholar in this field operates in this light or something closely resembling it while larger-scale theory construction falls somewhat outside the discipline.

Largely under the influence of postmodern thinkers, a major current in this field, as Sarah Joseph explains, "has been towards studying culture in action, towards a theory of how collective meanings and shared experiences help to construct subjectivity, how power is discursively constructed and how a primary level of politics is about contestations about meanings. It is assumed by such thinkers that reality can be known only through its representations and that, therefore, no authoritative accounts of reality are possible. Any attempt to provide such an account itself becomes a mode of power and to avoid this, a politics of difference should be pursued."[10] Subjectivity—likewise identity, knowledge, power, meanings, and culture itself—are one and all constructions, and we are back to the constructivist hypothesis we discussed in chapter 1. While methodological questions, as we have seen, have not received a great deal of attention in cultural studies, one does find a lively debate regarding the nature of knowledge, a major current of which has it that language constitutes more or less everything in our world or that signifying practices which are inseparable from power underlie our cultural representations and meanings in general. Nothing here is given or determinate but has the status of a discursive construction; there is no truth, meaning, subject, or identity marker that is outside of language or language games which themselves are conventions. On anti-essentialist and anti-realist views, it is constructions all the way down. Subjects are not found but produced, including by a culture industry that supplies them with products the consumption of which forms them as bearers of a particular identity.

Once again, the distinction between construction and discovery tends to be categorical. Knowledge throughout this domain consists in interpretations that are constructed and pass for true without "corresponding" or relating to anything that has being outside of our constructions. The individual is an imagined being, a product of historical and cultural discourses which bear no relation to anything so metaphysical as "human nature" or anything purported to be universal. Particularism and linguistic constructivism predominate here, while notions of ethnicity, race, gender, meanings, and so on are not existing realities but in every case productions of our contingent modes of speaking. Whether we are speaking of cultural meanings themselves or our knowledge of them, language is the medium in which they are fashioned or produced but not discovered. Since such production is in every case steeped in power, the business of scholarly interpretation includes the important matter of participating in the struggle to legislate meanings that are never more than fictions.

Fictions of what? If the postmodernists' answer is language—the ways in which cultural products and meanings are conventionally talked about, categorized, represented, and internalized in our discourses or language games—this is sometimes broadened out to include social imaginaries. Culture, not nature, is the source of everything in the human world, and where culture is invariably local and bound up with a narrative for which there is neither grounding nor reasoning, for reasoning is a late arrival and in no case antecedent to the imagination and its workings. Among that which imagination produces is reasoning itself—also truth, subjectivity, identity, and meaning, where each of the latter has been configured by language or an imaginary that is creative rather than reproductive. Every culture has—one might say is—an *imaginaire* which operates pre-reflectively upon everything that passes for thought within it and affords thinking a trajectory and an orientation that seldom comes into question. As an operative mode of thought, it is more tacit than explicit, more preunderstanding than understanding.

Our own view begins once again by refusing any dichotomy of construction versus discovery. The constructivist position has a good deal to recommend it, and Cornelius Castoriadis' hypothesis that "Each society [one may say culture] creates its own forms" bears a truth that is important to retain (so long as we are not attributing agency to either society or culture). "These forms," he continued, "in turn bring into being a world in which this society inscribes itself and gives itself a place. It is by means of them that society constitutes a system of norms, institutions in the broadest sense of the term, values, orientations, and goals of collective life, as well as of individual life. At their core are to be found in each instance social imaginary significations, which also are created by each society and which are embodied in its institutions."[11] Significations and forms of this order have no Prime Mover but are a chain of constructions without beginning or end, and it is within this chain that we find ourselves. What can be said of history can be said equally of culture: as beings-in-culture we are located in an imaginative schema that precedes and constitutes us even as we incessantly re-narrate the beings that we are and the circumstances that we find about us. We are speaking and storytelling animals, and the cultural world in which we find ourselves has shaped our experience in general while remaining subject to ongoing reinterpretation and reconstruction. Like historical facts, cultural meanings and truths are not unearthed in fully determinate form but are productions of an active imagination and change in the manner of a living past.

The human past does and does not sit still: historians are beholden to sources and evidence which also do not speak for themselves but require a mode of organization and synthesis that is in every case creative, and scholars in cultural studies find themselves in a similar hermeneutic situation. They too are beholden—not, it is true, to any hard cultural facts but to some matters that are difficult to describe as constructions. What we have spoken of as common sense empiricism plays a comparable role in area studies as in history and must be distinguished in similar fashion from subjectivism, myth-making, propaganda, and related notions. Like history or any field of inquiry that deals with evidence, research in cultural studies is constantly beholden to evidentiary material which exercises an authority over everything that scholars write. To characterize any such investigation as rational means in the first place that we are not making things up but are engaging in a comparable activity to joining a conversation or a game that precedes us and which it falls to us to take further—and not in any way we wish but in a way that is evidentially indicated. To organize, synthesize, or otherwise imagine is not to legislate but to show, and we are back to some familiar hermeneutic themes: the perspectivity, pre-structure, and historical embeddedness of interpretation, the dialectic of universal and particular, and the revelatory nature and contextual structure of understanding. All of these factors are in play in any inquiry into culture that is at once imaginative and rigorous. Here as well we may describe the scholar as a detective of sorts, examining the myriad texts, meanings, and artifacts that make up a culture with an eye to their interrelations and dynamics as well as any larger narrative to which they give rise.

What cultural interpreters do must be thought together with what happens to them in the course of their work, and here Mitscherling's concept of tracking intentionality warrants mention once again. Subjectivity and objectivity are relata, and as such any constitution of which we may speak can only be mutual and dynamic. Any process of investigation is less a constructing or legislating than a following along, noting how one cultural product or meaning relates to another, identifying connections and dynamics that are not limited to power relations but extend to the larger tendings and undercurrents that belong to a given culture at a given time. Everything we may speak of as cultural exists in a continual state of becoming or activity, and understanding it requires that we see it not as any thingly being frozen in time but in its myriad relations with what is around it, for a relatum is what it fundamentally is.

Let us speak of culture, then, following Geertz (and Weber), as a web-like configuration comprised in the main of meanings all of which are subject to ongoing interpretation and contestation: "Believing, with Max Weber, that man is an animal suspended in webs of significance he himself has spun, I take culture to be those webs, and the analysis of it to be therefore not an experimental science in search of law but an interpretive one in search of meaning. It is explication I am after, construing social expressions on their surface enigmatical."[12] Geertz was not a cultural studies scholar but an anthropologist, however his definition affords a rather good starting point and is much preferable to some alternatives, including Raymond Williams' "'social' definition of culture, in which culture is a description of a particular way of life, which expresses certain meanings and values not only in art and learning but also in institutions and ordinary behaviour."[13] Culture as a way of life, a constellation of ideas or information, a domain of aesthetic expression, worldview, system of values and behaviors, and similar notions all capture aspects of a phenomenon that is encompassing and goes to the heart of the kind of beings that we are. As an ontological matter, we are at once historical, cultural, and imaginative beings from the ground up—or this is the ground, the web in which we find ourselves always already existing and endeavoring to understand our world. As we saw in chapter 2, Mitscherling changes the metaphor to a "glass globe, within which are radiating lines, like strands of a web, thousands of them, all intersecting and going every which way," and where the strands are intentions in a non-materialist and also non-idealist sense of the term. Importantly, they are not constructions or projections of consciousness but belong to an order of "intentional being," and it is in the midst of such a world that *Homo sapiens* is invariably located.

Along related lines, Johan Fornäs likens culture to "an everchanging flux" and "a web of flows, multiplying, converging and crossing. Some of the interconnecting whirls of culture are clearly visible on the surface, others are hidden deep below. Some are strong and irresistible, others local and temporary. They flow in various directions and intersect at different levels." He adds, "Cultural processes are communicative practices. We do not passively submit to pre-existing frames, rules and codes, but reshape and recreate ourselves, each other, our worlds and our symbolic forms in an at least potentially open, active and creative process."[14] The accent on communication is well placed, for the web or globe of which we are speaking is nothing object-like but more like a conversational network in which the principal elements include meanings, practices, language, affinities, ideas, symbols, values, expressions, technology, institutions, identity, and (lest we forget) power. Culture is all these things, the totality of which run in a thousand directions and variously intersect, cohere, clash, jostle for position, form lasting structures, repeat themselves, become transformed, and in a near infinity of ways enter into the lives of populations. Some of the more visible and fleeting are surface phenomena while others constitute undercurrents that can be seen only by plumbing depths in the manner of Nietzsche's "cultural physician." A culture may divide into any number of subcultures, each of which may be conceived as a more concentrated or specialized conversation which never loses an organic connection to a larger interlocutionary order. Culture includes a vast array of material products while being itself neither material nor ideal but an intersubjective phenomenon whose elements and dynamics exist not inside heads but out there in the social world. The conversation metaphor harkens back to Michael Oakeshott's "conversation of humankind," although in a less universalist connotation. While some cultural elements may turn out to be universal, what we typically designate as cultures and what is commonly investigated in cultural studies are relatively local conversational webs which are differentiated while also having a tendency to overlap and to remain porous. Oakeshott's metaphor highlights the being-in-motion of a phenomenon that is living, whose dynamics are complex and changeable, and which is variously rational and steeped in power.

Let us speak of human beings at a basic level of analysis as participants in a conversational order that precedes and forms us, and where our capacities of participation are free while also conditioned by the imaginative schema that is our historical inheritance. Our hermeneutic situation is to be embedded in a cultural web the strands of which are neither discovered nor constructed but are relata with which we are in continual dialogue and which remain subject to an interpretation and contestation that is unending. To describe us as imagining beings entails that we are not the legislators but the detectives of the world, poets of a kind who are forever reweaving past, present, and future while following trails that are not projections but that have being in a sense that is neither material nor ideal. Geertz's notion of the human being as "an animal suspended in webs of significance he himself has spun" must therefore be qualified: we do not spin webs as spiders do, from threads of our own creation, but get about our culture by navigating and disentangling a myriad intentions or tendings that comprise every human environment while also adding to them and making moves that are not determined but are in some instances indicated by the conditions in which we find ourselves. We are at once inheritors of the artifacts and meanings that we live by and agents capable of exercising our freedom and rationality over an environment that never holds us captive.

A good part of the business of human existence so conceived involves an incessant search both for understanding our cultural world as a totality as well as the particular meanings or subcultures around which our lives are organized and for self-understanding, and where these two matters dissolve into one. Who one is is never distinguishable from where and when one is and the significations that one finds about one, for we are relational beings from root to leaf. Cultural meanings and artifacts generally are themselves relational and subject to a conversational agonism that is interminable in principle. As Geertz noted, "the human brain is thoroughly dependent upon cultural resources for its very operation; and those resources are, consequently, not adjuncts to, but constituents of, mental activity."[15] We think and converse and act with constant reference to some matter or other that may be broadly designated as cultural, for it is primarily culture rather than nature that constitutes our human world. Language, symbols, meanings, practices, and such things are not outward expressions but ingredients in the mental life of a species whose brain evolved in good measure in constant interchange with a myriad cultural elements which stand to minds in a chicken and egg relation or as relata which are what they are only with constant reference to what they are not. A work of art is not a mind, but apart from the latter it is not a work of art but a mute thing, and the same can be said of every other cultural artifact. It is not alive apart from its interactions, while minds too are not Hobbesian mechanisms which enter into culture as one might enter a shopping mall but cultural interlocutors from the ground up. Thought and culture are ultimately inseparable for all thinking is a thinking-about some matter that is a constituent of a humanly significant environment.

In the introduction we cited Ricoeur that "there is no human experience that is not already mediated by symbolic systems and, among them, by narratives," and that "we might speak of an implicit or immanent symbolism" animating thought and experience in general. This "immanent symbolism" or imaginative schema is operative in human experience in general and from the outset and is at the heart of a culture. Anyone studying culture or some aspect of it, then, faces what Geertz called "a multiplicity of complex conceptual structures, many of them superimposed upon or knotted into one another"—which we might qualify by noting that any such structure is neither conceptual alone nor indeed a structure in any strict sense but a concatenation of cultural elements which more closely resembles a conversation than a closed system.[16] The scholar, whether of cultural studies, anthropology, or what have you, is tracking a narrative and getting in on a conversation with a view to participating in it and is in no way an outsider gazing upon it from a vantagepoint of epistemic privilege. What Geertz called the anthropologist's "thick description" might better be described as a hermeneutic interpretation which is no pure construction but a reconstruction which supplements the meaning of what it sees and so modifies it. Cultural studies is an interpretive art whose object may be the larger imaginative schema in which a given population lives and moves and has its being or more likely a particular dimension of this. It is an art that follows along more than it "critiques" if by this word we intend a mode of knowledge that is epistemically authoritative and standing at some remove from its object. Like historians again, cultural interpreters do not construct what they see so much as follow a trail to which neither metaphysical materialism nor constructivism does justice. Neither the model of discovery nor invention applies to the manner in which any of us stands to and knows a culture, be it critically or otherwise. One approaches it as one approaches any narrative whether fictional or nonfictional, which is with an eye to what it has to say, how things stand for those who inhabit it, and the internal dynamics that animate it.

The fundamental aim of cultural studies so conceived is to converse with a given culture and to engage in critical interpretation when indicated, which is not to say always and everywhere. "Finding our feet" was Geertz's phrase, and it is a good one—finding one's way around a particular culture or subculture, seeing what things mean, what is at stake and how things work, who is who and what is what, which does not always mean engaging in ideological combat.[17] While political motivations undoubtedly drive a sizeable portion of the research that issues from the discipline of which we have been speaking, it remains that scholarly investigation is distinguishable from a phenomenon that one might call political apriorism. Power may reach into all aspects of culture and subjectivity, but so too does reason and some other forms of intentionality not all of which point in a unified direction but many and various ones, all of which are worthy of the attention of the student of culture. The legacy of Marxism is a factor here no doubt, but enthusiasm aside, there is more to a culture than its emancipatory struggles and more to its analysis than a participation in the same which too often looks to be coming from on high. Some hermeneutic humility is in order here and possibly some moral humility as well. Social criticism, whether it takes domination as its object or anything else, and as I have argued elsewhere, is no expertocratic bestowing of enlightenment but an interpretive rendering that is in every case questionable.[18] Becoming conversant with a culture or any region of it is about as multidimensional as the citizens who populate it, and such efforts are hampered by an apriorism which legislates more than it comprehends.

Cultural studies on this view of it is neither an objective science nor its antithesis, whether this be an interpretive free-for-all or an exercise in straightforward partisanship. It is a form of hermeneutic inquiry into the intricate and frequently opaque dynamics, tendencies, forces, undercurrents, interrelations, and meanings that belong to a culture and the imaginative schema that every culture has. Like any inquiry that reckons with evidence, scholarship here is a dialogical interchange which selects, synthesizes, and narrates what it sees in constant communication with the human beings who are embedded in the culture one is studying. It follows a trail that is not of its own devising or an extension of the scholar's own proclivities. A similar hypothesis could be extended to a good many disciplines of the humanities and social sciences; however, our concern in this chapter has been with a rather embattled field the methodological basis of which has long been a subject of debate. Our suggestion has been that history and culture lie at the heart of our existence, and that our human and hermeneutic situation is to be suspended in a web of imaginative elements that are inherited while also subject to ongoing refashioning. The scholar of cultural studies is not differently situated than ordinary members of a culture, for all of whom much of the business of life is to negotiate our way through the web that has us all by identifying relations, understanding meanings, revaluing values, and creating artifacts all of which amount to so many participations in the life of a culture to which all of us stand in a relation of belonging. No matter what theoretical knowledge one brings to bear, one does not make the evidence fit the narrative but allows a story to tell itself—critically when indicated, but our overriding posture is of openness to what has unfolded and the terms on which we may become conversant with it.

CONCLUSION

Insofar as historical inquiry or a given line of it can ever be said to begin, it begins in the midst of an historical world, with researchers who are themselves beings-in-history, participants in a lifeworld that has already supplied them with a fundamental orientation which precedes and makes possible whatever investigations they will conduct. What historians do cannot be disentangled from what has happened to them, where the latter signifies a number of things: historians have inherited a tradition which variously informs, structures, limits, and makes possible whatever interpretations they will fashion; they have inherited a cultural-historical narrative which is steeped in power and interests and which shines a particular light upon the human past while also casting a shadow; they are the bearers of an imaginative schema that is historically emergent, affectively charged, and largely prereflective; and they have appropriated a range of professional standards and norms within which they work and from which any departures must be rigorously defended. What historians do may be conceived as making moves within a game that precedes them and in which they are simultaneously free and unfree. Whatever knowledge they gain is a consequence at once of historians' particular activities and of the general framework in which those activities are carried out, and where the latter seldom comes into question in the course of day-to-day research. Questioning such matters leads by a short route from history proper to historiography and the philosophy of history, and it is a land to which practicing historians largely prefer not to go. We have ventured this in the foregoing chapters wherein our premise has been that we get a clue to the nature of historical knowledge through an examination of a few time periods during which our hold on the past and anticipations of the future were considerably altered by movements of historically-minded thinkers each of whose reconceptions were reimaginings which in turn shed light upon the capacity of historical imagination itself. Any understanding of a capacity profits by examining the thing itself in action, and it is for this reason that we have spent some time recalling the historical reimaginings that were early Christianity, the renaissance, and the enlightenment. All imagining is a reimagining, but there are times when the latter is conducted on a more ambitious scale, and it is these that have been our focus in chapters 3 through 5. During each of these relatively active phases in the imaginative history of the west, the past, present, and future of humanity were all being reconceived in the sense of renarrated; historians are storytellers, as so many have brought to our attention, but what manner of storytelling is this and how free is the telling?

We are speaking of an activity, and a very complex one. Without beginning at the beginning, the historical imagination goes to work synthesizing a myriad of traces of the past into a coherent account of what occurred and what it may be understood to have meant. If the story's elements or many of them are given, the arrangement is not but must be actively configured and sometimes reconfigured by scholars whose operative relatedness to an historical world is largely presupposed. The arranging itself is simultaneously an activity and a passivity; it is an active ordering of ideas and evidence, a grasping of connections and a seeing-in-relation of particulars that do not speak for themselves, in the same gesture that it is receptive and beholden to what it sees. From the side of the subject, imagining is a work of detection that brings to bear upon whatever evidentiary material it encounters an interpretive schema, a nomenclature, a disciplinary framework, and a historian's point of view, and the range of cognitive acts it deploys is notably similar to what is associated with other modes of thought that deal with evidence and the art of detection: gathering, selecting, organizing, classifying, questioning, hypothesizing, judging, showing, and in the end narrating. Where constructivists speak of a subjectivity that actively constitutes the manifold and of a past that tolerates whatever narrative subjectivity projects onto it, our own view regards this as an overcorrection of an objectivism that commits the opposite error of underestimating the hermeneutic artfulness of historical research. Historians in every case bring an imaginative framework to bear upon whatever material they encounter, and such schemas accomplish a good deal of the preliminary work (presupposing, prejudging, preformatting) of interpretation. As Gadamer in particular taught us to see, understanding is invariably based upon a preunderstanding that is an inheritance and which locates us within an historical world. The activity of interpretation is a working through of the prejudicial structure that accompanies and precedes it, where this includes an immanent critique of the anticipations themselves.

In the Christian imagination of late antiquity, we find a movement of thinkers actively displacing a received worldview while borrowing heavily from the same, in a manner that would be repeated during both the renaissance and the enlightenment. A novel reiteration of cultural elements gave rise over time to a new constellation, in the first instance in the form of a wide array of concepts, metaphors, and narratives that were repurposed to suit their audiences and the monotheists' drive for legitimation. Some old ideas needed to go, including the Greek cyclical model of historical time and of course the polytheist divinities, while a great many others were Christianized. The new schema was no revolutionary development but a synthesis of received cultural ideas not limited to Jewish monotheism, Greek and Roman philosophical concepts, stories of heroic lives and noble death, and let us not forget Roman politics and its endless machinations. The work of the late antique imagination was to weave together philosophical and religious ideas that were largely traditionary into a new arrangement that served at once the spiritual needs of the time and the will to power of the imitators of Christ. Christian historical consciousness looked no longer to a heroic past but forward to a coming kingdom; the past was the fall and one long prelude to the arrival of the savior, although this was sacred history while the profane variety lost much of its importance.

The renaissance imagination again witnessed no rabbit being pulled from a hat but a creative reintegration of received cultural notions and a consequent transformation of historical consciousness. The Greek and Roman past was regarded no longer as an age of pagan error but an apex of cultural achievement and an exemplar for a movement of artists and humanists who were promising no wholesale revolution but a selective rehabilitation of ancient models and a novel synthesis of the latter with a still Christian worldview. The new schema was not a rejection of the modern but a syncretism of modern and ancient ways, and it was not without medieval predecessors. Not birth but rebirth was the watchword of a movement the general trajectory of whose labors was in the direction of making what was old new again, retrieving and improving upon ancient ideas without abandoning the religious tradition in which they stood and its temporal authorities. Teleological history was imported from the sacred to the profane with the introduction of the ancient-medieval-modern triad, with the second term now regarded as a valley between the peaks that were the Rome of Augustus' time and fourteenth- through sixteenth-century Italy. The concept of progress itself would take full root in the seventeenth and eighteenth centuries with an enlightenment movement that would appropriate the ancient-medieval-modern scheme while echoing the judgment of civilizational stagnation that renaissance figures had attributed to the middle ages. History was on the march and possessed a vanguard and a rearguard, or such was this movement's conviction. A new age of reason had replaced a long period of unreason and cultural backwardness, so the story went, and the fruits of the new schema included the scientific method and technology, rationalism, empiricism, utilitarian rationality, and a host of cognate ideas which spread among the upper and middle classes of the west. Here again we find a displacing of an older imaginative schema with a new one, and less radically and more gradually than some of its more triumphalist proponents maintained. Enlightenment was no crossing of a cultural Rubicon but a creative reweaving of ideas both received and new and a modification of the *zeitgeist* which was as much attitudinal as doctrinal. Reality would now appear through a scientific and materialist lens, and the new worldview would become as totalizing as the monotheistic ancestor to which it bore an unmistakable resemblance.

To characterize historical imagination as an activity entails not that individual historians set about selecting and arranging traces of the past in sovereign fashion while bracketing a hermeneutic framework which is their inheritance as historical beings but that the particulars with which they concern themselves must be synthesized in a way that is at once rational and artful. The business of weaving together the disparate strands of narrative and evidentiary material with which the past presents us is never presuppositionless but involves in every case the application of a schema which itself is modified in the same gesture in which it prearranges and preinterprets such material. We are speaking of a dialectic of activity and passivity, a creative doing which already follows a trajectory that precedes and conditions such activity. Historians are storytellers, but the stories they tell are less constructions than reconstructions which are beholden to both the sources and evidence of which historians have long spoken as well as the prenarrative quality of the particulars themselves and the framework in which such particulars appear to us. As is the case with imaginative activity in other realms of experience, we must speak of the pre-and the re- as belonging to it in a fundamental way: historical particulars come to us in no case as raw data but as prenarrative elements and bearers of meanings which stem from a cultural-historical framework, while the business of inquiry is to apply such a framework and to configure and reconfigure the particulars in a way that is both rigorous and compelling. We tell the story not as we wish but as it demands to be told—"as it was" or, better, as it virtually was. Any re-presenting is not a copying but an activity that is intermediate between projecting and discovering, a certain midwifery in which our imagining is an active receptivity of a historical record that speaks to us provided both that we are informed and that we have an ear for what it says to us. By the late eighteenth century, it was unsurprising that an enlightenment historian should speak of "the decline and fall of the Roman empire" and of the centuries of barbarism and superstition that purportedly followed, just as an earlier renaissance narrative conditioned the perception of the middle ages as an unfortunately long ebb to the flow of the present and its ancient precedent. Christians of late antiquity had pronounced different judgments while practicing a similarly artful reconfiguration of a pagan past. In each instance, the past appeared as the schema allowed it to, while the work of historical interpretation was to bring to bear upon the sea of particulars an arrangement and an order that was conceived in advance while subject to ongoing modification.

If modern historians do not practice their craft in the manner of an Augustine or a Hegel and regard such figures not as historians but philosophers of history and ideologues of a kind, it is owing to the relation of imagination and rationality which, we have argued, is best regarded as internal and dialectical. A narrative goes off the rails when due to ideological commitments or insufficient evidence it is projected onto the phenomena rather than found in them, and it is on grounds of hermeneutic violence and apriorism that we are likely to consider such writers not historians in an authentic sense but historical thinkers of a different kind. What is problematic in ideological history is that we are interpreting the past within a schema that is not indicated by the evidence so much as read into it, and the basis of many a critique is that a given account constitutes such an imposition. If constructivism is without sufficient resources to articulate this critique or to sustain a principled distinction between actual history and ideological, fictional, or otherwise dubious varieties, what is needed is a conception of rationality that affirms the narrative hypothesis without abandoning all talk of investigative rigor and historical truth. Something resists us when we say of the past something that either lacks an evidentiary basis or amounts to a misarrangement and distortion. It is more than a preference or an aesthetic judgment to say that there was a renaissance (a few of them) and an enlightenment, that they occurred at particular times and places, and that they changed the conversation of the west in important ways, just as it is dubious to speak of wholesale civilizational collapse in the period of late antiquity and of the middle ages as a childhood of the mind. The latter are modern idealizations that are a function of a progress narrative which passes only given commitments that are ideological rather than historical. Barbarians, pagans, infidels, and artless medievals are long-imposed categories that shed light upon the imaginative schema of the speaker and little more, and the same may be said of the ancient-medieval-modern triad itself.

What is historical rationality but an imaginative synthesis that displays narrative coherence, evidentiary rigor, insight, and faithfulness to the phenomena, a practice of hermeneutic configuration which is a refiguring of what has been prefigured and a transition from chronicle to narrative where the latter in a non-fanciful sense relates itself. Whether we are speaking of fiction or nonfiction, good stories tell themselves in a sense that we have outlined in chapter 2. A mark of a rich historical interpretation—also a rational one—is that it participates in both *mythos* and *logos* in the general manner set forth in the first two chapters above. What historians do, we have argued, is (in some measure re-) configure a narrative that strives to encompass relevant evidence from the past while integrating it into a temporal framework that is both richly imaginative and rational, and where the latter values are conceivable as a following along and a taking direction from a story that relates itself. Historians are detectives, and like all who do this kind of work a good part of their labor is to follow a trail that is not constructed but exhibits a mode of being that is intentional rather than material or ideal. The trail of evidence is no projection of consciousness but is there—it has being—and it is precisely when it becomes such a projection that it leaves the track and veers into ideological, theological, or unduly speculative history. In arguing thus, we have incorporated Mitscherling's phenomenological analysis of intentionality where he speaks in the context of aesthetics of fictional narratives and works of art generally as creating themselves in a particular sense of this phrase; the activity of artistic production is neither a representing of a preexistent entity nor a Yahweh-like creation ex nihilo but an imaginative tracking of intentional structures that are not constructions of consciousness. Imaginative activity in general follows a trail that is there; one does not "make it up" but follows along as a detective follows a trail of evidence or a songwriter takes direction from the song and its inner *logos* or directionality in the very act of composing it. Although aesthetics is not our concern here, a similar principle is at work in the case of both fictional and historical narratives: fashioning either is an activity that is not sovereign but beholden to the thing itself. Historians and novelists are not bound in the same way; the former are beholden to evidence which the latter, including writers of historical fiction, need not worry about (although they might) while both are on a trail that must be followed in the same process by which the narrative is configured.

Rationality is a question of faithfulness to the things themselves or to the sources and evidence of which historians have long spoken as well as the kind of coherence that narratives in general must exhibit. Historical accounts must be true in more than an aesthetic connotation of the word: they need to fit the evidence in the sense of take direction from it even as there is creativity in the telling. Historians select and arrange particulars even while the latter in some ways govern the arrangement; there is a reciprocity here, a tensional circularity of objectivity and subjectivity where particulars neither speak for themselves nor tolerate hermeneutic violence. Constructivists and empiricists have both grasped half of a complex picture: historians are storytellers, and they also do not make things up—or if they do, they are no longer historians but thinkers of another kind. This form of narrating involves following leads, identifying relations, placing in context, reconciling universals and particulars, and organizing the whole in a way that is faithful to the reality of a past that is living and in which historians and the rest of us participate. Imagination, then, is an art of making contact with an extant past, an active synthesizing of elements which is also a tracking of intentionality that is implicit to them and a rendering actual of a potentiality. It is a mode of participating in an historical reality to which consciousness always belongs and opens onto lifeworlds that are never wholly beyond reach.

What has occurred when a narrative relates itself is that the historian has tracked an intentionality that belonged to the phenomena from the outset as a potentiality and rendered it actual, and not in the manner of a construction. If from the side of the subject imagining is a creative ordering that brings a schema to bear upon whatever evidence it encounters, such ordering is also a detecting which must be faithful to the phenomena as they present themselves. What counts as evidence and the manner of its appearing are likewise contingent upon the imaginative schema that historians bring to bear, but the other side of this is that something pushes back when historians' interpretations fail, as they sometimes do, to do justice to the past as it happened. Examples of the latter include the notion popularized by a variety of renaissance and enlightenment figures that the period of late antiquity constituted a large-scale civilizational collapse in the west from which it would take over a millennium to recover. This judgment accords with modern narratives of rebirth and progress while contemporary historians largely paint a different picture of the centuries that followed the end of the Roman era in Western Europe. The decline and fall story was a function of early modern partisanship both for their own times and for the ancient models they were endeavoring to revivify and surpass, just as Christians of late antiquity were more than slightly partisan it their estimation of their pagan predecessors and competitors. Such assessments served their proponents and the predominant ideology of the times while being a bit rich when regarded as historical hypotheses.

Historians work in the space between discovery and creation. Imagination— the activity and the schema in which it operates—is there from the beginning, and the modes of appearing that it makes possible are a function of an arrangement that is at once selective, aspectival, self-serving, shot through with power and interests, and more than occasionally true. It made hermeneutic sense to speak of a renaissance and an enlightenment as fundamental turning points in the history of the west, and if the whole truth is never captured in such statements, this is no more unique to historical interpretation than that the light it sheds casts a shadow and that it is impossible to disentangle entirely the elements from the arrangement. The particulars appear as an imaginative schema has allowed them to, and the schema itself is nothing separate and apart from the particulars but is in a fundamental way responsible to the latter in the manner of a dialectic in which subjectivity and objectivity, also past and present, are mutually constituted. Each is a relatum that comes to be what it is in constant dialogue with its respective other, and where the latter is better spoken of as a counterpart than an oppositional force. Historical investigators deploy a schema that also deploys them, often behind their back, and cultural studies finds itself in the same hermeneutic situation—not outside of the conversation but an interlocutor within it. Such a schema is the umbilical cord connecting each of us to an historical world that has claimed us even as we endeavor to bring parts of that world ever more into view.

History comes alive and speaks to us in the transition from chronicle to narrative, in the essential being-in-motion and in-relation that characterizes everything in the human world. Historical self-understanding is never more than a reflection of where we are in a scheme of things that is indivisibly temporal and cultural, operative and questionable, notional and real. The past is no blank canvas but an interpretive field inexhaustible in meaning and abounding with particulars all of which are historical not in themselves but in their contribution to a story that claims us still.

Notes

INTRODUCTION

1. This is my variation of Geertz's remark that "Doing ethnography is like trying to read (in the sense of 'construct a reading of') a manuscript—foreign, faded, full of ellipses, incoherencies, suspicious emendations, and tendentious commentaries, but written not in conventionalized graphs of sound but in transient examples of shaped behavior." Clifford Geertz, *The Interpretation of Cultures* (New York: Basic Books, 2000), 10.

2. Hans-Georg Gadamer, *Reason in the Age of Science*, trans. Frederick G. Lawrence (Cambridge: MIT Press, 1982), 111.

3. Paul Ricoeur, *Time and Narrative* vol. 1, trans. Kathleen McLaughlin and David Pellauer (Chicago: University of Chicago Press, 1990), 74, 3.

4. Ibid., 57, 58, 54, ix–x.

5. Ibid., 164–65.

6. Richard Kearney, *Poetics of Imagining: From Husserl to Lyotard* (London: Harper Collins, 1991), 158. Throughout this book, all italics in quoted material are in the original.

7. Richard Kearney, *On Stories* (New York: Routledge, 2001), 3, 133, 130.

8. Kearney, *Poetics of Imagining*, 1.

CHAPTER 1

1. Eric S. Nelson, "Wilhelm Dilthey and the Formative-Generative Imagination" in *Stretching the Limits of Productive Imagination*, ed. Saulius Geniusas (Lanham, MD: Rowman and Littlefield, 2018), 30.

2. Rudolf A. Makkreel, "Dilthey's Typifying Imagination" in *Productive Imagination*, eds. Saulius Geniusas and Dmitri Nikulin (Lanham, MD: Rowman and Littlefield, 2018), 87.

3. W. H. Walsh, *An Introduction to Philosophy of History* (New York: HarperCollins, 1977), 34.

4. Hayden White, *Metahistory: The Historical Imagination in Nineteenth-Century Europe* (Baltimore: Johns Hopkins University Press, 1973), ix.

5. Ibid., 6–7.

6. Louis O. Mink, "History and Fiction as Modes of Comprehension" in *New Literary History* 1, 557.

7. White, *Metahistory*, xi.

8. Paul Ricoeur, *Time and Narrative* vol. 1, trans. Kathleen McLaughlin and David Pellauer (Chicago: University of Chicago Press, 1990), 178–79.

9. Keith Jenkins, *At the Limits of History: Essays on Theory and Practice* (New York: Routledge, 2009), 137–38, 8.

10. Jean-François Lyotard, *The Postmodern Condition: A Report on Knowledge*, trans. G. Bennington and B. Massumi (Minneapolis: University of Minnesota Press, 1984), 36.

11. Clifford Geertz, *The Interpretation of Cultures* (New York: Basic Books, 1977), 5.

12. Jouni-Matti Kuukkanen, *Postnarrativist Philosophy of Historiography* (New York: Palgrave Macmillan, 2015), 40.

13. Cited in Robert Doran's "Editor's Introduction: Choosing the Past: Hayden White and the Philosophy of History" in *Philosophy of History After Hayden White*, ed. Robert Doran (London: Bloomsbury, 2013), 15.

14. Willie Thompson, *Postmodernism and History* (New York: Palgrave Macmillan, 2004), 1.

15. Jenkins, *At the Limits of History*, 4.

16. Hayden White, "The Historical Text as Literary Artifact" in *History and Theory: Contemporary Readings*, eds. Brian Fay, Philip Pomper, and Richard T. Vann (Malden, MA: Blackwell, 1998), 28.

17. White, *Metahistory*, xii.

18. Jenkins, *At the Limits of History*, 12.

19. Friedrich Nietzsche, *Beyond Good and Evil*, trans. Walter Kaufmann (New York: Vintage, 1989), sec. 2, p. 10.

20. George H. Taylor, "Foreword" in *Social Imaginaries: Critical Interventions*, eds. Suzi Adams and Jeremy C. A. Smith (Lanham, MD: Rowman and Littlefield, 2019), xii, xvi.

21. Saulius Geniusas, "Editor's Introduction" in *Stretching the Limits of Productive Imagination*, ed. Saulius Geniusas (Lanham, MD: Rowman and Littlefield, 2018), xvi.

22. John Dewey, *Knowing and the Known* (1949), Later Works volume 16, ed. Jo Ann Boydston (Carbondale: Southern Illinois University Press, 1990), 248.

23. John W. M. Krummel, "Rethinking the History of the Productive Imagination in Relation to Common Sense" in *Social Imaginaries: Critical Interventions*, eds. Suzi Adams and Jeremy C. A. Smith (Lanham, MD: Rowman and Littlefield, 2019), 45.

24. Richard Kearney, *Poetics of Imagining: From Husserl to Lyotard* (London: Harper Collins, 1991), 157.

25. Richard Kearney, *On Stories* (New York: Routledge, 2001), 5.

26. Fyodor Dostoevsky, *The Brothers Karamazov*, trans. Richard Pevear and Larissa Volokhonsky (San Francisco: North Point Press, 1990), 589.

27. Martin Heidegger, *Being and Time*, trans. Joan Stambaugh (Albany: State University of New York Press, 2010), 148.

28. Nietzsche, *Beyond Good and Evil*, sec. 5, p. 12.

29. Allan Megill, *Historical Knowledge, Historical Error: A Contemporary Guide to Practice* (Chicago: University of Chicago Press, 2007), 5.

30. Geoffrey Elton, "Return to Essentials" in *The Postmodern History Reader*, ed. Keither Jenkins (New York: Routledge, 1997), 176.

31. See Hans-Georg Gadamer, *Truth and Method*, second revised edition, trans. J. Weinsheimer and D. G. Marshall (New York: Continuum, 1989).

32. Marc Bloch, *The Historian's Craft* (New York: Vintage, 1964), 65.

33. Kearney, *On Stories*, 136.

34. Ricoeur, *Time and Narrative*, 66.

35. Willie Thompson, *What Happened to History?* (London: Pluto Press, 2000), 123.

36. Friedrich Nietzsche, *On the Genealogy of Morals*, ed. W. Kaufmann, trans. W. Kaufmann and R. J. Hollingdale (New York: Vintage, 1969), III sec. 24, p. 151.

37. Jean Granier, "Perspectivism and Interpretation" in *The New Nietzsche: Contemporary Styles of Interpretation*, ed. David Allison (New York: Delta, 1977), 190, 191.

38. Kuukkanen, *Postnarrativist Philosophy of Historiography*, 67, 96.

39. Walsh, *An Introduction to Philosophy of History*, 18.

CHAPTER 2

1. Richard Kearney, *On Stories* (New York: Routledge, 2001), 149.

2. Alun Munslow, *The New History* (New York: Routledge, 2018), 186.

3. Allan Megill, *Historical Knowledge, Historical Error: A Contemporary Guide to Practice* (Chicago: University of Chicago Press, 2007), 4.

4. Maurice Merleau-Ponty, *Phenomenology of Perception*, trans. Colin Smith (New York: Routledge, 2013), 475–6.

5. Jean Granier, "Perspectivism and Interpretation" in *The New Nietzsche: Contemporary Styles of Interpretation*, ed. David Allison (New York: Delta, 1977), 190, 191.

6. Leopold von Ranke, *The Theory and Practice of History* (New York: Routledge, 2011), 86.

7. F. R. Ankersmit, *History and Tropology: The Rise and Fall of Metaphor* (Berkeley: University of California Press, 2021), 123, 102, 107.

8. John Dewey, *Reconstruction in Philosophy* (Middle Works vol. 12: 1920), ed. Jo Ann Boydston (Carbondale: Southern Illinois University Press, 2008), 144.

9. Ankersmit, *History and Tropology*, 102.

10. F. R. Ankersmit, "'Presence' and Myth," *History and Theory* 45, no. 3 (2006), 328.

11. Perez Zagorin, "Historiography and Postmodernism: Reconsiderations" in *History and Theory: Contemporary Readings*, eds. Brian Fay, Philip Pomper, and Richard T. Vann (Malden: Blackwell, 1998), 201–2.

12. W. H. Walsh, *An Introduction to Philosophy of History* (New York: HarperCollins, 1977), 89.

13. Robert Stein, "Literary Criticism and the Evidence for History" in *Writing Medieval History*, ed. Nancy Partner (London: Bloomsbury, 2010), 69.

14. Peter Novick, *That Noble Dream: The "Objectivity Question" and the American Historical Profession* (Cambridge: Cambridge University Press, 2009), 1–2.

15. G. R. Elton, *Return to Essentials: Some Reflections on the Present State of Historical Study* (Cambridge: Cambridge University Press, 2002), 30. Marwick is equally dismissive of another caricatured version of hermeneutics; he objects in particular to "the total misunderstandings of such philosophers as Paul Ricoeur, who first insists that history is essentially the same as novel-writing, and then draws absurd conclusions from his illegitimate contention." Arthur Marwick, *The New Nature of History: Knowledge, Evidence, Language* (London: Palgrave Macmillan, 2001), 263. It is curious when those who in doctrinaire fashion proclaim the need for careful and rigorous grounding of statements in the evidence proffer critical interpretations of their opponents that are not even loosely grounded in their texts.

16. Louis O. Mink, "History and Fiction as Modes of Comprehension," New Literary History 1 (1970), 557.

17. Alasdair MacIntyre, *After Virtue: A Study in Moral Theory* (Notre Dame: University of Notre Dame Press, 1984), 197.

18. Kearney, *On Stories*, 130.

19. Paul Ricoeur, *Time and Narrative* vol. 1, trans. Kathleen McLaughlin and David Pellauer (Chicago: University of Chicago Press, 1990), 58, 55–56.

20. David Carr, *Time, Narrative, and History* (Bloomington: Indiana University Press, 1986), 169.

21. Ricoeur, *Time and Narrative* vol. 1, 52.

22. Merleau-Ponty, *Phenomenology of Perception*, 454, 446.

23. Ibid., 444, 440, 439.

24. Carr, *Time, Narrative, and History*, 43.

25. Jeff Mitscherling, Tanya, DiTomasso, and Aref Nayed, *The Author's Intention* (Lanham, MD: Lexington, 2004), 106, 114. The same theme is discussed further in Mitscherling's *Aesthetic Genesis: The Origin of Consciousness in the Intentional Being of Nature* (Lanham, MD: University Press of America, 2009) as well as Jeff Mitscherling and Paul Fairfield, *Artistic Creation: A Phenomenological Account* (Lanham, MD: Lexington, 2019). See also Mitscherling's earlier work, *Roman Ingarden's Ontology and Aesthetics* (Ottawa: University of Ottawa Press, 1997).

26. Mitscherling and Fairfield, *Artistic Creation*, 139–40.

27. Mitscherling, private correspondence.

28. Mark Twain, "Those Extraordinary Twins" in *Pudd'nhead Wilson* (New York: Penguin, 1987), 229.

29. Munslow, *The New History*, 18. The interesting example of historical fiction is something of a hybrid form in which the novelist is constrained in similar ways to the historian, in those works anyway that endeavor to be true to life.

30. Merleau-Ponty, *Phenomenology of Perception*, 472, 483.

31. Gary Brent Madison, *The Phenomenology of Merleau-Ponty: A Search for the Limits of Consciousness* (Athens: Ohio University Press, 1981), 14.

32. Ibid., 210.

33. Mitscherling and Fairfield, *Artistic Creation*, 27.

34. Wilhelm Dilthey, *Gesammelte Schriften* 8 (Stuttgart: Teubner, 1957), 226.

35. Merleau-Ponty, *Phenomenology of Perception*, 141.

36. Kearney, *On Stories*, 137; Kearney, *Poetics of Imagining: From Husserl to Lyotard* (New York: Routledge, 1991), 38, 17.

CHAPTER 3

1. Peter Brown, *The World of Late Antiquity* (New York: Thames and Hudson, 1989), 102.

2. Donald Harman Akenson, *Saint Saul: A Skeletal Key to the Historical Jesus* (Montreal: McGill-Queen's University Press, 2000), 46–47.

3. Peter Brown, *The Making of Late Antiquity* (Cambridge: Harvard University Press, 1993), 99, 100.

4. Timothy D. Barnes, *Constantine and Eusebius* (Cambridge: Harvard University Press, 1984), 249.

5. Charles Freeman, *A New History of Early Christianity* (New Haven: Yale University Press, 2011), 318.

6. Karl Löwith, *Meaning in History* (Chicago: University of Chicago Press, 1957), 168.

7. Cited in ibid., 176.

8. Matthew V. Novenson, *The Grammar of Messianism: An Ancient Jewish Political Idiom and Its Users* (Oxford: Oxford University Press, 2017), 17.

9. Averil Cameron, *Christianity and the Rhetoric of Empire: The Development of Christian Discourse* (Oakland: University of California Press, 1994), 21.

10. Cited in Joseph Vogt, *The Decline of Rome: The Metamorphosis of Ancient Civilization* (London: Orio, 1993), 159.

11. Ernst Cassirer, *An Essay on Man* (New York: Bantam, 1970), 42.

12. Charles Odahl, *Constantine and the Christian Empire* (New York: Routledge, 2010), 250.

13. George E. Demacopoulos, *The Invention of Peter: Apostolic Discourse and Papal Authority in Late Antiquity* (Philadelphia: University of Pennsylvania Press, 2016), 75.

14. Peter Brown, *Authority and the Sacred: Aspects of the Christianisation of the Roman World* (Cambridge: Cambridge University Press, 2002), 40.

15. Vogt, 254.

16. Eamon Duffy, *Saints and Sinners: A History of the Popes* (New Haven: Yale University Press, 2006), 2.

17. Demacopoulos, *The Invention of Peter*, 38.

18. Cited in ibid., 55.

19. Miriam Griffin, *Nero: The End of a Dynasty* (New York: Routledge, 1987), 18.

20. Vogt, 167.

21. *International Standard Version of the Bible*.

22. Brown, *The World of Late Antiquity*, 65.

23. Peter Brown, *Augustine of Hippo: A Biography* (San Francisco: University of California Press, 2000), 219.

24. Candida Moss, *The Myth of Persecution: How Early Christians Invented a Story of Martyrdom* (San Francisco: HarperOne, 2013), 245, 14.

25. Ibid., 19–20.

26. Cameron, *Christianity and the Rhetoric of Empire*, 56.

27. Thomas Sizgorich, *Violence and Belief in Late Antiquity: Militant Devotion in Christianity and Islam* (Philadelphia: University of Pennsylvania Press, 2009), 118.

28. Cited in Jonathan Riley-Smith, *What Were the Crusades?* (San Francisco: Ignatius Press, 2009), 66.

CHAPTER 4

1. Jacob Burckhardt, *The Civilization of the Renaissance in Italy*, trans. S. G. C. Middlemore (New York: Penguin, 1990), 120.

2. Gene Brucker, "The Italian Renaissance" in *A Companion to the Worlds of the Renaissance*, ed. Guido Ruggiero (Malden: Blackwell, 2007), 24.

3. Alison Brown, *The Renaissance* (New York: Routledge, 2021), 40.

4. Peter Burke, "The Circulation of Knowledge" in *The Renaissance World*, ed. John Jeffries Martin (New York: Routledge, 2007), 192.

5. James S. Amelang, "Social Hierarchies: The Lower Classes" in *A Companion to the Worlds of the Renaissance*, ed. Guido Ruggiero (Malden: Blackwell, 2007), 248.

6. John Jeffries Martin, "The Renaissance: A World in Motion" in *The Renaissance World*, ed. John Jeffries Martin (New York: Routledge, 2007), 23.

7. Gombrich writes, "A 'movement' is something that is proclaimed. It attracts fanatics, on the one hand, who can't tolerate anything that doesn't belong to it and hangers-on who come and go; there is a spectrum of intensity in any movement just as there are usually various factions or 'wings.' There are also opponents and plenty of neutral outsiders who have other worries. I think we can most effortlessly describe the Renaissance as a movement of this kind." E. H. Gombrich, "The Renaissance—Period or Movement?" in *Renaissance Thought*, ed. Robert Black (New York: Routledge, 2001), 35.

8. Quoted in Nicholas Mann, *Petrarch* (Oxford: Oxford University Press, 1987), 28.

9. Ibid., 108, 19.

10. Robert Black, "Introduction" in *Renaissance Thought*, ed. Robert Black (New York: Routledge, 2001), 5.

11. Burckhardt, *The Civilization of the Renaissance in Italy*, 129.

12. Quoted in Brown, *The Renaissance*, 111–12.

13. Walter Isaacson, *Leonardo da Vinci* (New York: Simon and Schuster, 2017), 519.

14. Gombrich, "The Renaissance—Period or Movement?" 44.

15. Hannah Gray, "Renaissance Humanism: The Pursuit of Eloquence" in *Renaissance Thought*, ed. Robert Black (New York: Routledge, 2001), 61.

16. Daniel Woolf, *A Global History of History* (Cambridge: Cambridge University Press, 2011), 185.

17. Burckhardt, *The Civilization of the Renaissance in Italy*, 98, 199, 198, 102.

18. Ibid., 199.

19. John Jeffries Martin, "The Myth of Renaissance Individualism" in *The Renaissance World*, ed. John Jeffries Martin (New York: Routledge, 2007), 208.

20. Brown, *The Renaissance*, 31.

21. Quoted in Brown, *The Renaissance*, 112.

22. Guido Ruggiero, "Renaissance Dreaming: In Search of a Paradigm" in *A Companion to the Worlds of the Renaissance*, ed. Guido Ruggiero (Malden: Blackwell, 2007), 8.

23. Conrad Leyser, "Late Antiquity in the Medieval West" in *A Companion to Late Antiquity*, ed. Philip Rousseau (Hoboken: Wiley-Blackwell, 2012), 30.

24. Nicholas Mann, "The Origins of Humanism" in *The Cambridge Companion to Renaissance Humanism*, ed. Jill Kraye (Cambridge: Cambridge University Press, 2004), 1.

25. Alexander Cowan, "Cities, Towns, and New Forms of Culture" in *The Renaissance World*, ed. John Jeffries Martin (New York: Routledge, 2007), 101–2.

26. Robert Black, "Humanism" in *Renaissance Thought*, ed. Robert Black (New York: Routledge, 2001), 81.

27. Rosamond McKitterick, *Charlemagne: The Formation of a European Identity* (Cambridge: Cambridge University Press, 2008), 370–71.

28. Quoted in Heinrich Fichtenau, *The Carolingian Empire: The Age of Charlemagne* (Toronto: University of Toronto Press, 1978), 102.

29. Brucker, "The Italian Renaissance," 26.

30. Robert C. Davis, "The Renaissance Goes Up in Smoke" in *The Renaissance World*, ed. John Jeffries Martin (New York: Routledge, 2007), 398.

31. James Hankins, "Humanism and the Origins of Modern Political Thought" in *The Cambridge Companion to Renaissance Humanism*, ed. Jill Kraye (Cambridge: Cambridge University Press, 2004), 125.

32. James Hankins, "The Significance of Renaissance Philosophy" in *The Cambridge Companion to Renaissance Philosophy*, ed. James Hankins (Cambridge: Cambridge University Press, 2007), 338.

CHAPTER 5

1. Samuel Fleischacker, *What Is Enlightenment?* (New York: Routledge, 2013), 19.
2. Ulrich Im Hof, *The Enlightenment* (Oxford: Blackwell, 1995), 220.
3. Immanuel Kant, *Political Writings*, ed. H. S. Reiss, trans. H. B. Nisbet (Cambridge: Cambridge University Press, 2016), 58, 54, 55.
4. Jack Lively, *The Enlightenment* (London: Longmans, 1966), 3.
5. Max Horkheimer and Theodor W. Adorno, *Dialectic of Enlightenment*, trans. John Cumming (New York: Continuum, 1998), 3.
6. J. B. Bury, *The Idea of Progress: An Inquiry into its Growth and Origin* (New York: Dover, 1960), 67.
7. Norman Hampson, *The Enlightenment* (New York: Penguin, 1990), 149.
8. Bury, *The Idea of Progress*, 144.
9. Marquis de Condorcet, *Sketch for a Historical Picture of the Progress of the Human Mind* (London: Weidenfeld and Nicolson, 1955), 4, 9.
10. Bury, *The Idea of Progress*, 285–86.
11. Condorcet, *Sketch for a Historical Picture of the Progress of the Human Mind*, 184.
12. Kant, *Political Writings*, 58–59.
13. Arthur Herman, *The Idea of Decline in Western History* (New York: Free Press, 2007), 29.
14. Hans-Georg Gadamer, *Reason in the Age of Science*, trans. F. G. Lawrence (Cambridge: MIT Press, 1989), 156.
15. Karl Jaspers, *The Origin and Goal of History*, trans. Michael Bullock (New York: Routledge, 2011), 96.
16. Jacques Ellul, *The Technological Society*, trans. John Wilkinson (New York: Vintage, 1967), 14, 43.
17. Charles Taylor, *A Secular Age* (Cambridge: Harvard University Press, 2007).
18. Bury, *The Idea of Progress*, 116.
19. Cited in Frederick Copleston, *A History of Philosophy* vol. 6 (New York: Doubleday, 1994), 45. Copleston is citing d'Alembert's *Éléments de Philosophie*.
20. Dorinda Outram, *The Enlightenment* (Cambridge: Cambridge University Press, 2006), 19.
21. Roy Porter, *The Enlightenment* (London: Palgrave, 2001), 68.
22. Hof, *The Enlightenment*, 141.
23. Porter, *The Enlightenment*, 6.

CHAPTER 6

1. Fred Inglis, *Cultural Studies* (Cambridge: Blackwell, 1995), 137.
2. Elizabeth Long, "Introduction: Engaging Sociology and Cultural Studies: Disciplinary and Social Change" in *From Sociology to Cultural Studies: New Perspectives*, ed. Elizabeth Long (Malden: Blackwell, 1997), 14.

3. Chris Barker and Emma A. Jane, *Cultural Studies: Theory and Practice* (London: Sage, 2016), 8.

4. Judy Giles and Tim Middleton, *Studying Culture: A Practical Introduction* (Malden: Blackwell, 2008), 10.

5. Simon During, "Introduction" in *The Cultural Studies Reader*, ed. Simon During (New York: Routledge, 2007), 2.

6. Inglis, *Cultural Studies*, 133.

7. Barker and Jane, *Cultural Studies*, 11.

8. Andrew Goodwin and Janet Wolff, "Conserving Cultural Studies" in *From Sociology to Cultural Studies: New Perspectives*, ed. Elizabeth Long (Malden: Blackwell, 1997), 130.

9. Michel Foucault, *Power/Knowledge: Selected Interviews and Other Writings 1972–1977*, ed. Colin Gordon, trans. Colin Gordon, Leo Marshall, John Mepham, and Kate Soper (New York: Pantheon Books, 1980), 82.

10. Sarah Joseph, *Interrogating Culture: Critical Perspectives on Contemporary Social Theory* (London: Sage Publishing, 1998), 13.

11. Cornelius Castoriadis, "The Greek and the Modern Political Imaginary," *Salmagundi* 100, 1993, 102.

12. Clifford Geertz, *The Interpretation of Cultures* (New York: Basic Books, 2000), 5.

13. Raymond Williams, *The Long Revolution* (New York: Columbia University Press, 1961), 57.

14. Johan Fornäs, *Cultural Theory and Late Modernity* (London: Sage Publishing, 1995), 1. Also see his *Defending Culture: Conceptual Foundations and Contemporary Debate* (London: Palgrave Macmillan, 2017).

15. Geertz, *The Interpretation of Cultures*, 76.

16. Ibid., 10.

17. Ibid., 13.

18. See my *The Ways of Power: Hermeneutics, Ethics, and Social Criticism* (Pittsburgh: Duquesne University Press, 2002).

Index

activity xv–xvi, xviii, 3, 10–11, 28, 39, 43, 47, 130, 138, 140, 143
Adorno, Theodor 100, 124
Akenson, Donald 53
Ambrose 68
Amelang, James 77
Ankersmit, Frank xi, 4, 33–34, 43
Annales school 20, 36
apriorism 18, 107, 134, 141
Aquinas, Thomas 80, 83, 93
argumentation ix, xii, 1, 3, 16–17, 23–24, 49, 138
aristocracy 61–62, 65, 67, 88, 92, 116–17, 126
Aristotle xiv, 83–85, 92, 110
Arius 58–9
arrangement, art of x–xii, 20–1, 24, 49, 96, 130, 132, 138, 140, 142–43
asceticism 71
Augustine 55–56, 59, 65–66, 68, 71, 79, 84, 90, 100, 103, 105, 141
Augustus 57

Bacon, Francis 99, 101, 109
Barker, Chris 123, 126
belonging x, 3, 38, 41, 46, 48
bishops 64–65, 70
Black, Robert 92
Bloch, Marc 19–20

Brown, Alison 77, 89
Brown, Peter 534, 62, 67
Brucker, Gene 76, 94
Burckhardt, Jacob 75–77, 81, 86–87, 90, 94
Bury, J. B. 101, 103–4, 110

Cameron, Averil 58, 71
Carr, David 40, 42
Cassiodorus 91
Cassirer, Ernst 60
Castoriadis, Cornelius 129
causality 32, 43
Charlemagne 93
Christianity xv, 10–11, 18, 51–73, 80–81, 84, 94–95, 101, 103, 117, 138–40, 143
chronicle ix, 5, 7, 12, 16, 19, 35, 40, 42, 86, 144
Collingwood, R. G. 4
Comte, Auguste 106–7
Condorcet 104
Constantine 53, 55, 57–61, 68, 70, 71
constructivism xi–xii, xvi–xvii, 1–25, 27, 33, 35, 42, 128–30, 138, 140–41, 143
context ix, 15, 17, 19, 38, 47, 142
contingency 24, 32
continuity xv, xvii, 51, 72, 97, 118

155

courts 88–89, 93–94, 113–15
critique ix, xii, 3, 16–17, 122–25, 133, 135, 141
crusades 71–72
cultural studies xvii, 121–35, 143
culture xvii, 45, 121–23, 125–34
cyclical model 52, 54, 100, 139

Danto, Arthur 4
Darwin, Charles 107
Davis, Robert 95
Demacopoulos, George 63
Descartes, René 38, 99–101, 103, 106, 108–11, 113–14, 118
detection ix, xi, 23, 28, 42–43, 45, 130, 132, 138, 142–43
Dewey, John 12, 23, 33
dialectic 3, 19, 46–48, 130, 140
Dilthey, Wilhelm x, xv, 2, 3, 48
Dostoevsky, Fyodor 13
During, Simon 125

education 54, 65–66, 84, 88, 92, 115–18, 123
Ellul, Jacques 109
Elton, Geoffrey 17, 36
empiricism ix, xii, xvi–xvii, 1–25, 27, 29–31, 33–37, 86, 108, 125, 130, 139
Encyclopedia 111, 116
enlightenment xv, xvii, 51, 97–119, 139–40, 143
Eusebius 55, 69–71
evidence ix, xi–xii, xvi, 2, 13–14, 19, 22, 24, 27–50, 130, 134–35, 138, 140–42

facts ix, xi, 4, 11, 13, 24, 29, 34, 129
Fleischacker, Samuel 98
Fornäs, Johan 131
Foucault, Michel x, 8, 16, 23, 124, 127
freedom 94–95, 102, 104–6, 112–13, 125, 132
Freemasons 116

Gadamer, Hans-Georg x, xv, 2, 19, 23, 25, 48, 97, 108, 138
Gallie, W. B. 4
gathering xii, 42, 46, 49, 138
Geertz, Clifford xiii, xv, 7, 40, 130, 132–33, 145n2
Geniusas, Saulius 10
Gibbon, Edward 51, 101
Giles, Judy 124
Gombrich, E. H. 77, 82, 150n7
Gramsci, Antonio 127
Gray, Hannah 85
Griffin, Miriam 64
Guicciardini, Francesco 90

Hampson, Norman 102
Hankins, James 95
Hegel, G. W. F. x, 9, 106–7, 141
Heidegger, Martin x, xv, 2, 15, 41
heresy 60, 68
Herman, Arthur 106
hermeneutics ix–xii, xiv, xvii–xviii, 2, 3, 15, 18, 34, 36–37, 148n15
Hobbes, Thomas 31, 45, 99, 102–3, 108, 112, 114
Hof, Ulrich Im 116
Hoggart, Richard 122
Horkheimer, Max 100, 124
humanism 55, 79, 83–86, 92, 94, 96
humility 122, 134
Husserl, Edmund x, 41–42, 45

idealism xvi, xviii, 7, 35, 46
ideology xviii, 16, 23, 29, 62, 65, 87, 105, 121–22, 125–27, 134, 141, 143
imagination 3
imagination, object side xvi, 2, 14, 28, 34, 37
imagination, subject side xvi, 2, 14, 22, 28, 37
imaginative history 51–52, 73, 91, 97, 107, 138
imaginative schema x, xiv–xviii, 2, 4, 8–12, 14, 19, 28, 48–49, 51–53, 57–58, 60–62, 65, 69, 72–73, 80–81,

88, 94, 96, 98–99, 105–10, 117, 122, 126, 129, 132–33, 137–41, 143
individualism 86–87, 94, 102–3, 128
Inglis, Fred 121–22, 125
intentionality xvii, 2, 14, 27–50, 134
intentionality, tracking viii, x–xi, xviii, 20, 24, 28, 43, 45, 49, 130, 132–34, 142–43
interests, knowledge as serving 9, 17, 22, 54, 56, 72, 96, 117, 126, 143
interpretation 1–25
Isaacson, Walter 82

Jaspers, Karl 109
Jenkins, Keith 6–8
Joseph, Sarah 128

Kant, Immanuel 98–99, 101, 105–6, 110, 114
Kearney, Richard xii, xiv–xv, 2, 12, 20, 22, 27, 39–40, 48
Krummel, John 12
Kuukkanen, Jouni-Matti 7, 24

late antiquity xvii, 18, 51–73, 143
legitimation 54, 56–57, 62, 69, 92, 96
Leo I 63–64
Leonardo da Vinci 82, 87
libraries 77–78, 82–83, 89, 93
Lively, Jack 100
Locke, John 31, 38, 102, 106, 112, 114
Long, Elizabeth 123, 125
Löwith, Karl 56
Lyotard, Jean-François 6

MacIntyre, Alasdair 38–39
Madison, Gary B. 47
Mann, Nicholas 79, 91
Martin, John Jeffries 78, 88
Marwick, Arthur 36, 148n15
Marx, Karl 106–7, 123–27, 134
materialism 101, 108, 118, 140
McKitterick, Rosamond 93

meaning viii–ix, xi–xiii, 3, 7–8, 12, 20, 24, 30–35, 37, 39, 42, 48, 57, 128–32, 134, 143
Megill, Allan 16–17, 30
Merleau-Ponty, Maurice xv, 30, 41, 46–48
middle ages 19, 45, 52, 77, 79–80, 89–90, 92, 98, 102–3, 110, 140
Middleton, Tim 124
Mink, Louis 4–5, 38
Mitscherling, Jeff xvii, 43–44, 47, 130–31, 142, 148n25
Montaigne, Michel de 114
Moss, Candida 69–70
Munslow, Alun 30

narrative, fictional xi, xvii, 4, 13, 19, 21, 27, 30, 36–38, 43, 45–46, 142
narrative, historical viii–xvi, xviii, 1–25, 27, 30–31, 33, 37–40, 49, 122, 127, 137–38, 140
Nietzsche, Friedrich x, xv, 2, 9, 11, 16–17, 22–23, 30–31, 34, 110, 131
Novenson, Matthew 57
Novick, Peter 36

Oakeshott, Michael xvi, 131–32
Odahl, Charles 60
Origen 55, 65
Orosius, Paulus 56

pagans xvii, 52–53, 56–57, 59–61, 66, 68, 72, 139–41, 143
Palmieri, Matteo 81
papal preeminence 63–64
past, historical x, xviii, 2–4, 7–8, 16, 22, 25, 28–30, 34–35, 37, 48–49, 86
Paul 66
periodization 77, 89–91, 102, 139, 141
persecution 68–70
Petrarch 75–80, 84, 88–90, 92, 94
phenomenology 3, 31
Plato 27, 66, 83–85, 92
Porter, Roy 114, 118

postmodernism xii, xvi, 7, 13–14, 16, 31, 33, 35, 37, 123, 128–29
power 17, 57–58, 61–62, 65, 72–73, 123, 126–28, 130–31, 134, 137
pre-structure x, xii–xiii, xviii, 3–4, 37–40, 43, 130, 138, 140
progress 99–102, 104–7, 109, 111–12, 117–18, 139, 141

questioning xii, 3, 23, 138

Ranke, Leopold von 31
rationality 16, 24, 27, 29–33, 37, 101, 130, 134, 140–42
relata xviii, 19, 44, 133
relations ix, xi, xv, 3, 6, 18, 21, 25, 28, 35–36, 38–39, 44, 46–47, 49, 142
relevance 20
renaissance xv, xvii, 19, 52, 55, 75–96, 101, 107, 139–40, 143, 150n7
representation 13, 30, 32–5, 42–43, 48
rhetoric 16–17, 24, 31, 54, 66, 79, 84–85
Ricoeur, Paul x, xii–xiv, 2–4, 6, 21, 27, 38, 40, 133, 148n15
Roman empire, eastern 82–83, 92–93
Roman empire, western 10–11, 32, 45, 51
Rousseau, Jean–Jacques 105–6, 112, 114
Ruggiero, Guido 90

sacred history 54, 56, 69, 71, 73, 86, 100
saints 70–71
science 99–102, 107–10, 112, 115, 117, 139–40
Schleiermacher, Friedrich 15
selection xi, 3, 20, 23, 42, 134, 138, 142

self-understanding xiv, 2, 9, 13, 25, 40
sequence 38–39
Sizgorich, Thomas 71
Socrates 69
Stein, Robert 35
subject and object xviii, 12, 34, 37, 46–48, 130
synthesis ix, 21, 42, 47–49, 129, 134, 138–39, 141

Taylor, Charles 110
Taylor, George H. 9
teleology xv, 52, 55–56, 98, 103–4, 110, 118, 139
temporality ix, xi, xiii, xv, 37, 40–42, 49, 96
Theodosius I 58–59, 61, 68
Thompson, Willie 7, 21
tradition xv, 109, 137
truth 2, 6, 10, 13–14, 20, 22, 27, 29–30, 36, 54, 62, 64, 69–71, 128–30, 142
Twain, Mark 45

universal and particular ix, xvi–xvii, 2, 15, 17–20, 39, 41, 47, 49, 130, 142
universities 82–85, 93, 114

Vasari, Giorgio 75
Vogt, Joseph 63, 65
Voltaire 100, 101, 113–14

Walsh, W. H. 4, 24, 35
White, Hayden xi, xii, 4–8, 33
White, Morton 4
Williams, Raymond 122, 124, 130–31
Woolf, Daniel 86

Zagorin, Perez 35

About the Author

Paul Fairfield is professor of philosophy at Queen's University, Kingston, Canada. He has authored, edited, or coedited numerous books in different areas of hermeneutics and phenomenology. His most recent book is *Philosophical Reflections on Antiquity: Historical Change* (Lexington, 2020).